THE BEST OF **Woodworker's Journal**

Tables You Can Make

From Classic to Contemporary

THE BEST OF **W**OODWORKER'S **J**OURNAL

Tables You Can Make

From Classic to Contemporary

from the editors of *Woodworker's Journal*

Fox
Chapel Publishing

1970 Broad Street • East Petersburg, PA 17520
www.FoxChapelPublishing.com

Our friends at Rockler Woodworking and Hardware supplied us with most of the hardware used in this book. Visit *rockler.com*. For subscription information to *Woodworker's Journal* magazine, call toll-free 1-800-765-4119 or visit *www.woodworkersjournal.com*.

Fox Chapel Publishing Company, Inc.

President: Alan Giagnocavo
Publisher: J. McCrary
Acquisition Editor: Peg Couch
Editor: Paul Hambke
Series Editor: John Kelsey
Creative Direction: Troy Thorne
Cover Design: Lindsay Hess

Woodworker's Journal

Founder & CEO: Ann Rockler Jackson
Publisher: Larry N. Stoiaken
Editor-in-Chief: Rob Johnstone
Art Director: Jeff Jacobson
Senior Editor: Joanna Werch Takes
Field Editor: Chris Marshall
Illustrators: Jeff Jacobson, John Kelliher

ISBN 978-1-56523-361-4

Publisher's Cataloging-in-Publication Data

Tables you can make : from classic to contemporary / from the editors of Woodworker's journal. -- East Petersburg, PA : Fox Chapel Publishing, c2008.

p. ; cm.
(The best of Woodworker's journal)
ISBN: 978-1-56523-361-4

1. Tables--Patterns. 2. Furniture making. 3. Furniture design. 4.Woodwork--Patterns. I. Woodworker's journal.

TT197.5.T3 T339 2008
684.13--dc22   0804

To learn more about the other great books from Fox Chapel Publishing, or to find a retailer near you, call toll-free 1-800-457-9112 or visit us at *www.FoxChapelPublishing.com*.

Printed in China
10 9 8 7 6 5 4 3 2 1

Note to Authors: We are always looking for talented authors to write new books in our area of woodworking, design, and related crafts. Please send a brief letter describing your idea to Peg Couch, Acquisition Editor, Fox Chapel Publishing, 1970 Broad Street, East Petersburg, PA 17520.

Introduction

The family gathers around the kitchen table, the couple dines at the restaurant table, the business team meets around the conference table, the artisan pounds on his worktable, and useful little tables grace every space where people gather. Where else could you park your coffee mug, your book, your remote control, or your reading glasses?

At the heart of daily life, you will always find a table. In most woodworking households, you will probably find two, three, or four. That is because tables are just about everybody's favorite shop project. Tables, at least in their most basic form, are among the most straightforward of woodworking projects. All you need is a top, three or four legs, and a clever woodworking method for joining them all together.

Kitchen tables need to be tough and sturdy. We offer two of them in this book, both with good-looking and hard-working butcher block-style tops. One has turned legs, while the other has drawers and a lower shelf that elevate it into an multi-purpose kitchen island.

Dining tables are always a winner, and there is no better place than the top of one for displaying those terrific planks you have been hoarding. You will find a rock solid trestle table by John English, with ingenious joinery that allows it to knock down flat just in case you wanted to free up the dining room for dancing or other activities. Plans for an outdoor table for the deck or patio, and a serving tray you can use to eat dinner in front of the TV also are here. As a bonus, we give you some hard-won professional advice on exactly how to assemble the tabletop so that you get the most out of those terrific planks.

There is always room in the house for a new coffee table, a sofa table or an end table, a side table, or a hall table, and there are several of each in this book. There's a reason why woodworkers love decorative table projects: they're relatively small, so you can complete them in a couple of weekends; they don't use a lot of material, and they're sure to win approval from the other folks in your household.

Be sure you don't miss the Collector's Coffee Table by Rick White, a smart piece that stores and displays your collectible treasures. Likewise, the Edo Table, by Tom Caspar, will teach you how to make ingenious joints that look a lot more intricate than they really are.

So, with this book you have a treasure trove of great table-making projects. Where else can you find so much satisfaction than down in your workshop, building something useful and beautiful for your family? For that matter, what am I doing writing the introduction to this book? I have a fabulous pair of cherry planks just waiting for me. Let's go pound out some tables!

Larry N. Stoiaken, Publisher

Acknowledgments

Woodworker's Journal recently celebrated its 30th anniversary—a benchmark few magazines ever reach. I would like to acknowledge both the 300,000 woodworkers who make up our readership and Rockler Woodworking and Hardware (*rockler.com*), which provided most of the hardware, wood, and other products used to build the projects in this book. Our publishing partner, Fox Chapel, did a terrific job re-presenting our material, and I am especially grateful to Alan Giagnocavo, Paul Hambke, John Kelsey, and Troy Thorne for their commitment to our content.

Larry N. Stoiaken, Publisher

Contents

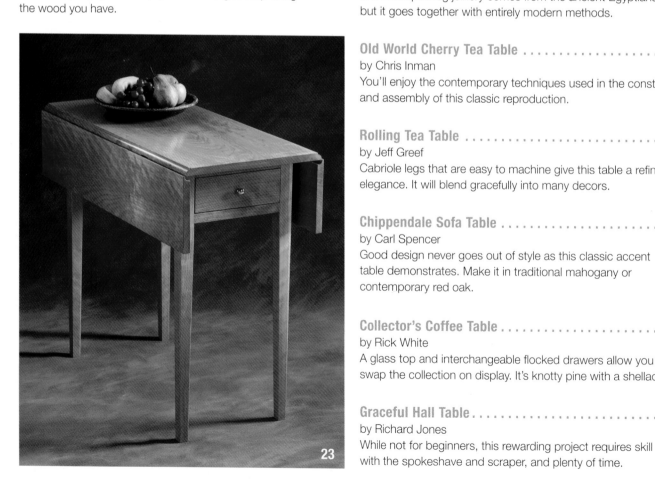

63

Butcher Block Kitchen Table

Kitchen tables serve as focal points for so many activities: dining, conversation, after-school homework, and as roomy work surfaces for food prep. A casual table, complete with maple butcher block top, is up to task for anything you need it to do. It even has a dual-action drawer that opens from two sides for storing silverware, placemats, or napkins. Pull it out far enough and you'll discover an added secret compartment, just for fun.

by Troy Johnson

Bordering the George Washington National Forest in beautiful northern Minnesota, our old cabin has been in the family so long that my warmest childhood memories are all of gatherings way up North. The best part of those occasions was the food: everything from burgers on the grill in summer to fresh walleye in the depths of winter. The table in the cabin served as both worktop and dining surface. Late afternoons, as the children played by the lake, its sturdy butcher block top was the scene of chopping, slicing, measuring, and pastry rolling. By six o'clock it would be cleared off, wiped down and set for the evening meal. If I was lucky, I got a seat halfway down one side—just the right spot to push the two-way drawer into my sister as she took a big gulp of milk.

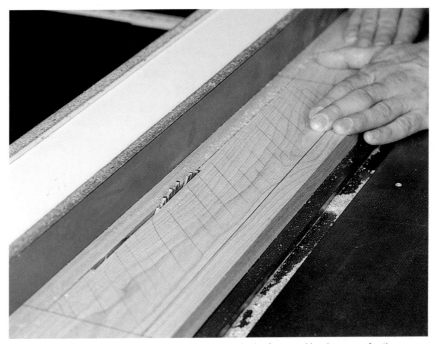

Figure 1: *Use your table saw to make the openings in the front and back aprons for the drawers, finishing up with a jig saw.*

Making the Legset

It's no surprise that, given all my fond memories, I knew exactly what to build when the old table finally needed replacing. Butcher block was the immediate choice for the top (piece 1), but the legset needed a little more thought. At a clan gathering, my family finally reached consensus: turned legs

with an authenticated historic green paint got all the votes.

Your first decision will be whether to turn the legs yourself or buy them as fabricated blanks. Many mail-order sources offer turned legs, or follow the profile on page 7 for shaping the legs yourself. With the legs in hand, begin the milling process by

cutting two mortises in each (see the Technical Drawings on pages 6 and 7 for locations and dimensions). It is an easy job on your router table, using a ¼" straight bit.

Drill a ¼" hole at each corner between the two mortises on your drill press, referring to the Drawings for the exact locations.

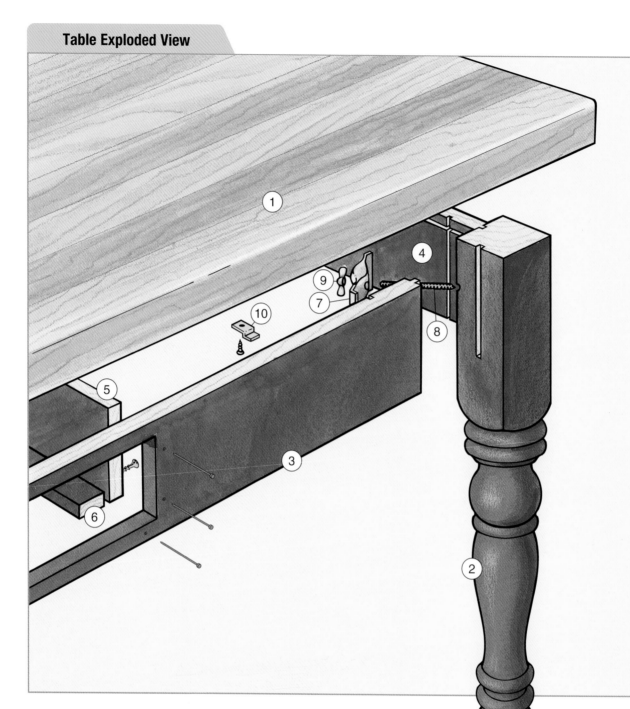

If you decide to paint your table base, you can use inexpensive poplar for the apron front and back, ends, dividers, and drawer supports (pieces 3, 4, 5, and 6). Refer to the Drawings when laying out the drawer openings in the front and back aprons, then make the long cuts on your table saw by raising the blade up through the piece, as shown in Figure 1 on page 1. Start and stop each cut by matching up pencil marks on the workpiece and fence.

Finish out the drawer openings with your jigsaw, then move back to the table saw to cut a ³⁄₁₆"-deep kerf along the length of each apron and a vertical kerf at each end (see Drawings for locations). You'll need the kerfs to attach the metal leg braces and tabletop hardware later. With that done, you can switch to a dado head to create tenons on the ends of the aprons (again, see the Drawings for details). Test-fit the aprons and legs, then temporarily install

the corner braces (pieces 7) with their hanger bolts and wing nuts (pieces 8 and 9) as shown in Figure 2.

When everything fits, disassemble the dry-fit and glue the tenons in place. Tighten the nuts on the bolts, check for squareness, and allow the subassembly to dry.

After a richly deserved coffee break, glue and screw the apron dividers to the

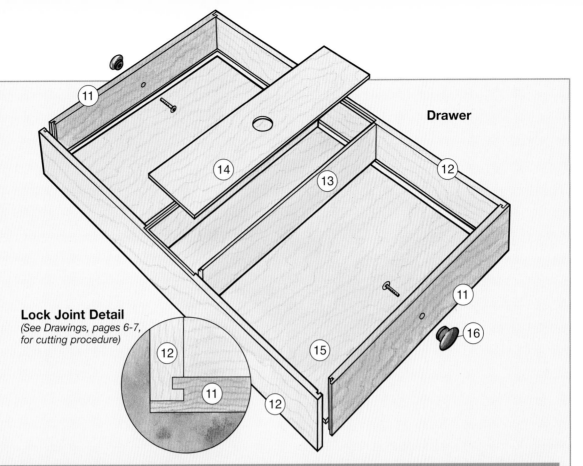

Drawer

Lock Joint Detail
*(See Drawings, pages 6-7,
for cutting procedure)*

Material List

	T x W x L			T x W x L
1 Tabletop (1)	1½" x 33¼" x 60"		10 Tabletop Fasteners (10)	Steel
2 Legs (4)	3½" x 3½" x 28¼"		11 Drawer Fronts (2)	¾" x 2¹³⁄₁₆" x 19¹³⁄₁₆"
3 Front and Back Aprons (2)	¾" x 4½" x 50½"		12 Drawer Sides (2)	¾" x 2¹³⁄₁₆" x 26⅞"
4 End Aprons (2)	¾" x 4½" x 23⁹⁄₁₆"		13 Compartment Sides (2)	¾" x 2⁹⁄₁₆" x 18⁵⁄₁₆"
5 Apron Dividers (2)	¾" x 4½" x 25¾"		14 Compartment Top (1)	¼" x 4¾" 19¹⁄₁₆"
6 Drawer Supports (2)	¾" x 2⁵⁄₁₆" x 25¾"		15 Drawer Bottom (1)	¼" x 18¾" x 26¼"
7 Corner Braces (4)	Steel		16 Knobs (2)	Beech, 1½" Diameter
8 Corner Brace Bolts (4)	Hanger Bolts		17 Low-Friction Tape (1)	Nylo-Tape ½" x 10'
9 Corner Brace Wing Nuts (4)	Steel		18 Glides (4)	Nickel, 1¹⁄₁₆" Diameter

*Quick*Tip

Ultimate Sanding Block

How can anything as basic as a sanding block be improved? Easily. Saw a ⅜" slot in one face, about ¾" from the side. Insert one edge of the sandpaper into the slot and wrap it around the block. Just your grip on the block will now keep the paper secure. Keep several sanding blocks on hand, some with square edges, others rounded to different radii. Depending on your application, it helps to have some sanding blocks made of hardwood, such as maple, and softer ones made of pine or poplar.

Figure 2: *The legs are secured to the aprons with mortise and tenon joinery that's reinforced by metal corner braces.*

Figure 3: *Specialty hardware is the key to quick assembly on this project. Tabletop fasteners hold the top securely to the base.*

drawer supports through pre-drilled holes. Attach them at the drawer openings (see the Drawings) using glue and 6d finish nails.

After setting the nail heads and filling them, refer to the sidebar on page 5 for guidelines on making the butcher block. When the top is ready, lay it face-down and center the legset on it, as shown in Figure 3, above. Attach the top with metal fasteners (pieces 10) designed to allow for any expansion and contraction that may occur in the glued-up top.

Building a Drawer with a Secret Compartment

Cut the drawer fronts (piece 11) from solid maple to match the tabletop. Both the drawer sides (pieces 12) and the compartment sides (pieces 13) can be made from less expensive yellow poplar.

With a ¼" dado head in the table saw, cut a rabbet in each drawer front and side (see Drawings) for the bottom. Staying with the dado head, turn your attention to the lock joints that secure the drawer sides to the fronts. I suggest trying out a test joint in scrap wood before milling the actual

*Quick*Tip

Sawing Thin Wood Safely

Cutting thin pieces on the table saw without some type of hold-down is dangerous. Here's a safe method to follow. First, lower the saw blade and install a zero-clearance insert. Next, position your thin stock over the blade, place the L-shaped hold-down on top of the stock and clamp it in place, as shown in the sketch. Then remove the veneer, turn on the saw, and raise the blade until you hear it just touch the hold-down. Back the blade down a bit and you're ready to begin feeding your thin stock through the blade.

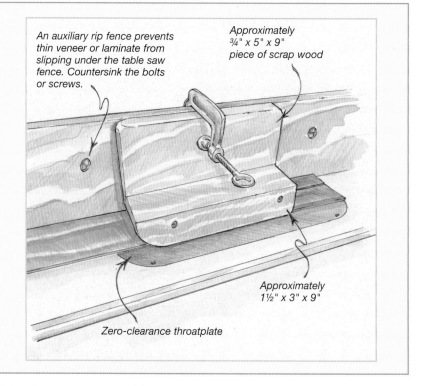

An auxiliary rip fence prevents thin veneer or laminate from slipping under the table saw fence. Countersink the bolts or screws.

Approximately ¾" x 5" x 9" piece of scrap wood

Approximately 1½" x 3" x 9"

Zero-clearance throatplate

Figure 4: *The center drawer slides in both directions and contains a nifty hidden compartment. Center the pulls on each front.*

workpieces, to refine your saw setups. It's also a good idea to use a tenoning jig to make the cuts in the ends of the long stock, and install a zero-clearance insert in your saw before proceeding with the joints.

Begin making the joints by cutting dadoes in the drawer sides (see Step 1 of the Drawer Joinery Detail Drawing on page 7), then cut the deep dadoes across the ends of the drawer fronts (Step 2). Finish up by milling rabbets in the drawer fronts.

Cut the compartment top and the drawer bottom (pieces 14 and 15) from ¼" plywood, then glue the drawer together. Glue and finish-nail the compartment sides in place next, then cut the rabbet around the top of the compartment for the lid (see the Drawings), using a router and a rabbeting bit. Square up the corners with a sharp chisel. Drill a 1⅛" hole in the center of the compartment top to serve as a finger pull, slightly rounding over the edges of the plywood with fine sandpaper.

Install the wooden knobs (pieces 16) on the drawer fronts (see Figure 4) before applying friction-reducing tape (piece 17) on the drawer supports. Or, wax them instead.

Finishing Up

After installing the glides (piece 18) in the bottom of each leg, remove the tabletop and drawer for finishing. I painted the apron and legs Windsor green after filling all the nail holes and applying a coat of good-quality latex primer. Put a clear, water-resistant finish on both sides of the maple top to enhance the traditional look, and match the drawer front to the top for a visually pleasing contrast with the green base. Then, be sure the person you like to tease sits right in front of the drawer at your next family gathering!

Gluing Up Butcher Block

While buying a glued-up slab of butcher block from a local lumberyard is a good option, it's not as much fun as building your own. If you decide to go this route, some issues to be aware of include moisture content, stock alignment, and the general challenge of surfacing a large glued up piece. Here are some tips to help the process go smoothly.

Use well-cured stock with low moisture readings. When you're ready to glue up the top, use biscuits or splines to help register the lumber, and watch the grain orientation. After the glue up, scrape all excess glue from the piece and belt-sand diagonally in opposite directions to remove material quickly and evenly. Use coarse sandpaper (36-grit) for this task.

Once the glued up panel is flat and even, cut the top to its final size and sand through the grits until it's as smooth as silk. Ease the top edge with a ¼" roundover bit and quickly seal the piece with an equal number of coats of finish on all surfaces. If a glued-up top remains unsealed for an extended period of time, it will start to move. Guaranteed.

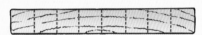

Cut plain-sawn 5/4 stock into little squares to create the right sized pieces for your tabletop.

Then flip each piece to get ready for glue up.

Using biscuits to ensure alignment, glue up the squares to create a top that will resist warping and checking.

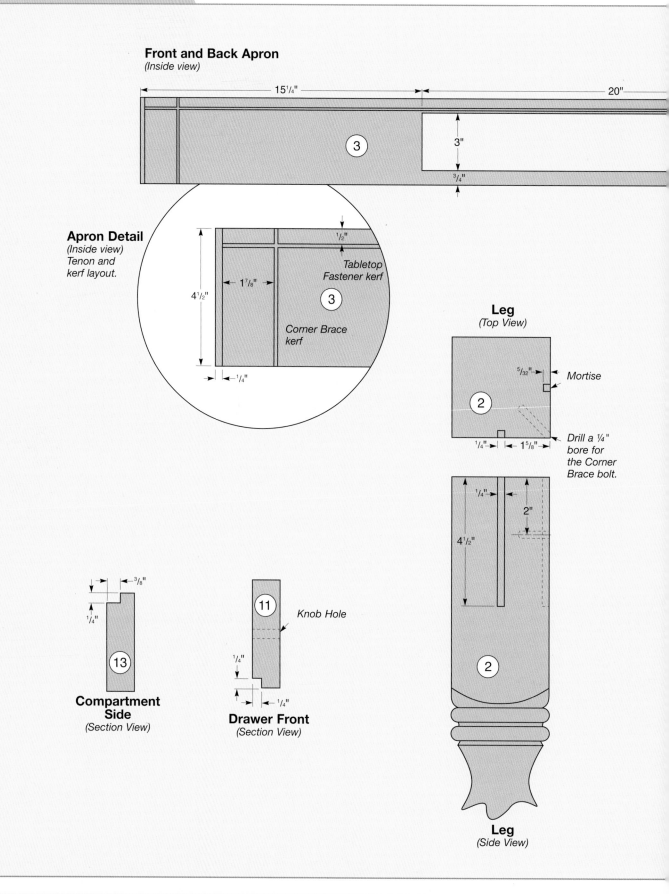

Front and Back Apron
(Inside view)

15¼"

20"

③

3"

¾"

Apron Detail
(Inside view)
*Tenon and
kerf layout.*

½"

*Tabletop
Fastener kerf*

③

1⁷⁄₈"

4½"

*Corner Brace
kerf*

¼"

Leg
(Top View)

⁵⁄₃₂"

Mortise

②

¼" 1⁵⁄₈"

*Drill a ¼"
bore for
the Corner
Brace bolt.*

¼"

2"

4½"

②

³⁄₈"

¼"

⑬

**Compartment
Side**
(Section View)

⑪

Knob Hole

¼"

¼"

Drawer Front
(Section View)

Leg
(Side View)

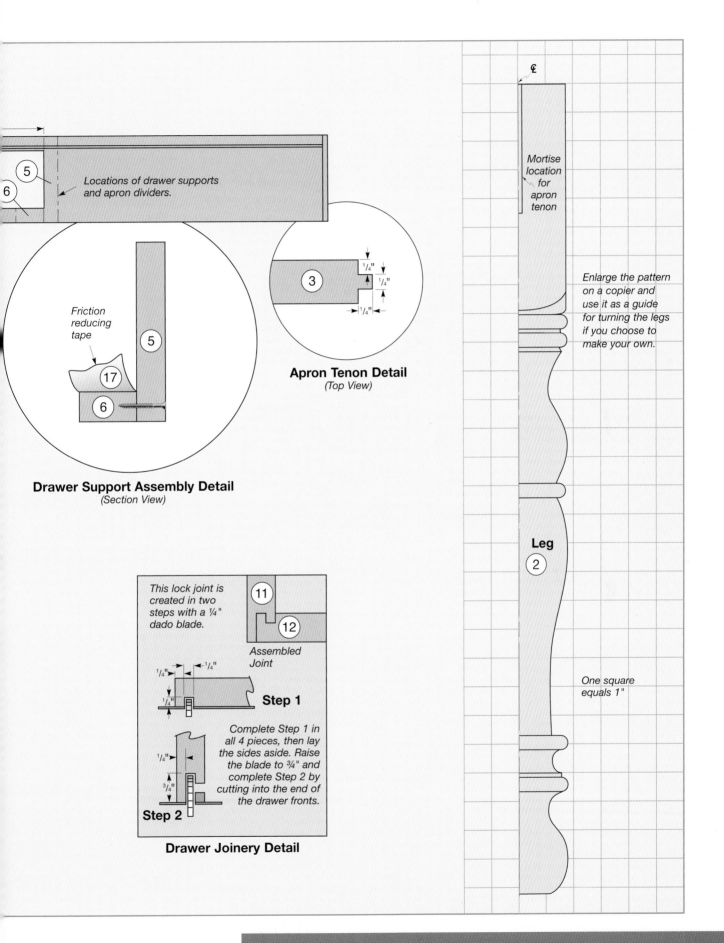

⑤

⑥

Locations of drawer supports
and apron dividers.

Drawer Support Assembly Detail
(Section View)

Friction
reducing
tape

⑤

⑰

⑥

③

¼"

¼"

¼"

Apron Tenon Detail
(Top View)

⊄

Mortise
location
for
apron
tenon

Enlarge the pattern
on a copier and
use it as a guide
for turning the legs
if you choose to
make your own.

Leg
②

One square
equals 1"

This lock joint is
created in two
steps with a ¼"
dado blade.

⑪

⑫

Assembled
Joint

¼"   ¼"

¼"

Step 1

Complete Step 1 in
all 4 pieces, then lay
the sides aside. Raise
the blade to ¾" and
complete Step 2 by
cutting into the end of
the drawer fronts.

¼"

¾"

Step 2

Drawer Joinery Detail

Classic Kitchen Island

Kitchen islands are just wonderful. The Classic Kitchen Island has a counter-height work surface where you can also eat, featuring ample storage as well as being good to look at. The project is reminiscent of an old-fashioned butcher's table, but it's a lot easier to build because the top is a slick, built-up assembly rather than a heavy chunk of hard maple.

by Rick White

Wrap-Around Top

To achieve the butcher block look and strength, I began by cutting two pieces of birch plywood (pieces 1) and glued and screwed them together to form the core. Next, I selected attractively figured hard maple lumber to glue up for the top (piece 2). Even though I purchased ¾"

S-4-S lumber, I still took the time to make sure the edges were dead straight with a pass on the jointer. After gluing up the top, I took it to a cabinet shop to have it sanded smooth and flat on a wide belt sander. You can flatten it yourself with a plane or hand-held belt sander…but I was in a hurry.

Once the top is flat, smooth and trimmed to size, glue the top edges (pieces 3), which provide an illusion of thickness, in place. Add to the illusion by making the end caps (pieces 4). Cut them to size and then plow a stopped groove on their inside faces (as shown in the

Top Exploded View on page 11). Slice biscuit slots into the top to match the grooves you just plowed. The biscuits must not stick out farther than the depth of the endcap grooves, or you'll have a big problem. Glue the biscuits in place, and make sure there are no excess glue drops to harden and get in the way. Put the top onto the plywood core: there needs to be a gap of at least ³⁄₁₆" between the core and the sides of the top, but the biscuited ends of the top must match the core exactly. Put the endcaps onto the top with the biscuits nestled in their grooves. Do not glue the piece on. Drill counterbored screw holes through the endcaps and screw them to the core. That will allow the laminated top to expand and contract with seasonal humidity without fracturing. Plug the screw holes, sand the top smooth, and set it aside for a bit.

The legs are a glued-up hollow construction. Because the plan was to paint the base, we used yellow poplar, a stable wood that accepts paint well.

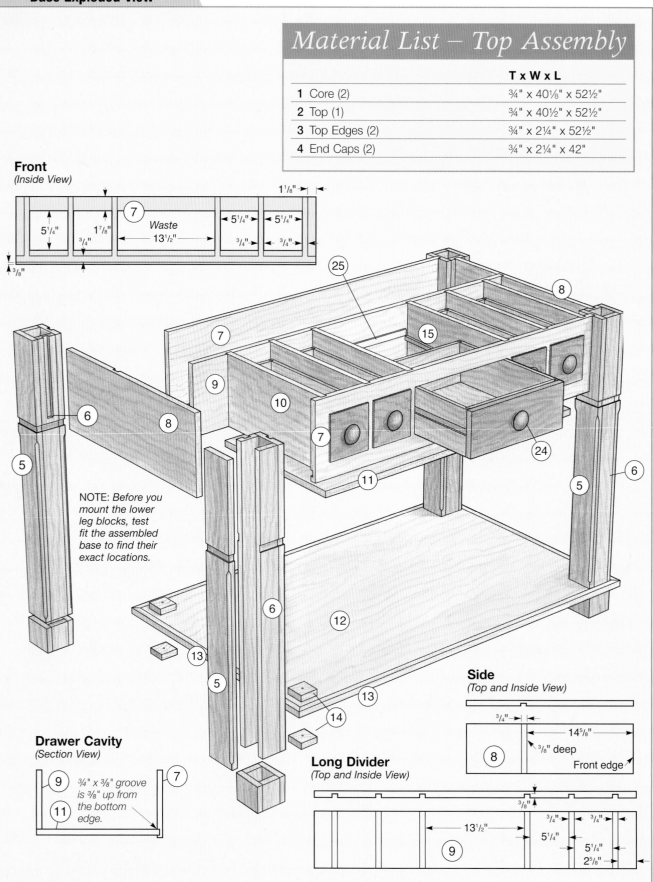

Material List – Top Assembly

		T x W x L
1	Core (2)	¾" x 40⅛" x 52½"
2	Top (1)	¾" x 40½" x 52½"
3	Top Edges (2)	¾" x 2¼" x 52½"
4	End Caps (2)	¾" x 2¼" x 42"

Front
(Inside View)

1⅛"

5¼" 1⅞" ⑦ Waste 13½" 5¼" 5¼"

¾" ¾" ¾"

³⁄₈"

NOTE: *Before you mount the lower leg blocks, test fit the assembled base to find their exact locations.*

Drawer Cavity
(Section View)

⑨ ¾" x ⅜" groove is ⅜" up from the bottom edge.

⑪ ⑦

Long Divider
(Top and Inside View)

⑨ 13½" ¾" ¾" 5¼" 5¼" 2⅝"

³⁄₈"

Side
(Top and Inside View)

¾" 14⅝" ⑧ ⅜" deep Front edge

³⁄₈"

The Basic Base

There is nothing tricky about constructing the base unit. Begin by creating the legs from the staves and fillers (pieces 5 and 6). Cut them to size, then glue and clamp together. The hollow construction will come in handy later. Once the glue has cured, sand them smooth and trim them exactly to length on the table saw. Go ahead and cut off the feet, and set them aside. Use the table saw to reveal the little decorative dado around the barrel of the leg. (See the Base Exploded View for details.) Use a router in a router table to plow the grooves into the upper faces of the legs. Square up the ends of the grooves so they are ready for the front, back and sides (pieces 7 and 8). Finally, use your router and a large chamfering bit to form the decorative leg bevels.

Cut the remaining sheet stock parts (pieces 9, 10, 11, and 12) to size. There are a number of dadoes and grooves to be cut into these pieces. Form them all on the table saw with a dado head installed. Again, the Exploded Views will specify the details.

Cut openings for the drawers in the face of the front after you form the dadoes and groove in its back face. Miter the shelf trim (piece 13) around the shelf (glue and finish nail it securely), and cut the leg blocks (pieces 14) and drawer slides (pieces 15) to size, but set them aside for the time being.

Now it's time to assemble the base. I glued and clamped it together on my work table with the legs pointed up in the air. That helped me align the upper edges of all the dividers, front, back, and sides, evenly. If you plan to paint the unit as I did, a finish nail here and there is no cause for worry. You might want to hold off on attaching the feet until you get it into your kitchen: that way it will clear a 30" door. I learned the hard way! Once the glue has cured, go ahead and glue the drawer slides in place to complete the

Material List – Base Assembly

		T x W x L
5	Leg Staves (8)	¾" x 3¾" x 33"
6	Leg Fillers (8)	¾" x 2¼" x 33"
7	Front and Back (2)	¾" x 9" x 41¼"
8	Sides (2)	¾" x 9" x 23¼"
9	Long Divider (1)	¾" x 7⅞" x 44¼"
10	Short Dividers (6)	¾" x 8¼" x 16½"
11	Bottom (1)	¾" x 16⅞" x 39"
12	Shelf (1)	¾" x 30" x 48"
13	Shelf Trim (1)	¾" x ¾" x 170"
14	Leg Blocks (12)	¾" x 2¼" x 2¼"
15	Drawer Slides (10)	⅜" x ¾" x 16½"

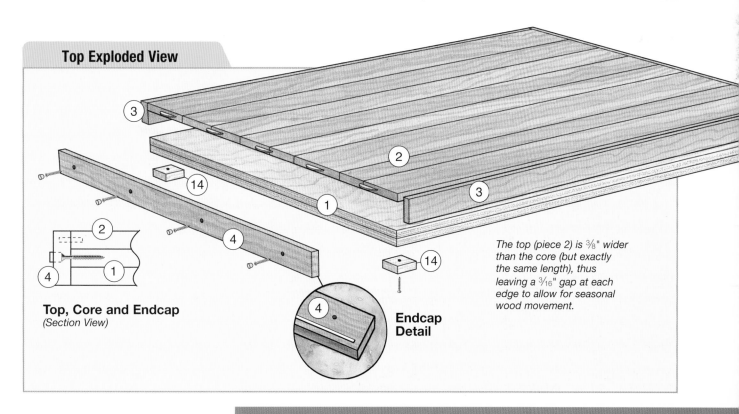

Top Exploded View

Top, Core and Endcap
(Section View)

Endcap Detail

The top (piece 2) is ⅜" wider than the core (but exactly the same length), thus leaving a ³⁄₁₆" gap at each edge to allow for seasonal wood movement.

Drawer Exploded View

Drawer Slide Locations

The ¾" grooves for the slides are ³⁄₁₆" deep, centered on the drawers and dividers.

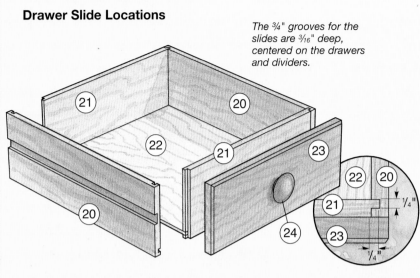

Material List – Drawers

		T x W x L
16	Drawer Sides (8)	½" x 5¼" x 15¾"
17	Drawer Fronts and Backs (8)	½" x 5¼" x 4¾"
18	Drawer Bottoms (4)	¼" x 4¾" x 15¼"
19	Drawer Faces (4)	¾" x 5¼" x 5¼"
20	Large Drawer Sides (2)	½" x 5¼" x 15¾"
21	Large Drawer Front and Back (2)	½" x 5¼" x 13¼"
22	Large Drawer Bottom (1)	¼" x 13½" x 15¼"
23	Large Drawer Face (1)	¾" x 5¼" x 13½"
24	Drawer Pulls (5)	2" Diameter
25	Spacers (5)	Trim to fit
26	Baskets (2)	Wicker, optional

Figure 2: *If you choose to use hanging wicker baskets, you may need to re-machine their hangers to match the inset drawing at right.*

Remove

Leg Block Locations
(Bottom View, Core)

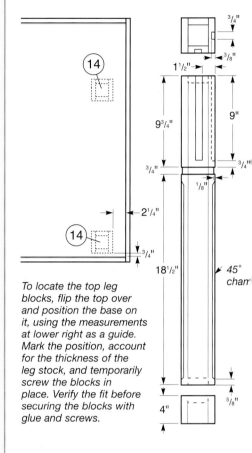

To locate the top leg blocks, flip the top over and position the base on it, using the measurements at lower right as a guide. Mark the position, account for the thickness of the leg stock, and temporarily screw the blocks in place. Verify the fit before securing the blocks with glue and screws.

base assembly.

The Drawers and Last Details

The simple corner joints on the drawers call for a bit of production woodworking. I machined all of the drawer parts (pieces 16 through 23) at once and took advantage of each setup on the table saw to do all similar pieces at the same time. Dry-fit the drawers to test their joinery and to see how they fit into the base. When you're satisfied, glue and clamp them up. Mount the drawer pulls (pieces 24) to the drawer faces before you mount the faces to the drawers with screws.

With drawer construction behind you,

sand them smooth and put two coats of clear finish on the drawers, inside and out.

Finishing Up

Use the drawer spacers (pieces 25) to adjust the drawer registration. I painted the base unit with white oil-based enamel so it would be easy to clean. As for the top, sand it to 600-grit, raise the grain with water and sand again with 600. Follow with several coats of butcher block oil.

Move the island to where you want to use it before you attach the top and feet (see notes on Leg Block drawing). Apply construction adhesive around the top of the legs to secure the top.

Add some sliding baskets to store spuds and onions down below, if you like. With that done, the only thing left is to screw the legs to the floor and get ready to start cooking. The project will delight your guests, no matter how good a chef you are.

Figure 4: *Form the island's feet by cutting them off the glued-up legs. Most of the machining on this project can be completed on a good table saw.*

Figure 3: *Before laminating the top, establish straight, square edges by jointing the hard maple stock.*

QuickTip

Table Saw Extension

After many years of using a radial arm saw, one reader wrote in to tell us the immediate weakness of table saws when he finally bought one: whatever he sawed went off the end of the table onto the floor. His answer was to make a sliding 24" x 24" plywood extension table attached to square aluminum tubing, as shown in the sketch here. When it's not in use, the outfeed table slides out of its telescopic tubes, and can be hung on a wall. For sawing heavy or extra-long stock, you may need to put a support under the table to prevent the tubing from bending. For greater rigidity, buy thicker-walled aluminum tubing, or switch to steel tubing instead.

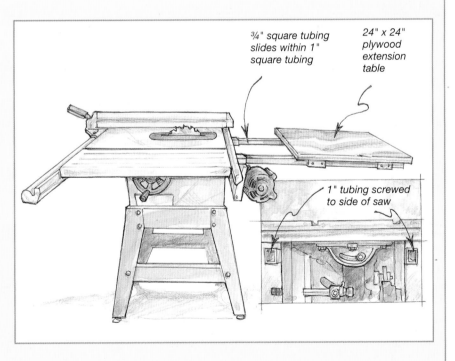

¾" square tubing slides within 1" square tubing

24" x 24" plywood extension table

1" tubing screwed to side of saw

Rock-Solid Trestle Table

My client wanted me to replace the family's three-generations-old dining room table. His requirements included doing something about the low, shin-banger beam that held the old table together. He also wanted it to knock down to clear the room for dancing.

by John English

The Rock-Solid Trestle Table incorporates several design elements the original lacked. It had to be large enough to seat six comfortably—eight in a pinch. The client also wanted a table that would come apart and go back together easily (because the dining room doubles as a dance floor on Thursday nights).

The client, Roger, wasn't ready to move away from the solid-oak trestle style to which he was so accustomed, but his wife Joan wanted a top that wouldn't feature crumb catchers and a slightly fancier look. Of course, both wanted to keep the cost way down. This last directive probably sounds familiar if you've ever built a project for a client!

The first thing I recommended was breadboard ends, for two reasons. First, the breadboard ends add a few inches of depth to the ends of the tables— additional leg clearance for anyone seated there—but more important, breadboard ends allow the legs to be moved further in without risking cupping at the ends. To address Joan's concern, they (along with a little extra router work) tend to upscale the overall appearance. I also kept the costs down by specifying readily available, ¾"-thick hardwood stock. If there's a lumberyard of any consequence near you, finding material for the table should pose no difficulties.

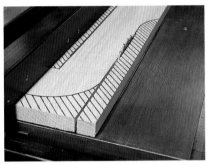

Figure 1: *Use your table saw to make the straight cuts in the feet, then switch to the band saw to complete the curved cuts.*

Figure 2: *A spacer clamped to the fence lines up the legs for tenoning and prevents binding by keeping the work away from the fence.*

Starting with the Feet

When it came to the large mortises in the feet, the decision to build with ¾"-thick stock made for easier work. The feet consist of three thicknesses of wood face-glued together, so making the large bottom mortises meant simply leaving a hole in the middle of each foot, as shown in the Foot Mortise and Leg Tenon Detail on page 19.

Start building the feet by cutting six laminations (pieces 1) to shape. Make the straight cuts on your table saw, as shown in Figure 1, then finish up each cut by band-sawing the curves to shape.

After the laminations have been cut to shape, remove the center sections of two of them (see Lamination Templates). The instant mortises will be a bit wider than the leg tenons, which allows the laminated legs to shrink and expand with seasonal changes in humidity.

Glue and clamp the feet together, making sure the ends and the top edges are flush as you tighten your clamps. When the glue is dry, scrape off any excess before jointing the top and bottom edges and drum-sanding the curved areas. Then run a bearing-guided chamfering bit along the top edge of each foot.

Making the Tenoned Legs

Each of the legs (pieces 2) is made from a pair of face-glued boards, edged with a custom molding. After cutting and jointing the boards to size, glue and clamp the bark sides together, as discussed in Lamination Templates on page 21. After the glue sets, joint the edges before rounding over the vertical edges of each leg with a ¼"-radius roundover bit.

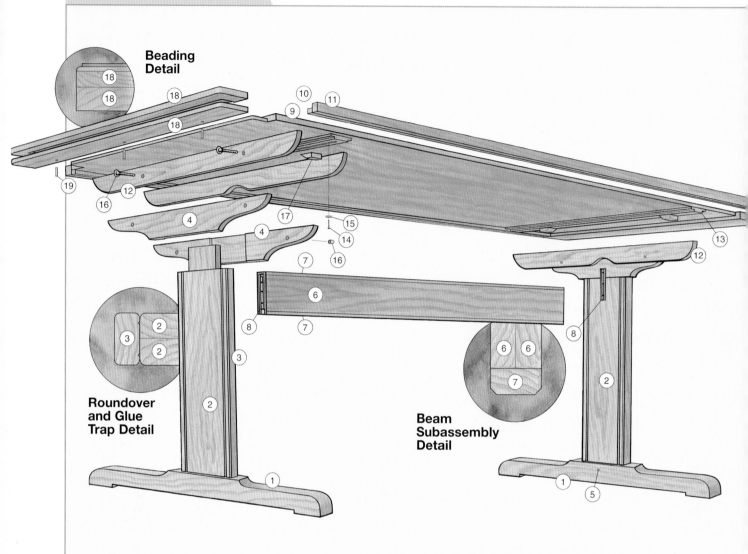

Beading Detail

Roundover and Glue Trap Detail

Beam Subassembly Detail

Material List

	T x W x L			T x W x L
1 Feet Laminations (6)	¾" x 4" x 38"		**11** Tabletop Moldings (2)	¾" x 1½" x 68⅞"
2 Leg Laminations (4)	¾" x 8½" x 26¾"		**12** Support Bracket Sides (4)	¾" x 3" x 38 ¼"
3 Leg Moldings (4)	¾" x 1½" x 18½"		**13** Support Bracket Bases (2)	¾" x 3⅜" x 38¼"
4 Tabletop Support Laminations (4)	¾" x 4⅞" x 24"		**14** Support Bracket Screws (20)	#6 x 1⅛"
5 Leg Dowels (2)	⅜" Diameter x 1¼"		**15** Support Bracket Washers (20)	Countersunk
6 Beam Laminations (2)	¾" x 5½" x 43⅜"		**16** Swivel Mirror Screws (4)	⅜" Brass
7 Beam Moldings (2)	¾" x 1½" x 43⅜"		(with threaded inserts)	
8 Tapered KD Fittings (2)	6" Steel		**17** Alignment Blocks (4)	¾" x 1½" x 2"
9 Tabletop (1)	¾" x 40" x 74⅞"		**18** Endcap Laminations (4)	¾" x 5⅞" x 41¾"
(includes tongues)			**19** Endcap Dowels (6)	⅜" Diameter x 1¼"
10 Tabletop Cleats (2)	¾" x ¾" x 68⅞"			

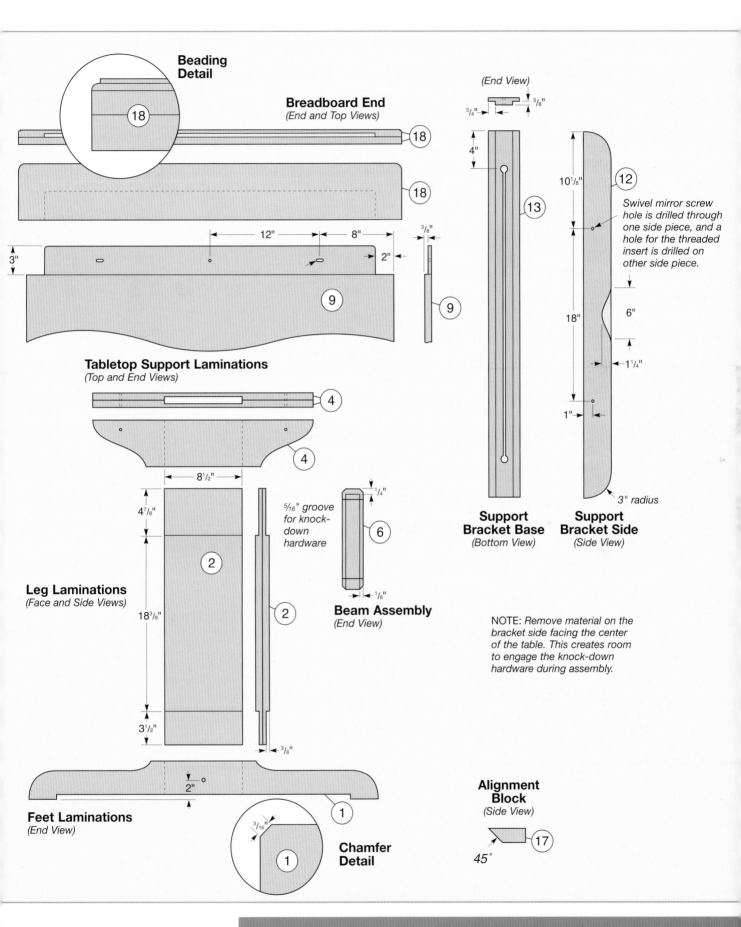

Beading Detail

(18)

Breadboard End
(End and Top Views)

18

18

(End View)

³/₄" ⊢ ↔ ⊣ ³/₈"

4"

13

10¹/₈"

12

3"

12" 8" ³/₈"

2"

9

9

Swivel mirror screw hole is drilled through one side piece, and a hole for the threaded insert is drilled on other side piece.

18"

6"

1¹/₄"

Tabletop Support Laminations
(Top and End Views)

4

4

8¹/₂"

1"

3" radius

Support Bracket Base
(Bottom View)

Support Bracket Side
(Side View)

4⁷/₈"

2

⁵/₁₆" *groove for knock-down hardware*

¹/₄"

6

2

Beam Assembly
(End View)

¹/₈"

NOTE: *Remove material on the bracket side facing the center of the table. This creates room to engage the knock-down hardware during assembly.*

Leg Laminations
(Face and Side Views)

18³/₈"

3¹/₂"

³/₈"

2"

1

Feet Laminations
(End View)

³/₁₆"

1

Chamfer Detail

Alignment Block
(Side View)

45°

17

Figure 3: *After rounding over all four long edges of the leg moldings, create two V-shaped glue control grooves in each back face.*

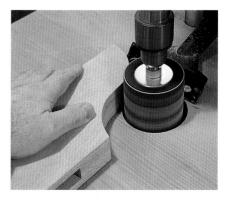

Figure 4: *After cutting the glued-up tabletop supports to shape, drum-sand the curved edges smooth and even.*

Now lay out the tenons on the ends of the legs (the top and bottom are different thicknesses). Cut them with a dado head, using your table saw's miter gauge and a spacer block (see Figure 2).

Rip and joint the leg moldings (pieces 3) to dimension, then use the same roundover bit you used on the legs to shape all four of its long edges. Stay at the router table a minute longer to mill two glue traps in the back face of each piece of molding (see Figure 3), using the tip of a V-groove bit.

Forming the Tabletop Supports

While the table's feet are three laminations thick, there is no structural or aesthetic reason for such a large build-up in the tabletop supports. To save time and materials, Rick went with just two laminations here.

Creating the tenons in the supports is a simple matter of cutting a ⅜"-deep dado in each lamination (piece 4), then gluing two pairs together. Use the same table saw technique you used for the leg tenons to create these dadoes. Dry-fit them to the legs as you go, to ensure a correct fit.

Enlarge and transfer the templates to each support lamination, then band-saw all of them to shape. Do so after cutting the dadoes, because this step is more forgiving—a slip here is easier to repair than a crooked mortise.

Glue and clamp the two sets of support laminations together in the correct orientation. After the glue dries, use your drum sander to remove the band saw marks, as shown in Figure 4.

Assembling the Legs

Dry-fit the leg tenons in the feet and tabletop support mortises. The fit should be snug on the wide faces and leave a ¹⁄₁₆" gap at either end to allow for movement (see Figure 5). When you're satisfied with the fit, glue the feet to the legs.

While the glue is wet, lock each tenon into its mortise with a ⅜"-diameter dowel (piece 5: See Lamination Templates, page 21, for hole and dowel locations). Each dowel should penetrate the inside foot lamination as well as the leg tenon laminations.

Before gluing the tabletop supports in place, trim the moldings to length. Glue and clamp them in place, keeping the glue between the traps you milled earlier. When the glue is dry, install the tabletop supports with glue and clamps.

Milling the Beam

The beam on the table is located high enough to avoid even the tallest diner's ankles. It is made from two face-glued laminations (pieces 6) edged with square moldings (pieces 7). Glue and clamp all four elements together. After the glue dries, ease the long edges with your chamfering bit.

Stay with the router to cut mortises in the ends of the beam for the tapered steel knock-down fittings (pieces 8) that hold the beam to the legs. Use a bearing-guided rabbeting bit to make the

Grain Orientation in Face-glued Boards

Through the ages, countless woodshop students have discovered, (often to their dismay), that wood retains a tendency to curl away from the center of the tree.

Christian Becksvoort explained it best in his excellent book, *In Harmony with Wood*: "On a plain sawn board, [cupping] is usually manifested in the concave surface forming away from the tree."

So, to put it simply, gluing the bark sides together, as shown here, will decrease the chance the edges will peel apart later. For rift- or quartersawn lumber, grain orientation is less of an issue for face-gluing because the growth rings run nearly perpendicular to the board faces.

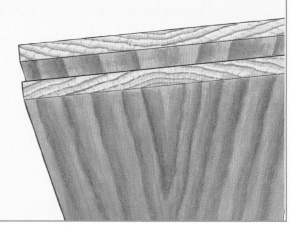

mortises, as shown in Figure 6. Take their dimensions from the actual hardware you purchase. To center the tapers in the mortises, I have found pairs of thin drill bits made perfect spacers (Figure 6, inset) while predrilling for the screw holes.

Making the Tabletop

While veneered plywood is one choice for the tabletop (piece 9), my clients opted for traditional solid oak. For a stable top, alternate the end grain of each board—but don't get religious about it. There's nothing sadder than an exquisite face of a board staring at the floor for a couple of generations because someone got carried away on a simple rule of thumb. After the glue has dried, scrape the excess and sand thoroughly. Use a straightedge and a straight bit in your router to trim the tabletop to its exact width and length, making each cut in several passes. To minimize tearout, use a fresh straight or spiral carbide bit.

Stay with your straightedge and router to cut the ⅜"-thick tenons on the ends of the tabletop. Remove 2" from the end of each tenon with your jigsaw, and smooth any tearout with a file.

Build up the tabletop's edges by gluing and clamping ¾"-square cleats (pieces 10) along each long edge. While the glue dries, use a beading bit to form the edge of the moldings (pieces 11). Glue and clamp the moldings in place, and, when the glue dries, scrape off the excess and belt-sand them flush. Before you leave the tabletop, sand a ⅜" radius on each of the four tenon corners.

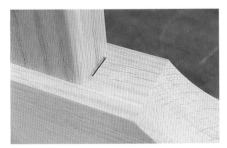

Figure 5: *Leave ¹⁄₁₆" play on either side of the legs when you glue them into their mortises, to allow for wood movement. Leg moldings will eventually cover these gaps.*

Forming the Tabletop Cleats

Use a pair of U-shaped support brackets to lock the top to the legsets. Each bracket is made up of two sides (pieces 12) and a base (pieces 13). Following the dimensions shown in the drawings, use a dado head in your table saw to create rabbets on the long edges of each base (see Figure 7).

Band saw and sand the ends of the support bracket sides to the shape shown in the drawings, then glue and clamp the brackets together. Drill a ¾" hole 4" from the ends of each bracket base, then chuck a ¼" straight bit in your router to cut a groove between the holes (see Figure 8). The large holes at the ends of the grooves will stop the base pieces from splitting.

Assemble the legs and beam and center them on the upturned top. Mark the locations of the legs, making sure they are perpendicular to the edges of the tabletop and remove the legset. Use your marks to locate the support brackets, then predrill for ten screws (pieces 14) in each bracket base. Use washers (pieces 15) to seat the screws along the groove: the washers will accommodate expansion and contraction of the 40"-wide top through the seasons.

Replace the legset, this time seating it upside down in the support brackets and centering it side to side. Drill two holes (see Lamination Templates) in each of the outside support bracket sides, continuing through the tabletop supports (don't go all the way through the inside support brackets). Remove the legsets and enlarge the holes in them—but not in the brackets—to receive the threaded

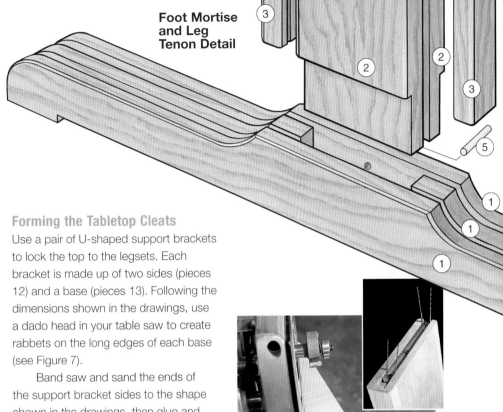

Figure 6: *Use a bearing-guided rabbeting bit to cut mortises for the steel tapers. Pairs of matched drill bits help center the tapers while you predrill for their screws.*

inserts that come with the swivel mirror screws (pieces 16). Screw the inserts home and tighten everything up with the swivel mirror screws. At this point, you can add the optional alignment blocks (pieces 17). They're handy for quickly lining things up if you'll be knocking down the table often. All that really remains now is the breadboard ends, and those are described on the next page.

Figure 7: *Use a dado head in your table saw to cut rabbets in the support bracket bases. Two support bracket sides will fit into the rabbets.*

Finishing Up

My clients wanted a clear finish that would showcase the white oak and still be impervious to spills, dropped silverware, and other dining room hazards. In the end it came down to

Figure 8: *Create the screw slots in the cleat bases in several passes, raising the ¼" bit ⅛" with each pass.*

satin polyurethane or Danish oil. While everyone loved the look and feel of the oil, I still advised the poly for its harder finish and greater durability.

I applied five coats of finish to the top and three to the legset. The top's underside received two coats—it's always smart to coat both faces of a top to keep moisture moving in and out of both faces evenly. First coats of finish on all the surfaces were cut with 25% thinner to act as a sanding sealer, and all but the topcoat were steel-wooled between applications. The end result was a smooth low-luster finish that was exactly what the clients were looking for: A classic piece of furniture completely at home in a 100-year-old rural farmhouse.

Figure 9: *This sturdy trestle table is ready to knockdown in minutes: it comes apart and sets up without tools.*

An Easy Approach To Building Breadboard Ends

Breadboard ends are caps employing grain running perpendicular to a tabletop. The warp-fighting joint typically features a mortise slightly wider than its tenon to accommodate wood movement. Start by laying out the ⅜"-deep mortises, and remove the waste with a straight bit chucked in your router. Clamp the two laminations (pieces 18) together, and dry-fit them to a tenon. When you've got a good fit, glue the laminations together. Be sure the mortises are perfectly aligned. After the glue dries, joint both long edges before sanding a ¾" radius on the outside corners of each endcap. The endcaps are intentionally ¼" longer than the tabletop is wide, to allow for expansion in the top. Shape the top outside edge of each breadboard end with the same beading bit you used on the tabletop edge molding. Then slide the ends onto the tabletop tenons and drill three ¼" holes up from the bottom, at the locations shown on the Pinup Shop Drawings. Remove the endcaps and elongate the two outside holes in each tenon, as shown here. Reinstall the ends and secure them by gluing the three dowels (pieces 19) in place. The slotted holes allow the tenons to move a little inside the endcaps' mortises.

Remove the endcaps and elongate the two outside holes in each tenon.

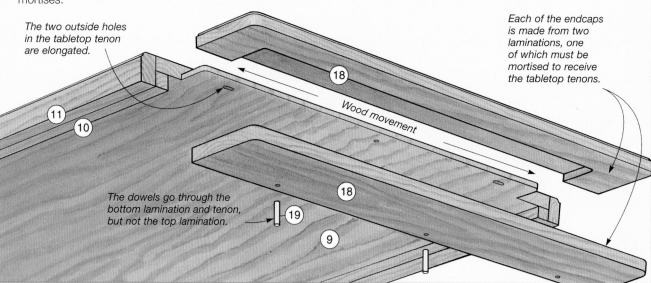

The two outside holes in the tabletop tenon are elongated.

Each of the endcaps is made from two laminations, one of which must be mortised to receive the tabletop tenons.

Wood movement

The dowels go through the bottom lamination and tenon, but not the top lamination.

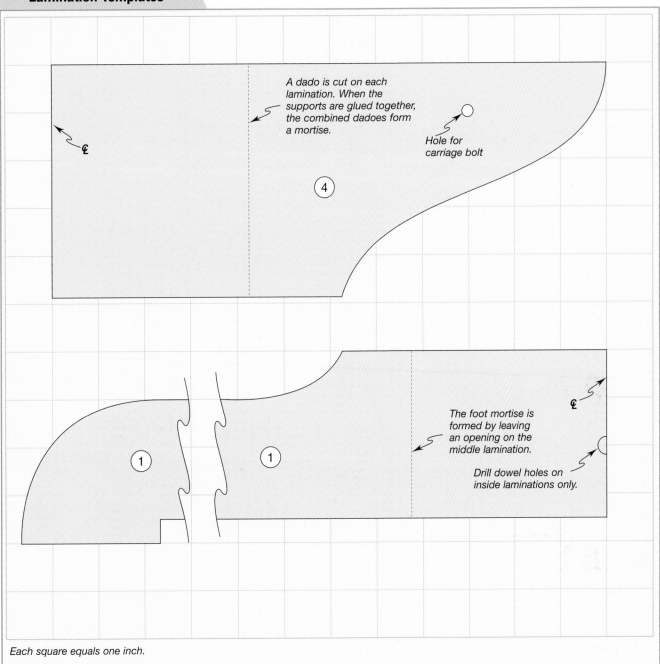

A dado is cut on each lamination. When the supports are glued together, the combined dadoes form a mortise.

Hole for carriage bolt

℄

4

1

1

℄

The foot mortise is formed by leaving an opening on the middle lamination.

Drill dowel holes on inside laminations only.

Each square equals one inch.

*Quick*Tip

End Caps Keep Panels from Buckling

Here's a way to keep solid-wood panels from buckling when they're edge-glued and clamped. Make custom end caps by plowing grooves the same dimension as the panel stock in a couple of 2 x 4s. Apply a strip of tape in each groove or use paste wax to prevent any glue squeeze-out from bonding the caps to the panel. Then, fit the end caps over the panel ends to keep everything lined up.

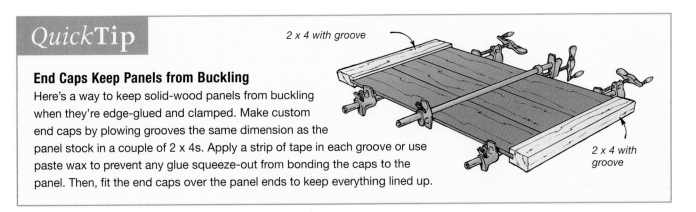

2 x 4 with groove

2 x 4 with groove

Drop-Leaf Table

This past summer I attended the Kelly Mehler School of Woodworking in Berea, Kentucky. The project my six classmates and I tackled was a Shaker-inspired Drop-leaf Table. Under Kelly's watchful eye, we milled, machined, and dry-fitted our tables together. It was a wonderful week of woodworking that taught us some subtleties of the craft.

by LiLi Jackson

A room really starts to come together when the furniture you've built for it matches. I recently built a Shaker-style pencil post bed out of cherry. At Kelly Mehler's School of Woodworking, I was about to tackle a Shaker drop leaf table. The expanse of flat surfaces on the table makes it the perfect project for showing off the beauty of your chosen wood.

Digging through Kelly's collection of cherry, I found some excellent stock for my table, particularly a 17"-wide board I quickly grabbed for the top. Likewise, a couple of highly figured 8"-wide boards were laid aside for my leaves. You might not be so lucky in your lumber search but remember, the success of a project like this is really tied to the beauty of your stock.

Start Your Milling and Machining

Once you have harvested your stock and given it a couple of days to acclimate to your shop environs, it's time to mill everything to overall size and begin machining your pieces. I started with the apron subassembly, which includes the side and back aprons (pieces 1 and 2), the upper and lower rails (pieces 3 and 4), the leaf supports and their stops (piece 5 and 6) and the leaf support track and its guides (pieces 7 and 8). You'll also need to cut the legs (pieces 9) to size, but hold off on tapering them until you've completed their mortises. Dimensions for all of these pieces are provided in the Material List (see page 25), while the Technical Drawings on the next page provide all the essential location and joinery details.

Kelly taught me a trick to help with lumber warping called "sticking." When I wasn't working with a piece, he had me sandwich it between long squared sticks with a heavy piece of lumber on top. Sticking allows the wood to breathe, while keeping it straight from the pressure on top. Sticking has seriously alleviated shop stress—I no longer come in the next morning and find the shop gremlin has magically warped my wood.

Start your machining by forming the tenons on the aprons and rails and the matching mortises in the legs (see photos, page 24). While you're handling the aprons and rails you may as well rout the ½"-deep mortises to accept the tabletop buttons. I put three along each side and two at each end. The final machining on the subassembly is to form the notches for the leaf supports and the mortises for the leaf track. Note: the leaf support openings on the two side aprons are offset— one goes to the left of a centerline, the other to the right, to accommodate the side-by-side sliding supports. Glue the guides to the sides of the track, leaving a ¼" of track sticking out at each end to form a tenon. The guides create a channel to keep the leaf supports in place. Next, glue the stops to the leaf supports. Follow the Technical Drawings on pages 24-25 for their locations. When the glue dries, use a ⅜" core box bit and your router table to shape their ends, as shown in the Drawings. Now you're ready to taper the legs, but before you move on, test all your matching mortises and tenons to ensure they all fit well.

A host of details are hidden until you view the table from the bottom. Leaf supports, guides, tracks and stops, drawer glides, supports and stops, and tabletop buttons all share the hidden space with a large drawer (not shown here).

Figure 1: *A hollow chisel mortiser or a drill-press mortising attachment allows you to chop a very clean and accurate square-ended mortise.*

Figure 2: *Saw the tenon shoulders using a crosscut box on the table saw, then clamp the parts in a tenoning jig to saw the cheeks.*

Figure 3: *Assemble the side aprons with their pairs of legs, then glue and clamp the rails in place to complete the base subassembly.*

Figure 4: *The base comes together nicely after the two side aprons and legs are glued up.*

Tapering the Legs

As you can see in Figure 3, I used a simple tapering jig on the table saw to taper the two inside aspects of each leg, starting 6½" from the top and cutting at an angle designed to leave the ends of the legs exactly 1" square. If your jig is like mine, you'll want to save your taper cutoff from the first cut to slip under the lower toggle clamp for your second cut (otherwise you have to reset the toggle nut with each cut, which is a pain). Work through the four legs, making sure to taper the two sides with the mortises.

Now you're ready for the first subassembly. First, glue and clamp each side apron to two legs, using a large square to keep things true. When you've finished, you're ready to glue the back apron and the two rails between the leg subassembly. Don't forget about your leaf support track. It isn't glued in, but it does have to be trapped in place as you bring the pieces together.

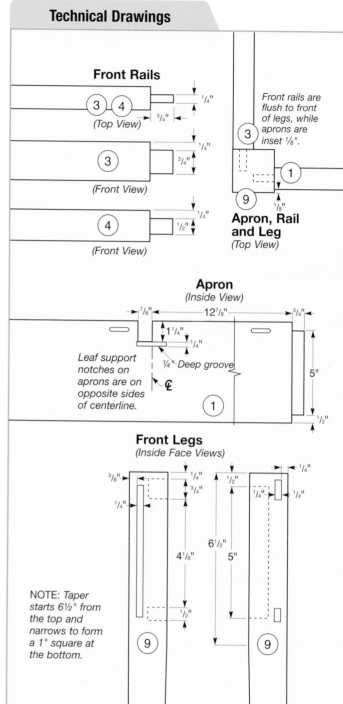

Technical Drawings

Front Rails

(Top View)

(Front View)

(Front View)

Front rails are flush to front of legs, while aprons are inset ⅛".

Apron, Rail and Leg
(Top View)

Apron
(Inside View)

Leaf support notches on aprons are on opposite sides of centerline.

¼" Deep groove

Front Legs
(Inside Face Views)

NOTE: Taper starts 6½" from the top and narrows to form a 1" square at the bottom.

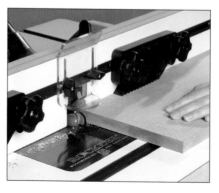

Figure 5: *If your router is variable-speed, slow it down when you tackle the cove cut for the rule joint. And, take a few passes or you'll suffer tearout at the worst possible spot.*

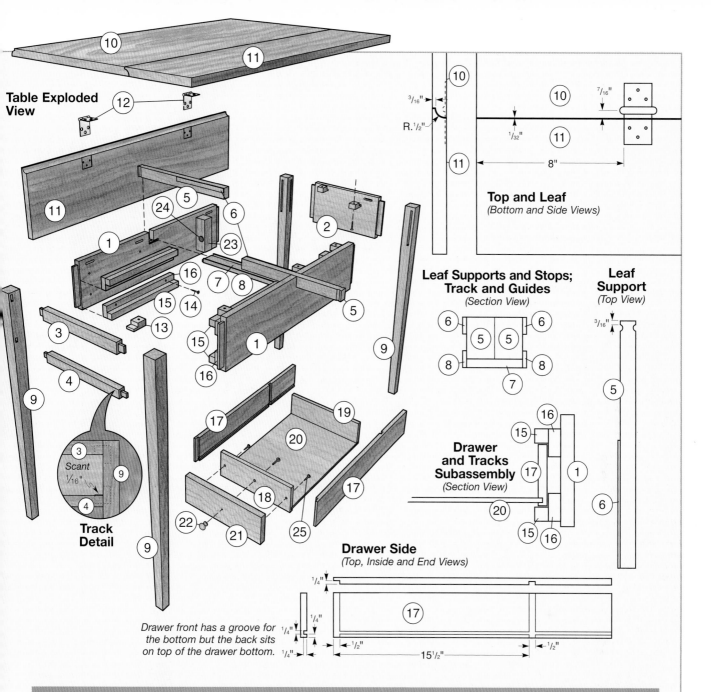

Table Exploded View

Top and Leaf
(Bottom and Side Views)

R.¹/₂"
³/₁₆"
¹/₃₂"
⁷/₁₆"
8"

Leaf Supports and Stops; Track and Guides
(Section View)

Leaf Support
(Top View)

³/₁₆"

Track Detail

Scant ¹/₁₆"

Drawer and Tracks Subassembly
(Section View)

Drawer Side
(Top, Inside and End Views)

¹/₄"
¹/₄"
¹/₄"
¹/₄"
¹/₂"
15¹/₂"
¹/₂"

Drawer front has a groove for the bottom but the back sits on top of the drawer bottom.

Material List – Table & Drawer

Table	T x W x L	Drawer	T x W x L
1 Side Aprons (2)	¾" x 6" x 27¼"	15 Tracks (4)	¾" x ¾" x 11¾"
2 Back Apron (1)	¾" x 6" x 12¼"	16 Guides (4)	¹¹/₁₆" x 1½" x 11¾"
3 Upper Front Rail (1)	¾" x 1¼" x 12¼"	17 Sides (2)	½" x 3⅜" x 22"
4 Lower Front Rail (1)	¾" x 1" x 12¼"	18 Front (1)	½" x 3⅜" x 10⅛"
5 Leaf Supports (2)	⅞" x 1¼" x 13½"	19 Back (1)	½" x 2⅞" x 10⅛"
6 Stops (2)	⅛" x ½" x 7"	20 Bottom (1)	¼" x 15¾" x 10⅛"
7 Track (1)	¼" x 1⅛" x 12½"	21 Face (1)	¾" x 3⅝" x 10⅝"
8 Guides (2)	⅛" x ½" x 12"	22 Knob (1)	¾" Diameter x ¾" brass
9 Legs (4)	1½" x 1½" x 29½"	23 Stops (2)	1½" x 1½" x 4½"
10 Top (1)	¾" x 16½" x 35½"	24 Dots (2)	¾" Diameter felt
11 Leaves (2)	¾" x 7¾" x 35½"	25 Washer Head Screws (2)	#8 x 1"
12 Drop Leaf Hinges (4)	1½" x 3¼"		
13 Tabletop Buttons (10)	⅝" x 1" x 1⅞"		
14 Flathead Screws (18)	#8 x 1¼"		

Figure 6: *Installing the hinges is a four-step process. First, using the locations given on the drawings, rout hinge knuckle grooves.*

Figure 7: *With the spacers in place, screw the hinge temporarily in place and score around it with a knife.*

Figure 8: *Mount a straight bit in your router and remove the waste from the hinge mortises.*

Figure 9: *Clean up to the lines of the mortises using a sharp chisel.*

The Top and the Leaves

Bringing the top (piece 10) and the leaves (pieces 11) together comes next. The first tricky part of the step is forming the rule joint. You will absolutely suffer terrible tearout if you're too aggressive with the cut, so take a few passes for this machining step...and if your router is variable-speed, slow its RPM down a bit as well.

Once the rule joints are made, toss a blanket over your workbench and lay the top on it, upside down. The second tricky part of this step is to rout the hinge knuckle grooves into the underside of the top.

Use the Technical Drawings to locate these grooves and the same ⅜" core box bit you used to shape the ends of the leaf supports. A guide attached to your router base with double-stick tape (Figure 6) will keep you on track. Surface screw the hinges (pieces 12) in place on the top's underside, but before doing the same for the leaves, trap ½₂" spacers between the top and each leaf (see Figure 7), to keep them from binding. With the hinges screwed in place, use a knife to outline their locations, remove them and use a router to create their mortises, to the thickness of the hinge (stay clear of the lines). Clean up to the lines with a sharp chisel, as shown in Figure 9. Now reinstall the hinges and, while the top is still upside down, place your leaf supports and the apron/leg subassembly on it. I use blue painters tape to center the top so it's easy to find the location again in case anything moves.

Turn back to the table saw to make the tabletop buttons (pieces 13). You can see from Figure 10 on page 27, upper left, that it's easiest to take a production approach to these 10 pieces, first forming a rabbet with the table saw, then drilling and countersinking for the screws (pieces 14) and then crosscutting them to size. Carefully place your buttons and predrill into the top. Be careful ... don't go too deep. With all 10 holes drilled, replace the buttons and screw them into place.

Final Building Steps

Hang in there, you're getting close. Pretty soon you'll assemble the drawer, but first create their tracks and guides (pieces 15 and 16). The simple subassemblies are glued together, drilled, and countersunk and then secured against the side aprons. Locate the two bottom track/guides first. One trick I learned is to install the track/guides a scant ¹⁄₁₆" higher than the opening so the drawer doesn't wear out its welcome on the bottom rail. Instead, it will slide back and forth on the track. That's a sweet trick. Finally, you may turn your table upright.

I kept things simple with my drawer (pieces 17-22). Just about everything you need to know for building it is shown in

Figure 10: *Try some simple production line techniques when making items like the tabletop buttons above.*

Figure 11: *Handmade detail makes all the difference, as you can see in these table buttons.*

Figure 12: *Finely detailed leaf supports, though hardly seen, are a delight to touch and operate.*

Figure 13: *Precisely fitted brass hinges add an elegant touch of craftsmanship.*

Figure 14: *Rock solid drawer guides and supports add real value to a simple yet elegant table.*

the Technical Drawings. Form a rabbet at the front of each drawer side, a dado on each side for the back and a groove to capture the bottom. The sides are extra long because I wanted to have a full extension drawer and my extra-long sides leverage against the upper track to prevent the drawer from sagging when it's fully opened. Assemble the drawer by gluing and clamping. Install the brass knob on the face and attach the face to the drawer, using washer head screws. Test the fit and use your hand plane to get the same size gap all the way around the drawer face. Finish installing the drawer by fitting its face perfectly flush to the front rails, and then marking a line at the end of the drawer sides on the inside face of the side aprons (pieces 1). Turn the table back upside down now, and glue two drawer stops with pre-mounted felt dots (pieces 23 and 24), right at your mark. Let the glue dry and retest the drawer's fit. If it's a little proud, you can slightly trim the back ends of the drawer sides with a block plane.

Shellac and Mica Finish

Disassemble everything you can and, after diligently sanding up through the grits, I suggest a few coats of shellac, sanding between every coat to keep things smooth. On my last coat I added some Sepp Mica Powder Inca Gold (www.artistcraftsman.com) to the shellac to create a little sparkle. It's a small thing, but I think everyone should have their own signature finish. I followed the shellac with a few coats of BriWax, which contains bee's wax and carnauba wax. After a few coats, you'll start to get a really nice luster on your table.

Now just kick back and enjoy an elegant yet practical table ... just as the Shakers intended!

Figure 15: *The author's signature finish combines shellac and gold mica powder. Here she applies a coat to Shaker-inspired pencil-post headboard.*

Guidelines for Making a Table Top

Creating an attractive, durable panel for a table top may seem like a walk in the park, but it has some pitfalls. These guidelines will help improve your odds for success.

by Tom Caspar and Tim Johnson

Putting together a table top is a lot like taking a family picture at a reunion. In both cases, you start with chaos and end up with an heirloom. If you think of the boards in your table top as individuals in a family portrait, it might help put a project in perspective. Like family members, each board has a unique personality. Your job is to organize them to look their best. Then, just like clicking the camera shutter, you freeze the boards for eternity in a glue up—you don't want to live with a hasty arrangement.

A successful table top has two qualities: it must be pleasing to look at and it must remain stable. Accomplishing both requires an artistic eye and good craftsmanship. Here are some guidelines for selecting and arranging boards in a table top. The rules aren't written in stone, but at the very least you'll become familiar with all the aspects of the challenge.

It's also important to mention not all boards belong in a table top. In a stack of lumber, each board has characteristics that make it suitable for different uses in a project. Woodworkers must learn to be harsh board critics for successful table top work.

1. Select Good Lumber

That is one rule you shouldn't bend. Choose boards likely to remain flat and straight. Look at the ring pattern at the end of a board. The more the grain lines curve, the greater the likelihood the board will cup. Wide boards are often tempting to use, but be careful—rip them in half or thirds if they come from too near the center of the tree, and separate them in the panel arrangement. Predicting wood movement is fundamental to making a successful table top.

2. Use Boards with Interesting Grain

Perfectly symmetrical or straight grain can be monotonous. Small knots, color streaks, squirrely grain, and other defects can be pleasing to look at if distributed throughout a top. The top should not look like bookmatched plywood. Avoid using widely spreading grain patterns at the end of a board. Don't cut or join boards too near a knot or crotch.

3. Plan Ahead

Unless you're working on a pretty small table, don't use boards narrower than 5". More narrow boards tend to make a top look like it's been chopped into little pieces.

4. Plane Carefully

Plane each surface of a board the same amount. Stop planing when your boards are ⅛" too thick, then stack the boards with stickers so all sides are equally exposed to the air. After three days see if they remain true.

5. Rip for Effect

Choose boards with similar widths, keeping the differences under two inches. A top is less interesting when all of the boards are exactly the same size, but widely varying board sizes are distracting. Balance similarly wide boards on either side of the center board to build up a symmetrical pattern.

A center board looks better than a center glue joint

Avoid using boards narrower than 5 inches. Blend grain where possible

Distribute interesting grain with balance in mind

Balance boards of similar width on either side of center board

6. Odd is Better than Even

Always use an odd number of boards. The eye is usually drawn to the center of a panel, and a center board looks better than seeing a glue joint here instead.

7. Create a Composition

Arrange interesting areas in a balanced, random pattern. Don't cluster knots or swirly grain at one end of the table top or in the middle. Consider disguising transitions from board to board by placing similar grain patterns together.

8. Arrange for Effect

Frame a top with straight-grained boards along both outside edges. Run-out grain at an edge carries the eye with it.

9. Color can be a Surprise

Check for color differences—neighboring boards shouldn't be dramatically different in color. Wet boards with water, alcohol or mineral spirits to get an idea of their finished appearance. Think twice before using sapwood or other distinctly different features.

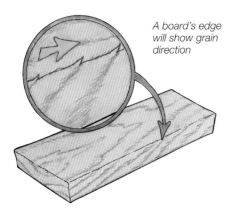

A board's edge will show grain direction

10. Make Planing Easier

Try to line up all the boards so the edge grain runs the same way. If you're successful, you'll avoid tearing out the wood when planing the top by hand.

11. Give it a Rest

This is important. Walk away from your best arrangement for a day or two, then come back later to have a fresh look. See if it's still pleasing to the eye.

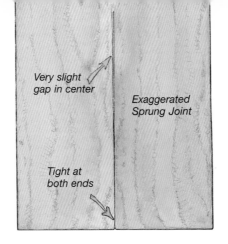

Very slight gap in center

Exaggerated Sprung Joint

Tight at both ends

12. Keep Joints Simple

For a table top, butt joints are fine. Biscuits, dowels, or splines will help align a top, but they will not make a well-fitted joint any stronger.

13. Joint with a Purpose

Long joints should be sprung. That means the edge will be planed or jointed in a slightly hollow manner. Two sprung boards will touch at their ends but have a minute gap in the middle. Since boards lose moisture from their ends faster than out their sides, unsprung joints can separate at the ends over time. Check for tight joints before you glue.

14. Know Your Limits

Don't try to glue up too much at once. Thick, unsightly glue lines result when there is too much open time. Consider gluing the top in halves. Be sure to apply glue completely to all edges about to be joined.

15. The Last Rule

Draw a zig-zag line down the length of each joint, then plane the panel by hand. When all the lines are removed the joints should be flush. Holding a light at a low angle will reveal any defects.

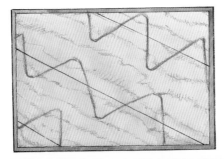

End Grain Debate

Like so many other things in life, woodworking is not always cut and dried. One controversy that divides many woodworkers has to do with orienting the end grain patterns in a panel made up of several boards, such as in a table top.

Wood moves with changes in seasonal moisture. Along with the expansion and contraction of the wood often comes some warping, which usually shows as a slight cupping of a board. The challenge for woodworkers is planning for the tendency of wood to cup so a panel will remain as flat as possible.

The adherents to the first school of thought might be called the "ripplers." Ripplers alternate the end grain pattern of every board so half of the boards have their bark side facing up and half have their pith side facing up. Typically, a board cups toward its bark side. In this panel configuration, as every board warps slightly, each one in the opposite direction from the one next to it, the panel looks like a series of ripples and the overall effect is minimal. Holding the panel with table top fasteners or breadboard ends will limit the distortion, but not eliminate it.

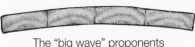

The "big wave" proponents orient all of their boards with the end grain repeating in the same direction. As the boards cup in the panel, the whole piece will distort into a uniform bowl shape, which can be controlled with just a few fasteners. The panel then feels smooth, even if it's not perfectly flat.

Both theories are right, but neither is foolproof. It's probably a sign that no matter how hard we try, we can't control everything.

Beam

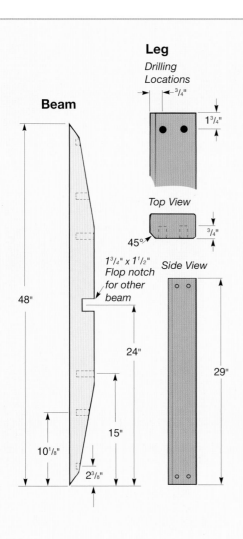

48"

24"

15"

$10^{1}/_{8}$"

$2^{3}/_{8}$"

Leg

Drilling Locations

$^{3}/_{4}$"

$1^{3}/_{4}$"

Top View

45°

$^{3}/_{4}$"

$1^{3}/_{4}$" x $1^{1}/_{2}$"
Flop notch for other beam

Side View

29"

Support Beam Assembly

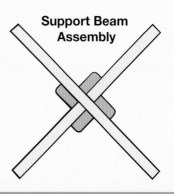

Material List – Table

		T x W x L
1	Foot Cores (2)	1½" x 3½" x 28"
2	Foot Appliques (Left) (4)	1¼" x 3" x 11½"
3	Foot Appliques (Right) (4)	1¼" x 3" x 9½"
4	Foot Pads (4)	¼" x 1½" x 2"
5	Support Beams (2)	1½" x 3½" x 48"
6	Legs (4)	1½" x 3½" x 29"
7	Top Slats (28)	1½" x 1½"
		(for lengths, see pg. 34)
8	Splines (28)	½" x 1" x 2" (White Oak)
9	Dowels (8)	¾" x 14" (White Oak)
10	Plywood Base (1)	½" x 12¾" x 12¾"
11	Marble Center Piece (1)	⅜" x 12" x 12"
12	Lag Screws (16)	⁵⁄₁₆" x 2"

this project. Each foot consists of a 2 x 4 core sandwiched between two smaller 1¼"-thick pieces. Begin by cutting two 2 x 4s to a length of 28" for the foot cores (pieces 1), then cut four 2 x 4s to a length of 11½" for the left foot appliques (pieces 2) and four more 2 x 4s to a length of 9½" for the right foot appliques (pieces 3). In two passes, rip the applique pieces to a thickness of 1¼". Cut the four foot pads (pieces 4) so they're ready to glue onto the assembly later.

Cut the two table support beams (pieces 5) to a length of 48" and lay out the half lap joint at the midpoint (see Drawings above). While you're at it, cut the half laps on the foot cores, remembering that for each pair, one

member is notched on its top edge, while the other is notched on its bottom edge. Mount a ½"-wide dado blade in your table saw and raise it 1¾", then, using a miter gauge for support, remove the waste in the dadoes by taking three passes with each piece. A snug fit is best for the joints.

One edge on the foot cores, the appliques and the support beams must now be cut at an angle on the band saw. Follow the Drawings to lay out each of these angles and, once the shapes are cut, belt-sand the surfaces smooth. Next, rout a ³⁄₁₆" roundover on the bottom edges of the beams, the top edges of the two foot cores and the outside top edge of the foot appliques.

The foot core and beam pieces are now ready for assembly. Epoxy is an excellent waterproof glue that provides a long set-up time and good gap filling properties, making it the best choice for this application. Mix only the amount you can use in a short period of time, then spread it into the half laps. Secure the half laps by driving two non-corrosive screws up into each joint.

For the legs (pieces 6), cut four 2 x 4s to a length of 29", and rout a ½" chamfer on one edge of every leg. Now prepare the legs for joining with the foot and beam assemblies by drilling counterbored pilot holes at the locations indicated on the Drawings shown above. First drill ½"-deep by

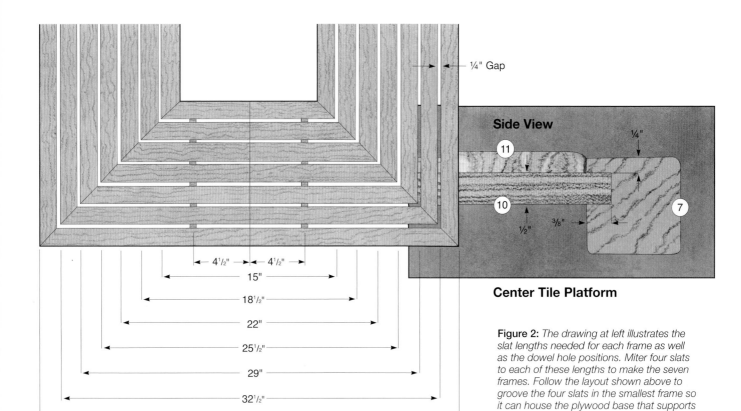

¼" Gap

Side View

⑪

⑩

⑦

¼"

½"

³⁄₈"

Center Tile Platform

4½" 4½"

15"

18½"

22"

25½"

29"

32½"

36"

Figure 2: *The drawing at left illustrates the slat lengths needed for each frame as well as the dowel hole positions. Miter four slats to each of these lengths to make the seven frames. Follow the layout shown above to groove the four slats in the smallest frame so it can house the plywood base that supports the marble insert.*

¾"-diameter counterbores and follow with ⁵⁄₁₆" pilot holes. Slip the legs into position with the feet to mark the screw locations, then remove the legs and drill ¼" pilot holes in the feet. Repeat the last procedure with the legs and the beams.

Mix a new batch of epoxy and spread it on the legs where they join the feet and beams. Place the legs into position and secure the joints with lag screws (pieces 12), remembering to put a washer on each one. Spread epoxy on the eight-foot appliques as well and clamp them to each side of the foot core pieces. Clean up as much glue as possible with a damp rag and later, when the glue has dried, scrape off remaining epoxy residue.

Machining the Table Top

You'll need 64 lineal feet of 1½"-by-1½" stock (pieces 7) to make the seven frames of the top. Each frame is joined at the corners with splines (pieces 8), and the frames are then joined to one

another with dowels (pieces 9). The center frame is filled with a piece of marble backed by ½"-thick plywood.

Rip 4 eight foot 2 x 4s into 1½"-square stock for the slats that make up the top. Roundover the edges on the eight-foot-long strips with a ³⁄₁₆"-radius bit. Next, miter the pieces to length with a power miter saw, a table saw or a radial arm saw. Follow the measurements shown above to cut four slats of equal length for each frame.

The slats are splined together at their mitered ends to give the top extra rigidity and to minimize any gaps that might occur due to the effects of humidity. A typical table saw jig for this operation is shown in Figure 1. The jig, which looks like a lower case "h" from the end, is made of plywood to wrap over the rip fence. Cut two pieces of 2 x 4 scrap to the shapes shown in the drawing and screw them to the jig at a 45° angle for supporting the slats as they pass over the blade.

Install a ½"-wide dado blade in your

table saw and raise it ½". Now clamp the rip fence so the face of the jig is ¾" from the center of the blade and you'll get perfectly centered dadoes.

Next, drill two ¾" holes into every slat for inserting the dowels that reinforce the top assembly. Chuck a ¾"-diameter bit in your drill press and, to ensure accuracy, make the alignment jig shown in Figure 3 by screwing a 1½" x 12" fence to a piece of scrap 1" x 8". Clamp the jig to your drill press table so the center of the bit is ¾" from the fence. Draw lines on the drill press fence 4½" to the left and right of the bit's center and put center lines on the longest edge of each slat. Match the center line of the slat with the mark on the left side of the fence and drill the first hole, then slide the slat to the right to align the marks and drill the second hole.

The slats for the smallest frame must be grooved on their inside edge to house the plywood base (piece 10) that supports the marble (piece 11). Set up a ½"-wide dado and raise it to ⅜". Plow the groove so it is set back ¼" from the top surface of the slats (see Figure 2).

The splines (pieces 8) are made of white oak for strength and weather resistance. Rip a ½" x 6" x 20"-long oak board into 2½"-wide strips. Cut the strips into 1"-long pieces. You'll notice the grain runs the short way on the splines, which is correct. If the grain of the splines runs parallel with the joint they are much more likely to break. You'll need a total of 28 splines.

The dowel rods (pieces 9) are also made of white oak. Cut four 36" dowels in half and sand them vigorously with 100-grit paper to slightly reduce their size so they fit into the slat holes easily. Now chamfer one end of every dowel with a belt sander.

Making the Top Assembly
Assembling the frames isn't difficult at all if you make yourself the special framing jig shown in Figure 4. Make four blocks from scrap 2 x 4 material, cutting each block 3½" square. Mark the center of the blocks and drill a 1½"-diameter hole through each one. Next, cut in from two sides to form a 90° inside corner. Place one block outside each corner of a frame and use a band clamp, running around the entire assembly, to pull the frame and blocks tight.

Glue up each frame by spreading epoxy in the spline grooves and on the mitered ends of the slats. Next, put the splines in place and assemble the frame. Now set up the band clamp and corner blocks to pull the frame together while the glue dries. Check for squareness by measuring diagonally across each frame, adjusting the frame until the two measurements are equal. Remember the plywood base (piece 10)

for supporting the tile should be installed at this time in the smallest frame.

The top is designed with ¼" gaps between each frame. In order to maintain the spacing, make a bunch of ¼"-thick spacers to place between the frames while you drive the dowels through the holes. Put some epoxy in the holes in the smallest and largest frames, then lay all the frames and ¼" spacers in sequence on your bench. Tap the chamfered ends of the dowels into the frames and continue until they contact the plywood center plate. Once all the dowels are driven, turn the assembly over and pin the dowels in every frame with a 1¼"-long brad. Drill pilot holes before driving the brads and, after countersinking them slightly, fill the hole with wood putty to minimize the effects of moisture. Finally, cut off the ends of the dowels and sand them flush with the outside frame.

Center the pedestal on the overturned top and mark three screw locations in each support beam where they solidly cross the frames (see Exploded View on page 37). Use a ½"-diameter bit to counterbore these positions. Since the width of the beams vary from one screw location to another, drill your counterbores deep enough

Figure 3: *Once the drilling jig is clamped to the drill press table, align the center mark on the slat with the left line on the fence to drill the first hole. Next, slide the slat along the jig to line up its center line with the right location mark on the fence and drill the second hole.*

to leave 1" of stock remaining from the bottom of the hole to the top edge of the beam. Now drill ⅛" pilot holes through the beam and ½" into the top. Join the assemblies with #10-2" non-corrosive wood screws. It's also convenient to now glue and pin the foot pads (pieces 4) onto the bottom of each foot core.

Set the table upright to install the marble. Run a thin bead of silicone caulk on the plywood where it meets the redwood frame, and add four evenly spaced dollops of caulk on the interior area of the plywood. Set the marble in place, wipe away any squeeze-out with a damp rag and let the caulk cure overnight.

Building the Benches
The benches are designed in a trestle style that incorporates many of the same elements as the table. As you did with the table, make the feet and support beams first. The patterns for the pieces are on page 37, so go ahead and cut out eight feet (pieces 13) and eight support beams (pieces 15) from 2 x 4 stock, and sixteen appliques (pieces 14) for the feet from ¾" redwood. Roundover all of the top edges of the feet, the outside top edges of the appliques, and all of the bottom edges of the beams with a ³⁄₁₆"-radius bit. Prepare the beams and feet for joining the legs by drilling ½"-deep by ¾"-diameter counterbores as shown in the Exploded View on page 37. Follow the counterbores by drilling ⁵⁄₁₆" pilot holes. Each beam also requires two ½"-diameter by 1¼"-deep counterbores on the bottom edge for securing the outside slats in the seat assembly (see page 37). Follow these counterbores with ⅛" pilot holes.

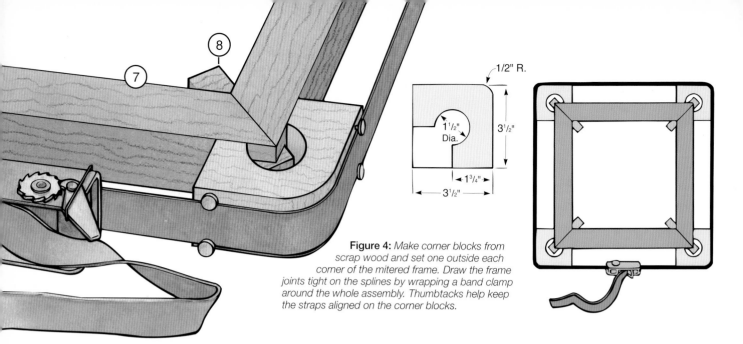

1/2" R.

1 1/2" Dia.

3 1/2"

1 3/4"

3 1/2"

Figure 4: *Make corner blocks from scrap wood and set one outside each corner of the mitered frame. Draw the frame joints tight on the splines by wrapping a band clamp around the whole assembly. Thumbtacks help keep the straps aligned on the corner blocks.*

All of the legs (pieces 16) are chamfered on their bottom edges and notched at the top to join with the stretchers. Cut the legs to length and chamfer the bottom edges on the table saw. Lay out the notches following the elevation on the next page and remove the waste with a jigsaw. Lay the feet and beams on the legs, then drill the pilot holes and join the pieces together with lag screws (pieces 20). Use epoxy to adhere the appliques to each foot.

The stretchers (pieces 17) span between the legs, giving the benches strength and acting as the middle slat in the seats. Use the pattern on the next page to lay out the stretchers, including the dowel hole locations. Cut them out with a jigsaw and round over the top and bottom edges with a 3/16"-radius bit. Slip the stretchers into the leg notches and equip your portable

drill with a 1/4" bit. Extend the center lag screw hole from each support beam into the stretchers for 2".

The slats (pieces 18) that make up the seat are the same as those on the table top, so you can rip four eight foot 2 x 4s into 1 1/2" x 1 1/2" strips and cut them into 24" lengths. Round over all of the slat edges with the 3/16"-radius bit. Now use the same drill press jig you made for the table top and drill two dowel holes 4 1/2" off-center on each slat. Remember to drill the holes through the slat portion of each stretcher also.

Cut two 13"-long dowels (pieces 19) for each seat and sand them with 100-grit paper so they slip into the slat holes easily. Now put epoxy in the stretcher holes and slip the dowels in place, leaving about 5 1/4" stick out on each side. Wipe the glue from the dowels and add two more slats on both

sides of the stretcher. Be sure to use 1/4" spacers between every piece and pin these slats with brads. Now put epoxy into the holes in the two outside slats and mount them onto the dowels. The finished width of the seat should be 12". When the glue is dry, cut off the ends of the dowels and sand them flush with the slats.

Set the seat assembly onto the legs, dropping the stretcher tenons into the notches and securing the joints with 3" lag screws (pieces 21). Now flip the entire bench over and drive #10-2" wood screws (pieces 22) through the beams into the outside slats to completely secure the seat to the leg assembly.

Redwood, as it ages, turns from its original red color to silvery grey. The only way to maintain the original reddish tone is to color the wood with an exterior wood preservative. Reapply the finish every season.

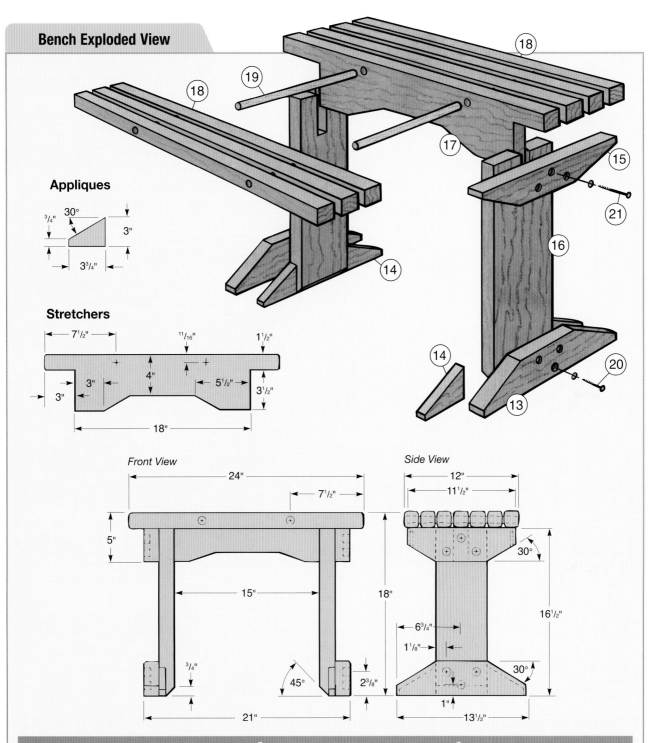

Appliques

30°
³/₄"
3"
3³/₄"

Stretchers

7¹/₂"
11/16"
1¹/₂"
4"
3"
3"
5¹/₂"
3¹/₂"
18"

Front View

24"
7¹/₂"
5"
15"
³/₄"
45°
2³/₈"
21"

Side View

12"
11¹/₂"
30°
18"
16¹/₂"
6³/₄"
1¹/₈"
30°
1"
13¹/₂"

Material List – Four Benches

		T x W x L			T x W x L
13	Feet (8)	1½" x 3½" x 13½"	18	Seat Slats (24)	1½" x 1½" x 24"
14	Appliques (16)	¾" x 3" x 3¾"	19	Dowels (8)	¾" x 13"(White Oak)
15	Support Beams (8)	1½" x 3½" x 11½"	20	Lag Screws (40)	⁵/₁₆" x 2"
16	Legs (8)	1½" x 5½" x 16½"	21	Lag Screws (8)	⁵/₁₆" x 3"
17	Stretchers (4)	1½" x 5" x 24"	22	Wood Screws (16)	#10 - 2"

Serving Tray

The simple and elegant lines on the Serving Tray are a study in positive and negative space. The X-shaped leg joinery's history is traceable to the ancient Egyptians, but the project uses entirely modern methods to execute the design.

by LiLi Jackson

While today's woodworkers have plenty of nineteenth- and twentieth-century motifs to look to for design inspiration, for this project, I turned to the distant past. Curule chairs were popular during the medieval period, but they actually can be traced even further back than that, to the dynasties of ancient Egypt. They're familiar enough, with their knuckle-jointed X-shaped bases, but the design element doesn't seem to find a lot of application in today's furniture. I wasn't particularly interested in making a curule chair, but the X-shaped legs seemed a fitting choice for a serving tray. I settled on mahogany for this project—it's a great species for a beginner, essentially knot-free and easy to mill and finish. Its fine grain also adds elegance.

Getting Started

Build the tray first, then move on to the base. An overriding concern for my initial design was the legs must be true and at perfect right angles to the base and floor. A slight skew in or out would result in a spindly, awkward look. If you construct the tray first, there's some room for tweaking the base rails to push the legs out or pull them in.

The first thing to do is cut the tray's stiles and end rails (pieces 1 and 2) to width but a bit long. The pieces get a

Figure 1: *After the tray stiles and rails are cut to width and rabbeted, they can be mitered to length. Use a fine-tooth crosscut blade to help minimize tearout on splintery mahogany.*

rabbet along their top edges, so use a straight bit in your router table or a dado blade in your table saw to form them, as shown in the Technical Drawings. Once the rabbets have been milled, miter the parts to length and lay out for the

matching notches on the inside of each stile for the two support rails (pieces 3).

Cut them by hand, if you're up to it. Setting up to make these cuts with a router is more hassle than it's worth. Grab your biscuit joiner and cut slots to help beef up the miter joints. The table may be handling a good amount of weight, so you'll want to ensure that the joinery will be as strong as possible. Dry-fit the frame to make sure that you've got clean miters. Shape the support rails (see the Drawings) and form the tenons at the ends. When they're ready, dry-assemble your tray again, for a final look. The tops of the support rails should be perfectly flush with the bottoms of the rabbets on the end rails and stiles. When everything matches up, go ahead and glue up the pieces and set them aside.

Making Handles and Rim

While the glue is drying, cut and shape the handles and form the miters on their ends, as well as on the ends of the back rim (pieces 4 and 5). The pieces all get a soft roundover and plenty of time under the sandpaper, as they are the showiest parts of the project and will be reflected by the mirrored top. When they're ready to install, pre-drill pilot holes from the bottom of the frame, three for each handle and five for the rim. Again, you don't want to short-change this piece on strength—you might be carrying some precious cargo on it. Form the miters at the corners of the rim and

Figure 2: *A biscuit or plate joiner is a great way to strengthen and align miter joints. The biscuits fit just under the tray's rabbet.*

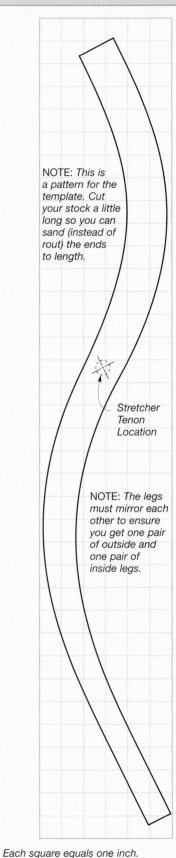

Tray Exploded View

NOTE: *This is a pattern for the template. Cut your stock a little long so you can sand (instead of rout) the ends to length.*

Stretcher Tenon Location

NOTE: *The legs must mirror each other to ensure you get one pair of outside and one pair of inside legs.*

Each square equals one inch.

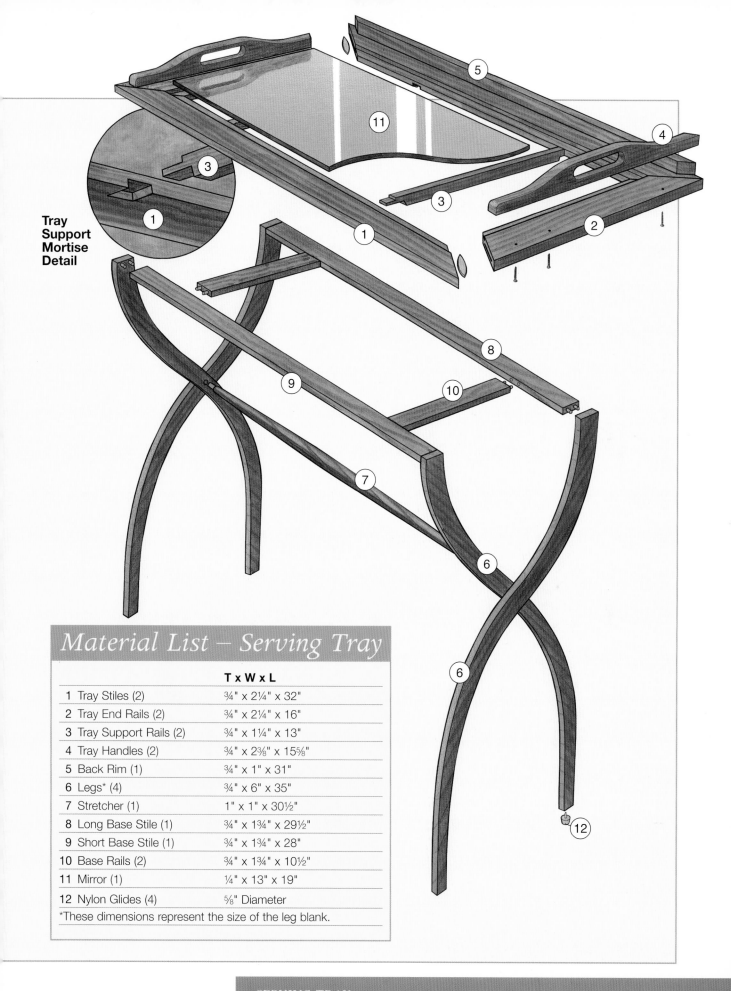

**Tray
Support
Mortise
Detail**

① ③ ① ⑤ ④ ③ ⑪ ② ⑧ ⑨ ⑩ ⑦ ⑥ ⑥ ⑫

Material List – Serving Tray

	T x W x L
1 Tray Stiles (2)	¾" x 2¼" x 32"
2 Tray End Rails (2)	¾" x 2¼" x 16"
3 Tray Support Rails (2)	¾" x 1¼" x 13"
4 Tray Handles (2)	¾" x 2⅜" x 15⅝"
5 Back Rim (1)	¾" x 1" x 31"
6 Legs* (4)	¾" x 6" x 35"
7 Stretcher (1)	1" x 1" x 30½"
8 Long Base Stile (1)	¾" x 1¾" x 29½"
9 Short Base Stile (1)	¾" x 1¾" x 28"
10 Base Rails (2)	¾" x 1¾" x 10½"
11 Mirror (1)	¼" x 13" x 19"
12 Nylon Glides (4)	⅝" Diameter

*These dimensions represent the size of the leg blank.

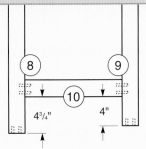

Base Subassembly
(Top View)

4³/₄"   4"

⑧ ⑨

⑩

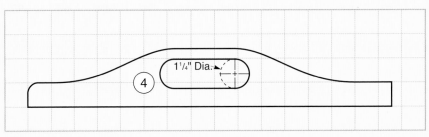

1¹/₄" Dia.

④

Each square equals one inch.

Tray Stile
(Top View)

①

³/₄"

5³/₄"   ³/₄"

**Tray Handle
Location**
(Front View)

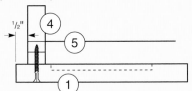

¹/₂"   ④

⑤

①

Support Rail and Tray Stile
(Side View)

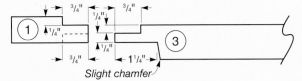

①   ³/₄"   ³/₄"

¹/₄"

¹/₄"   ③

¹/₄"

³/₄"   1¹/₄"

Slight chamfer

Laying Out and Forming the Legs

Figure 3: *Use the scaled drawing to help create a fair and true template of the tray leg. The next step (in preparation for template routing) is to transfer the shape to the hardwood leg blank.*

Stretcher
(Side View)

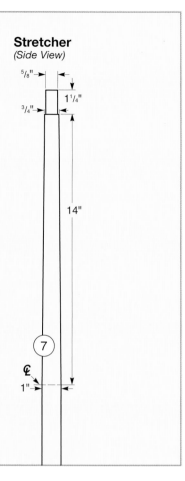

5/8"

1 1/4"

3/4"

14"

⑦

℄

1"

handles and glue them up. Once the glue dries, you can screw the assembly in place on top of the frame—just be sure to keep the rim flush with the back and the handles ½" shy of each end.

Before moving on to assembling the base, I recommend creating a cardboard template for ordering your mirrored top. I used full ¼" mirror glass for mine—it's not cheap, and it doesn't sand or plane well, either. Take the template to your glass shop and let them create the top directly from it, rather than from a set of measurements. It's the best way to eliminate any possibility of dimensional errors.

Creating the X Factor

The legs (pieces 6) are created using a template. No method ensures uniformity better, and as was mentioned earlier, perfectly even and matching legs are a real key to the success of the tray project.

Spend some extra time refining your template, lightly sanding it until it is true and smooth all around. Then, as you can see in Figures 3, 4, and 5, it's a simple matter of transferring the shape to your stock, cutting the stock slightly oversized on the band saw and then applying your template. I installed one small screw at the middle (which would later be hidden by the stretcher tenon) and turned to double-sided tape for the ends. One word of caution: Once you start the final pass with your flush-cutting bit, you may want to stay away from the ends. End grain will often fracture if you try to cut across it in this manner. It's not an inevitable occurrence, of course, but mahogany isn't priced like pine. You may want to take a conservative approach and protect your lumber investment from the scrap bin. A way around the end grain problem is to leave a little stock at each end and use a disk sander

Figure 4: *Take the leg blank to your band saw and cut within ¹⁄₁₆" of the line you marked onto the blank. Don't cut into the line; you need to leave some material for the router bit to remove. This will ensure uniform legs.*

Figure 5: *Use double-sided tape and one screw at the tenon mortise location to attach the template to a roughed-out leg. A flush-trimming bit shapes the legs. Don't attempt to rout across the end grain on the legs. Use a disk sander to do the final shaping here to prevent router mishaps.*

Figure 6: *Since there are only four mortises to chop, lay them out and cut them by hand. The support rail's top edge must align perfectly with the rabbet on the tray stiles and rails.*

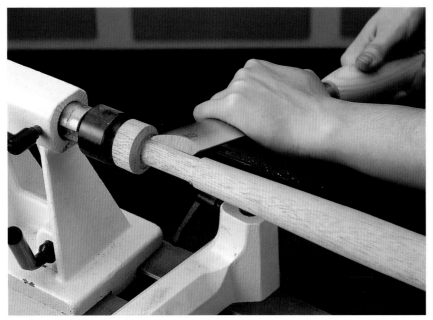

Figure 7: *The turned tenons on both ends of the stretcher need to be long enough to engage both legs, on each side of the table, as you assemble the project. Use a skew chisel at the lathe to perfect their length and diameter.*

(while the template is still attached) to bring the stock flush to the template at each end. Sand your legs and lay them aside for now. You'll want all of your base pieces ready to go before you assemble any of them.

Turning the Stretcher

I toyed around with using square stock for the stretcher (piece 7), but the idea never actually made it off the drawing board. Clearly, the tray calls for a round base stretcher—and it was a great chance to get an hour or two in on the lathe. Once you give spindle turning a try, the lathe will quickly become one of your favorite tools.

Start by locating the centers on the ends of your turning blank. Machine your square stock into an octagonal profile by cutting off the corners on your table saw. Mount the blank between centers and use a gouge to rough out a cylindrical shape. Switch to a skew to bring the blank down to about 1" in diameter. Find the center (from end to end) and from there, lay out your tenon shoulders. Reduce them down to ⅝" in diameter. It's critical that the stretcher's length from shoulder to shoulder matches the length of the shorter stile (piece 9) above it, otherwise you'll end up with a pigeon-toed table. The stretcher tenons will end up being 1¼" long, but when you're turning, you'll want to allow a little extra for paring off. Gradually create an arc that starts with the 1" diameter in the center of the piece and gracefully reduces to ¾" at each shoulder. Sand the stretcher all the way through to 320-grit (but not the tenons) while it's still on the lathe, and then trim the tenons to length.

Creating the Tray Support

The next step is to mill the stock for the tray support (pieces 8, 9, and 10). You'll notice that the stiles are different lengths, due to the offset created by the relative position of the legs. Cut the pieces to size, use the Elevation Drawings to locate your dowel holes, and glue the subassembly together, making sure to keep things square as you carry this process out.

Bringing it Together

The first assembly step is to bring the sets of legs together. You'll be drilling right through two inner legs, but on the other two, you'll limit your depth to ½". Remember, the legs mirror each other, so be sure to lay everything out before you start drilling. Next, locate and drill the dowel holes (I used a doweling jig and dowel-centers to make the task a bit easier) at the tops of the legs and pilot holes for the glides at their bottoms. With the machining done, you can dry-assemble the legs, the stretcher, and the base subassembly. Check to ensure all is square and proceed to your final glue-up.

Finishing Up

Test-fit the mirror (piece 11) and tap the glides (piece 12) in place. After sanding everything down to 320-grit, I applied a custom stain concocted by mixing (half and half) Zar's® Rosewood Stain with Carbon Black Woodburst®.

Next, apply a coat of sanding sealer and two coats of lacquer, with a light 320-grit sanding between each coat. The final step is to carefully drop the mirror into place.

QuickTip

Shaving-Free Lathe Tool Caddy

To work efficiently at the lathe, it helps if your woodturning tools are sharp, near, and clean. Here's a simple caddy you can build from scrap wood and wire mesh to hold them. It hugs the lathe bed securely with a dozen ring magnets embedded in its underside. Just slide this caddy close to your work, and the tools remain clean as the chips fall through the wire mesh bottom.

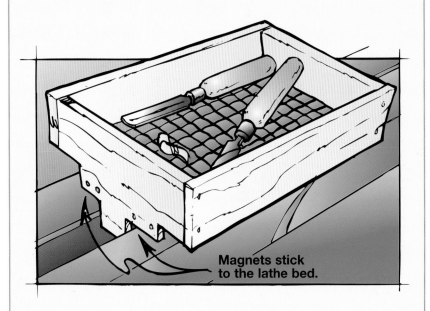

Magnets stick to the lathe bed.

Old World Cherry Tea Table

Antique collectors will appreciate the humble heritage of a classic reproduction. Woodworkers will enjoy the contemporary techniques in its construction and assembly. And everyone will enjoy an elegant spot for tea.

by Chris Inman

You may never serve high tea in the afternoon, but that doesn't mean you won't find a use for a classic table. As a matter of fact, if you look through many of today's leading decorating magazines, you'll find tea tables are as popular as ever.

The most elaborate tea tables were produced in Philadelphia during the mid-1700s. The Chippendale tables had richly carved legs and pillars, and elaborately detailed pie crust tops—unlike their restrained Shaker counterparts of the same era. Generally speaking, round tops were favored, although rectangular topped tables also were common. Some of the tea tables featured tilting tops that made them easier to store near a wall when not in use. Tables of this type often were called snap tables due to the distinctive sound the catches made when the top was let down. Since tilting tables were designed to save space, they were usually pulled out for serving tea in the afternoon, then put away for the rest of the day. Tables with fixed tops were used for displaying fine tea services.

This tea table is a reproduction. The original was probably designed by a rural colonial craftsman who simplified the styles he saw in the city. The bevels and scallop on each leg, the lack of carving on the pillar and the overall sparseness of the design are clues to this humble heritage.

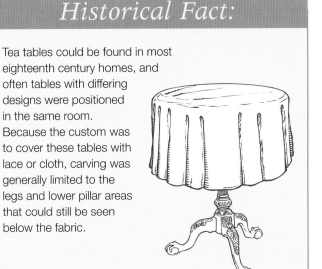

Historical Fact:

Tea tables could be found in most eighteenth century homes, and often tables with differing designs were positioned in the same room. Because the custom was to cover these tables with lace or cloth, carving was generally limited to the legs and lower pillar areas that could still be seen below the fabric.

Turning the Pillar

Historically, tea tables were made with many kinds of cabinet woods, including native birch, maple, walnut and cherry, as well as imported mahogany and rosewood. Imported woods were used mainly for formal and ornate designs, while native species often were specified for simpler applications. Cherry is the perfect choice. It shows off the simple lines of the design, maintains the flavor of the period and comfortably fits into both casual and formal surroundings.

Begin making your tea table by selecting a 2"-thick plank of cherry and cutting two 4" x 23" pieces for gluing into the pillar (piece 1). Make sure the joint is tight and as inconspicuous as possible. If you have a single piece of cherry thick enough for the whole pillar, by all means use it. Once the glue dries, trim the blank to a length of 22½" and draw pencil lines connecting the diagonally opposite corners on each end. The centering points that you get from the crossing pencil lines will come in handy when mounting the stock in your lathe. Before moving on to that step, however, use a compass to draw a 3¾" circle on one end of the blank and rip the corner waste off the stock with your table saw blade tilted 45° (see Turning the Pillar on page 51). Making the cuts will remove lots of material with

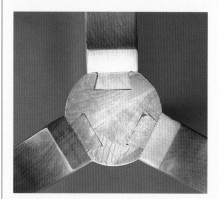

Figure 1: *Snug-fitting joints are the key to this table's stability. If your joints are sloppy, try slipping veneer next to the tails to fill the gaps.*

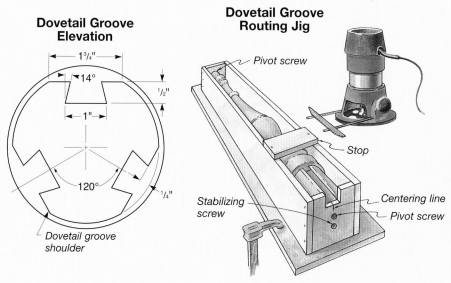

Dovetail Groove Elevation

1³/₄"

14°

1"

½"

¼"

120°

Dovetail groove shoulder

Dovetail Groove Routing Jig

Pivot screw

Stop

Stabilizing screw

Centering line

Pivot screw

less effort than if you turn the blank from scratch. Now you can mount the blank in your lathe and use a roughing gouge to turn a 3¾" diameter cylinder.

By the time you finish roughing in the blank, you'll already be standing ankle deep in wood shavings, so take a break and trace the pillar shape off the Technical Drawings, page 52. Enlarge the pattern to full size and glue it to a piece of plywood—3M Spray Mount works well for this application—to make a storyboard that displays all the design details of the pillar. Use the storyboard to lay out the high and low spots of the pillar on the blank and turn the profile to

shape. To accurately size the pillar tenon, first turn it slightly oversize and test its fit in a 1½" hole drilled in scrap wood. Then, if need be, remount the pillar on the lathe and shave the tenon down until you have a perfect slip-fit in the test hole. Complete the turning by sanding it in the direction of the grain with 220-grit paper. For safety, make sure you unplug the motor.

Routing the Dovetail Grooves

The three sliding dovetail grooves in the pillar base are routed 120° apart with the help of a jig. Build the dovetail groove routing jig shown in Figure 2 to fit snugly around your pillar (the interior jig box

dimensions should match the largest diameter and length of your pillar).

Now mark the groove locations using the dovetail groove layout found on page 52. Install your turning in the jig, making sure the pivot screws enter the pillar at the indents left by the lathe's drive and tail centers. Align one groove layout with the centering mark on the jig, then drill a pilot hole and drive the stabilizing screw.

Before routing the dovetail grooves, rout a shoulder at the opening of each joint, as shown in the Dovetail Groove Elevation above. Chuck a ⅝" straight bit in your router and adjust the depth of cut to ¼". The set-up will result in a 1¾"-wide shoulder. If the diameter of your base is not exactly 3", adjust the cutting depth so you still end up with 1¾"-wide shoulders. Screw a stop to the jig to prevent the bit from cutting into the base shoulder, then rout away the waste for the groove shoulders (see Figure 2).

Once you've completed the shoulders you can rout the grooves. Given that dovetail bits are not very robust, make the first pass in the groove with the ⅝" straight bit. Mount a fence to your router's base, center the bit on a groove location, and make one ½"-deep

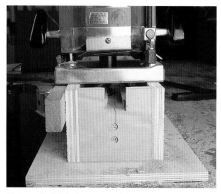

Figure 2: *Before routing the dovetail grooves, use a ⅝" straight bit set for a ¼"-deep cut and rout shoulders for each joint location.*

Figure 3: *With the router fence riding against the jig, center the first cut, then adjust the fence ¼" closer to the bit and rout each groove wall again.*

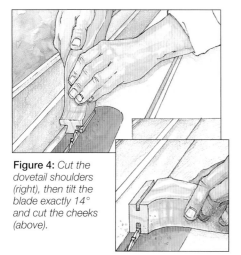

Figure 4: *Cut the dovetail shoulders (right), then tilt the blade exactly 14° and cut the cheeks (above).*

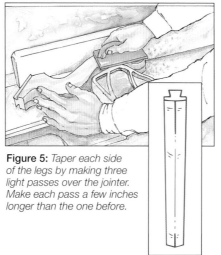

Figure 5: *Taper each side of the legs by making three light passes over the jointer. Make each pass a few inches longer than the one before.*

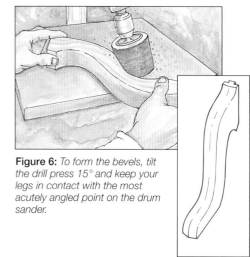

Figure 6: *To form the bevels, tilt the drill press 15° and keep your legs in contact with the most acutely angled point on the drum sander.*

pass to establish the center of each groove. Switch to a ½" diameter, 14° dovetail bit and set the cutting depth to ½". Adjust the fence and rout the grooves to their full 1" width (see Figure 3), making a pass along each wall with the same fence setting. The routing sequence ensures the grooves are centered on the pillar. Finish up by using a chisel to pare the ends of the grooves flush with the base shoulder.

Making the Legs

The key to making strong legs (pieces 2) is having the wood grain running parallel with the narrowest part of each piece. Enlarge and trace the pattern of the leg (see page 52), cut out your pattern and position it on your 1¾"-thick stock so the grain pattern of the wood follows the leg as much as possible. Trace each leg and cut them out with your band saw, then sand the shaped edges smooth.

Now use your table saw and cut the dovetail on each leg (see the Dovetail Elevation on page 50). You'll cut the shoulders with the fence clamped ½" from the blade and the blade height set at ⁷⁄₁₆" (so it grazes the dovetail cheek), as shown in Figure 4. Be sure to cut some scrap wood first to test the set-up, then cut the shoulders on the legs. Tilt the blade exactly 14° and raise it to meet the

shoulder cuts. Set your fence and cut a 1"-wide dovetail on a scrap piece (see Figure 4). Clean out the corner of each shoulder with a chisel and test the fit of the tail in a groove. Continue cutting test tails until you get a perfect slip fit, then complete the tails on the legs.

The finished legs are thicker at the hip than at the toe. You can plane the tapers by hand or get a jump on the job using a jointer. Center a line down the top edge of each leg to use as a guide and set the depth of cut on your jointer at ¹⁄₃₂". Using a push paddle for safety, make the first pass on each side only as long as the foot, then make two more passes, each one a few inches longer than the pass before, to reach the knee (see Figure 5). Three passes on both sides of each leg should do it. Blend the jointer marks together with a hand plane or belt sander.

Chuck a 3"-diameter drum sander with a coarse sleeve in your drill press and form the bevels on the front edge of the legs. Depending on the style of your machine, tilt the drill press table or head 15° and sand the bevels on the legs until they meet the center line (see Figure 6). Always keep the point of contact between the legs and drum square with the tilting angle — if you slip to either side you'll lose the angle and end up sanding a nearly flat bevel. Sand the edge of

each leg except for the sharp curve in the hip area, which you can leave until after assembling the base. Once all of the bevels reach the center lines, switch to a finer sanding sleeve and refine the curves.

The Top, Block and Braces

Glue-up a panel for the top (piece 3), preferably using an odd number of boards that look uniform in color and grain pattern, and balanced in width. Plane the panel after the glue dries (see Figure 7), then rout the top into a 24"-diameter circle using a trammel jig like the one shown in Figure 8. Soften the edges with a ½" roundover bit (see Figure 9) and sand them smooth.

For the block (piece 4), cut some 1¾"-thick stock and drill a 1½" hole through its center. Use the ½" roundover bit to rout the bottom edge at each end of the block, routing with the full curve of the bit this time.

Enlarge and cut out a full-size pattern of the brace onto your material. Drill a pair of ⅜"-diameter holes in one side of each brace (pieces 5), as shown on the drawing, and band saw the pieces to shape. Slip dowel points (short steel dowels with a point on one end) into the holes, center the braces on the block, and press the braces against the block to transfer the hole locations. Drill ⅜" holes

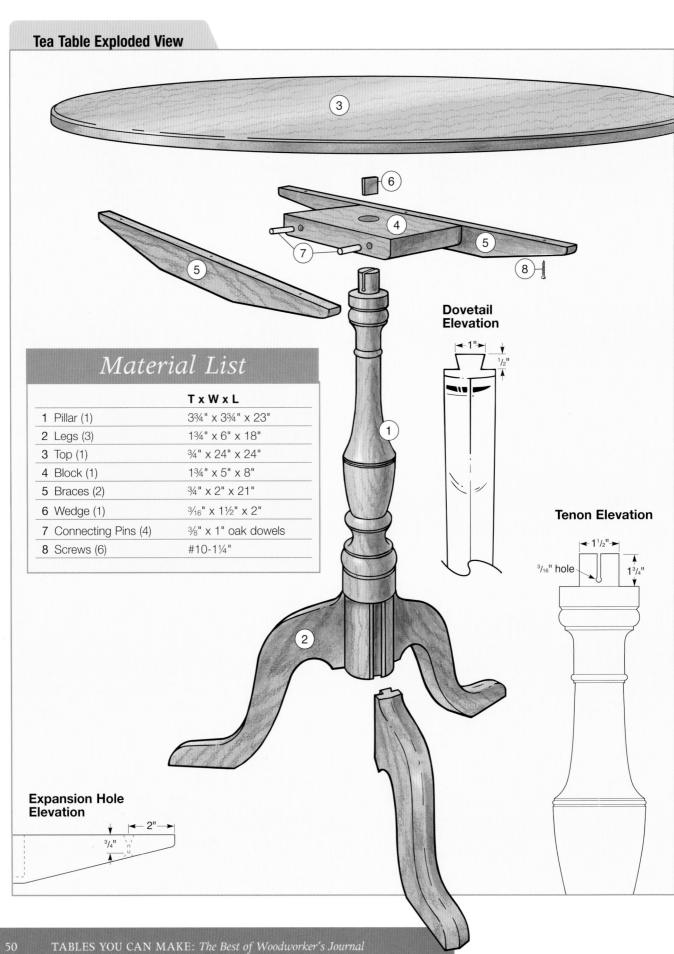

Material List

	T x W x L
1 Pillar (1)	3¾" x 3¾" x 23"
2 Legs (3)	1¾" x 6" x 18"
3 Top (1)	¾" x 24" x 24"
4 Block (1)	1¾" x 5" x 8"
5 Braces (2)	¾" x 2" x 21"
6 Wedge (1)	3/16" x 1½" x 2"
7 Connecting Pins (4)	3/8" x 1" oak dowels
8 Screws (6)	#10-1¼"

Dovetail Elevation

1"

½"

Tenon Elevation

1½"

3/16" hole

1¾"

Expansion Hole Elevation

2"

¾"

Turning the pillar for this tea table requires a set of basic turning tools including a roughing gouge, spindle gouges, a skew chisel, and a parting tool.

To make a story board, enlarge the half-pattern given in the Technical Drawings to full size and glue it onto a piece of thin plywood. Rough the blank into a cylinder, then use the story board as a guide for laying out and sizing the turning. Mark the major points of the pillar, then blend the shapes by eye.

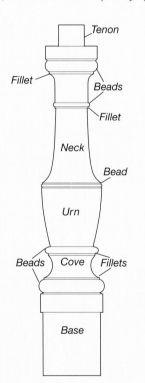

Tenon
Fillet
Beads
Fillet
Neck
Bead
Urn
Beads Cove Fillets
Base

Step 1: *Trimming the corners of the blank at a 45° angle will quickly reduce the amount of wood you have to remove during the turning process.*

Step 2: *Mount the blank in your lathe and, with the wood revolving at a slow speed, turn a 3¾"-diameter cylinder using a large roughing gouge.*

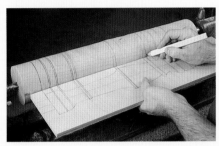

Step 3: *Make a full size pillar pattern and glue it to a piece of plywood to make a storyboard, then lay out the turning details on the cylinder.*

Step 4: *Using a parting tool and a caliper, define the major high and low points of the pillar by taking your measurements off the storyboard.*

Step 5: *Shape the inside curves with a set of spindle gouges, making the final passes with the bevels firmly contacting the wood for smooth cuts.*

Step 6: *Use your skew chisels to form the beads, base, tenon and urn, and to plane the flatter areas of the pillar to their finished size.*

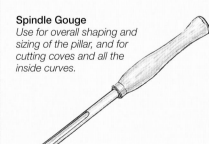

Spindle Gouge
Use for overall shaping and sizing of the pillar, and for cutting coves and all the inside curves.

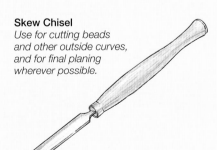

Skew Chisel
Use for cutting beads and other outside curves, and for final planing wherever possible.

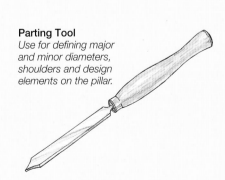

Parting Tool
Use for defining major and minor diameters, shoulders and design elements on the pillar.

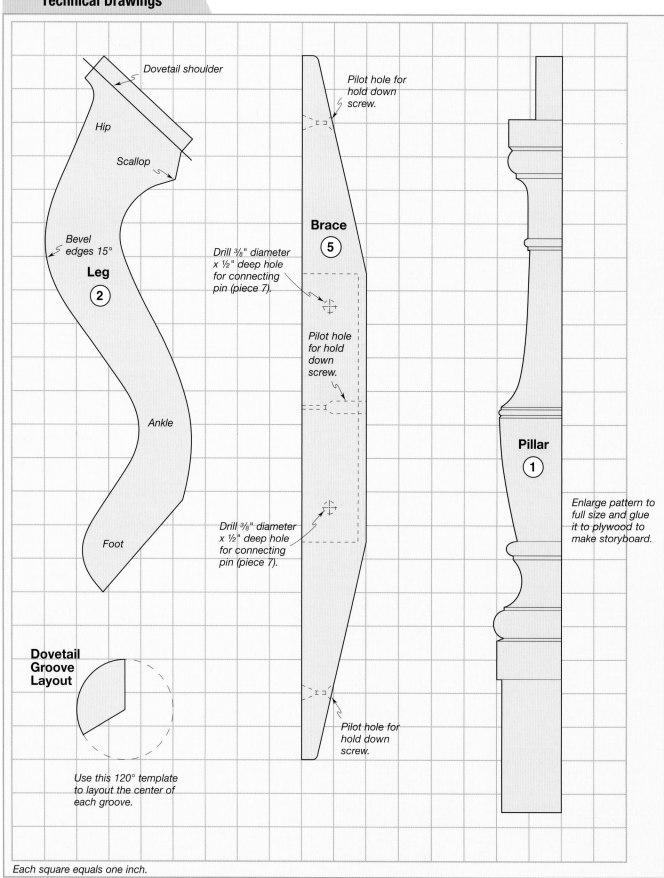

Dovetail shoulder

Hip

Scallop

Bevel
edges 15°

Leg
②

Ankle

Foot

**Dovetail
Groove
Layout**

Use this 120° template
to layout the center of
each groove.

Pilot hole for
hold down
screw.

Brace
⑤

Drill ³⁄₈" diameter
x ½" deep hole
for connecting
pin (piece 7).

Pilot hole
for hold
down
screw.

Drill ³⁄₈" diameter
x ½" deep hole
for connecting
pin (piece 7).

Pilot hole for
hold down
screw.

Pillar
①

Enlarge pattern to
full size and glue
it to plywood to
make storyboard.

Each square equals one inch.

in the block at the indentations, then drill expansion holes into each brace for screwing the top to the base (see the Expansion Hole Elevation on page 50).

The last step before assembling the table base is making a wedge (piece 6) for securing the block to the pillar. Slice the wedge off a piece of 1½" thick scrap wood with your table saw's miter gauge tilted 5°.

Assembling the Base

Cut your pillar to its finished length by trimming off the waste at each end with a hand saw, then use the saw to cut a kerf in the tenon, as shown in the Tenon Elevation on page 50. Now drill a ³⁄₁₆" relief hole at the bottom of the kerf to help keep the pillar from splitting when you drive the wedge, and glue the block onto the tenon. Turn the block so its ends are parallel with the tenon kerf, then glue and tap the wedge into place. Sand the tenon and wedge flush.

Gluing the legs to the pillar shouldn't require any clamps if the joints fit properly. If your joints are a little sloppy, you may find old bicycle inner tubes make good clamps for an awkward glue-up. Spread glue in the grooves and slide the leg tails into place, then wrap the assembly with the inner tubes if they're needed. After the glue dries, use a rasp and a carving gouge to refine the sharp curve at the top of each leg, then sand the entire table to 220-grit.

Now lay the top upside-down on your workbench and center the block on it—the grain of the block crosses the grain of the top. Cut connecting pins (pieces 7) and press them into the block holes, then press the braces onto the pins. Next, mark the pilot hole locations for screwing the top to the braces. Remove the base assembly and drill the pilot holes carefully so you don't drill too deeply.

After sanding the table one more time for good measure, finish the cherry with four coats of oil/varnish finish. Lightly sanding between each coat with 400-grit wet or dry paper will give you surfaces as smooth as silk. When you assemble the base with the top, leave the connecting pins unglued in case you ever need to repair the table.

Undoubtedly, your tea table is just as finely crafted as the originals were more than 200 years ago. It seems a shame that the custom then was to keep the tables covered with a piece of cloth. Luckily, fashions change, so put your table out where your craftsmanship will be appreciated. Just be sure to cover it at tea time.

Figure 7: *Surface the panel for the table top with a well-tuned and sharpened hand plane after the glue joints are thoroughly cured.*

Figure 8: *To rout the top round, make a trammel jig from ¼" plywood and mount it to your router base. Use a ½"-long wood screw for the pivot point.*

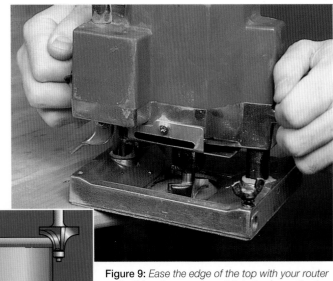

Figure 9: *Ease the edge of the top with your router and a ½"-radius roundover bit, but only use the lower half of the cutting edges to form a partial roundover.*

Rolling Tea Table

Don't let the shaped pieces scare you off. A little patience and some power tool tricks will take your woodworking to the next level. Cabriole legs give the table a refined elegance that will blend gracefully into many decors. Choose a fine-grained hardwood for your project lumber — mahogany, cherry or walnut are excellent choices.

by Jeff Greef

The Rolling Tea Table is about shaping curves. At first glance it may look like a project only for woodworkers with exceptional skills, but it's approachable for anyone with a little experience and a fair amount of patience.

Sculpting the legs and curved top frames of the table is different from cutting elaborate and complex joints where every angle must be exact. To look good, a rounded shape doesn't necessarily have to follow a precise geometric pattern—it just needs to be consistent. If you shape a surface slightly oversized you can go back and take a wee bit more off to make it look right.

Using machines helps make a lot of the shaping go faster. A band saw cuts away most of the waste on the legs, and a stationary sander does the bulk of the rest of the shaping. The curved top frames get their start on the table saw—with a regular blade, no molding heads are necessary. The balance of the shaping is done with carving chisels, spokeshaves and hand sanding. The shaping takes patience and time, but the reward for the effort is a look that beats straight table legs hands down.

Getting Started

The legs of this project require 8/4 stock. Don't laminate the legs because glue lines will detract from the graceful elements of the cabriole style. Remember, it's important to allow thick hardwood time to adjust to your shop's climate before you start to shape the legs.

Figure 1: *Use an 8"-high fence on the router table when forming the dovetails. Be sure the fence is set at exactly 90°. A little wax helps keep the pieces moving smoothly along as you cut them.*

Creating Shapely Legs

Start by machining the leg blanks (pieces 1), then cut the bevels and dovetails on the inside corner of each, as described in the sidebar on page 57. It's a good idea to make an extra leg out of scrap wood to use for test making cuts and machine setups. Be sure the finished bevel width matches the thickness of the aprons.

The leg style is referred to as cabriole with a splat foot. Follow the steps shown in the sidebar on page 60 to form the legs, using the "sand-a-little, look-a-lot" approach. Sight down the length of the legs to find bulges that need to be brought down and recesses that need to be faired in. Make all of the legs at once, comparing them as you go through the steps, to ensure you shape them consistently.

Take great care when using the spokeshave, and again when you start your finish-sanding. At both stages, it is easy to form a flat spot or a depression that will stand out like a sore thumb when you apply varnish to the completed project.

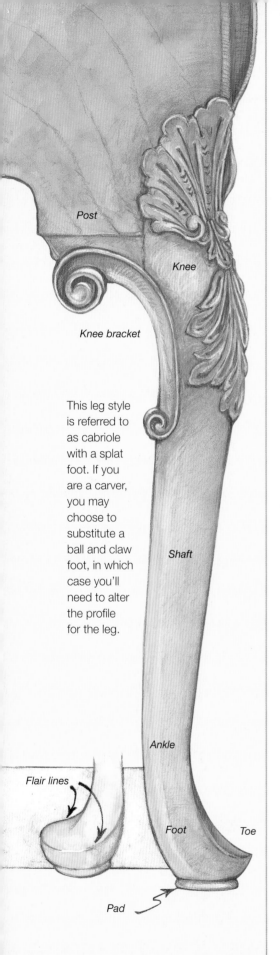

Post

Knee

Knee bracket

This leg style is referred to as cabriole with a splat foot. If you are a carver, you may choose to substitute a ball and claw foot, in which case you'll need to alter the profile for the leg.

Shaft

Ankle

Flair lines

Foot   Toe

Pad

Forming the Aprons

Your apron stock (pieces 2 and 3) must be uniform in thickness or the sliding dovetails won't be consistent. Get started by planing all of the stock at the same setting. Once again, make an extra apron for test cuts and machine setups. You also should sand or scrape the stock prior to forming the joints. It's easier to do now, and you risk rounding the shoulders of the dovetails if you sand later.

Once the apron stock is sanded, mount a high vertical fence on your router table, as shown in Figure 1. Be sure the vertical face of the fence is square to the table, and give yourself at least 8" of height for stability. You will notice in Figure 1, I fixed a strip of plywood to the table, adjacent to the bit. Doing so prevents the frame ends from dipping into the hole in the router table top as they pass by the bit. Complete the setup by waxing the strip and vertical fence to ensure smooth movement.

Figure 2: *Slight bows could rock the aprons while the tails are being formed. Attach guide runners to a high fence to allow for any imperfection in the aprons.*

If your stock is slightly bowed, it may rock against the fence, leaving you with inconsistent dovetails. Solve the problem by fixing two runners to the fence, at the top and bottom, as shown in Figure 2. These will allow any bows to bend inward without contacting the fence.

Set the dovetail bit height $\frac{1}{32}$" or so less than the depth of the slots on the legs and experiment with your extra apron to find a fence location that will give you tails that fit the slots well. Remember, any change in the distance of the fence from the bit will double the

*Quick*Tip

Shop-made Flocking Dots

When making small boxes or jewelry chests, you may decide to line the interior with decorative flocking material. Here's a way to make the most of it and add another detail to your project. Before sweeping up the excess flocking, vigorously press one side of a piece of double-sided carpet tape into the surplus flocking until the tape is completely covered. A light brushing with a soft brush will leave you with a felt-like tape. Punch the tape into circles or cut it into furniture protectors for the bottom of your boxes. With this technique, you'll know that the color will exactly match the interior of the box.

change in thickness of the tail, because the cut is made on both sides. The tails should slide snugly into their grooves, but you shouldn't have to use a mallet to persuade them into place.

Use the same basic setup to trim the bottom of the dovetails to match the 2½" slots in the legs, as shown in Figure 3. Back up these cuts with a support block to keep the aprons at 90° to the fence.

Now lay out the curved lines on the lower edges of the aprons. Enlarge the pattern on page 58; trace the curve on one long apron and one short apron and then band saw the shapes on the matching aprons, two at a time. Smooth the curves with a spokeshave or a small drum sander mounted in a drill press. Follow up with sandpaper and a sanding block and, as with the legs, compare the curves to be sure you have the shapes you want.

Adding Strength to the Leg Assembly

To strengthen the leg-apron joints, use screw blocks (pieces 4) made on the table saw. Cut the blocks so their grain direction is parallel with the aprons—so they'll expand and contract at the same rate. With the legs and aprons temporarily assembled, trim the blocks to a length that holds them about 1⁄16" from the rear surface of the legs, as shown in the Corner Block Detail on page 58. That ensures the screws will pull the block onto the aprons, rather than onto the legs, making for a considerably stronger joint.

Clamps won't be necessary for the joint because snug dovetails will hold themselves well, and the screw blocks will pull it all together. The blocks also serve to square up the assembly, but if you're off by a little bit you always can coerce the assembly into square by pulling across the corners with twine. Assemble each joint individually. Before you start, seal the mitered surfaces of the screw blocks with glue so the end grain will not absorb glue faster than the face grain during assembly. Next, use tapered bits with countersinks to drill holes for the two screws (pieces 5) that hold each block to its leg. Once the screws are installed, plug (pieces 6) the holes over the screws. Remember, the table has a glass top. The screw blocks and plugs will be readily visible from the top, so be sure to do a neat job plugging the screw holes.

Shaping the Top Frame

The edge of each frame component (pieces 7 and 8) has a curved lip that droops downward, away from the plane of the table top. It takes several steps to make the profile, as shown

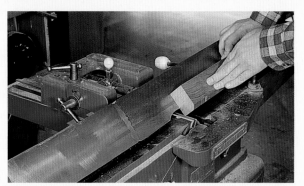

A jointer lets you sneak up to the bevel width on the legs and eliminate sanding.

The leg joinery is formed in two passes. Use a straight bit to hog out the waste and then turn to a dovetail bit to complete the joint. A stop block limits the length of the cut.

Bevels are cut on the two inside corners of each leg at 45°. Form the bevels on a jointer (as shown above), or on a table saw. The finished bevels must match the ½"-thick aprons exactly.

Next, step to the router table and set up a 45° fence to form the dovetail cuts. To produce a smoother cut, rout the slots in two passes. First, hog out the waste with a ¼" straight flute bit. Then, follow up with a 3⁄8" dovetail bit, setting the depth to 3⁄8". Center the slot along the width of the leg bevel, clamping a stop on the router table to limit the length of the cut to 2½". Square up the slot with a chisel to complete the joint.

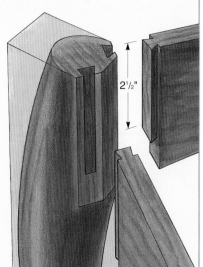

2½"

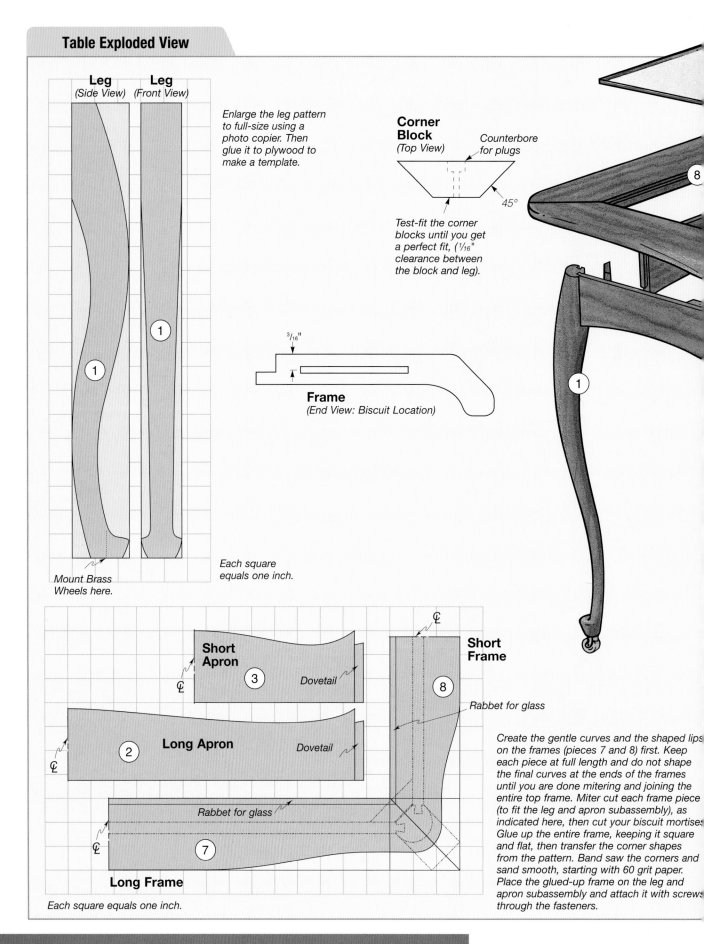

Leg
(Side View)

Leg
(Front View)

Enlarge the leg pattern to full-size using a photo copier. Then glue it to plywood to make a template.

Corner Block
(Top View)

Counterbore for plugs

45°

Test-fit the corner blocks until you get a perfect fit, (1/16" clearance between the block and leg).

3/16"

Frame
(End View: Biscuit Location)

①

①

①

Mount Brass Wheels here.

Each square equals one inch.

Short Apron

③ *Dovetail*

Short Frame

⑧

Rabbet for glass

Long Apron

② *Dovetail*

Rabbet for glass

⑦

Long Frame

Each square equals one inch.

①

⑧

Create the gentle curves and the shaped lips on the frames (pieces 7 and 8) first. Keep each piece at full length and do not shape the final curves at the ends of the frames until you are done mitering and joining the entire top frame. Miter cut each frame piece (to fit the leg and apron subassembly), as indicated here, then cut your biscuit mortises. Glue up the entire frame, keeping it square and flat, then transfer the corner shapes from the pattern. Band saw the corners and sand smooth, starting with 60 grit paper. Place the glued-up frame on the leg and apron subassembly and attach it with screws through the fasteners.

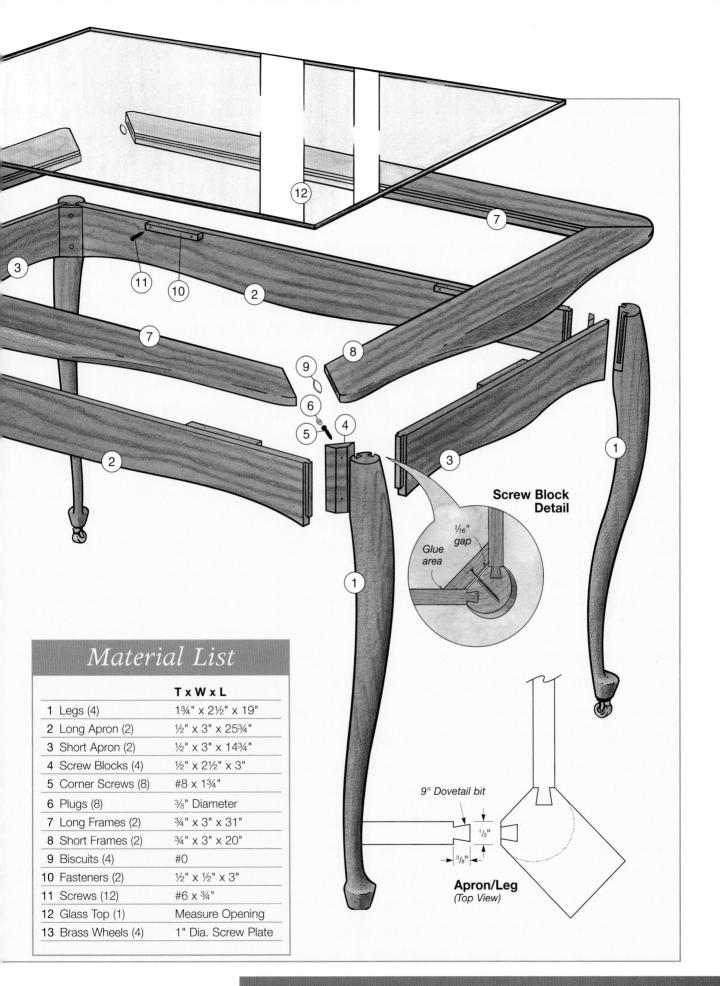

Material List

		T x W x L
1	Legs (4)	1¾" x 2½" x 19"
2	Long Apron (2)	½" x 3" x 25¾"
3	Short Apron (2)	½" x 3" x 14¾"
4	Screw Blocks (4)	½" x 2½" x 3"
5	Corner Screws (8)	#8 x 1¾"
6	Plugs (8)	⅜" Diameter
7	Long Frames (2)	¾" x 3" x 31"
8	Short Frames (2)	¾" x 3" x 20"
9	Biscuits (4)	#0
10	Fasteners (2)	½" x ½" x 3"
11	Screws (12)	#6 x ¾"
12	Glass Top (1)	Measure Opening
13	Brass Wheels (4)	1" Dia. Screw Plate

Screw Block Detail

1/16" gap

Glue area

9° Dovetail bit

½"

⅜"

Apron/Leg
(Top View)

Be careful not to sand the dovetail joint area.

Watch out for depressions or flat spots. Your finish will exaggerate any flaws.

Cabriole legs needn't be identical, simply consistent. Use a sharp spokeshave to bring the legs to their final shape.

Sandpaper can be a handy carving tool when shaping the feet.

Step 1: *Use the fifth scrap wood leg you made earlier for testing. Trace the leg patterns onto adjacent sides of the leg blanks. Cut the first profile on your band saw.*

Step 2: *Tape the cut-off pieces back in place for the second cuts. Doing so replaces the tracings cut off on the first step and gives the bottom of the blank a flat surface to ride against the table.*

Step 3: *The band saw will leave a roughly shaped leg with a square cross section that must be rounded. A stationary belt sander with a 60-grit belt is excellent for the task. Compare all legs as you work on them to ensure they are shaped similarly.*

Step 4: *After sanding and carving the curves to your satisfaction, begin smoothing the legs with a sharp spokeshave. You could do all shaping of the legs with spokeshaves if you don't have a stationary belt sander. Finishing with a spokeshave helps smooth the curves.*

Figure 3: *You'll have to switch to a straight bit to knock off the bottom of the apron's tails. Be sure to use a tall support block when trimming the bottom of the apron dovetails.*

in Shaping the Frame on page 61. Once the outer edge is shaped, use your table saw to form a rabbet on the inside edge of these pieces for the glass top to fit into. Check with your glass dealer before making the cut to verify the exact thickness of the plate glass they stock— it will probably be $7/32$". Don't order the glass until you glue up the frames. It's easier to order glass to fit a top than it is to make a top to fit a pre-cut piece of glass.

Only the center of each piece will retain the curved lip, so use the band saw to cut away the lip on the ends of each piece, using the drawings as a guide. Next, begin final shaping of the curved frame on each piece with the stationary sander. The flat platen of the sander will only let you go so far before you will need to turn to a spokeshave to complete the process. Watch carefully as you shape to ensure all of the curves flow evenly. Finish shaping the underside of the frame with 60-grit sandpaper.

Get set up to cut your corner miters now, carefully following the instructions on the Technical Drawings. The pieces are specified slightly oversized in the Material List. For clean miters, use a sliding cut-off jig on the table saw, as shown in Figure 4. The jig needs to be built up to accommodate the edge lip.

Join the frame pieces with biscuits (pieces 9) as shown in the Elevation Drawings. Test-fit the joints and when everything fits well, glue and clamp them together: measure diagonally and adjust the frame to square. When the frame is dry, transfer the rounded shape to all four corners of the top, then use your band saw to cut the corners and round them over with 60-grit sandpaper.

Completing a Few Final Steps

Install the four fasteners (pieces 10) with screws (pieces 11). Measure the opening for the glass top (piece 12) and order it, asking them to knock off (swipe) the edges so they won't be sharp. Install the brass wheels (pieces 13) to the end of each leg.

That's about it. Now finish-sand the entire project and apply your finish of choice. As you apply finish, remember the inside of the leg and apron assembly will be visible.

Figure 4: *A sliding cutoff jig forms the miters at the ends of the table's frame components. Secure the miters with biscuits located in the remaining ³⁄₈"-thick stock.*

Shaping the Frame

The frames (pieces 7 and 8) consist of moldings created in several steps. Make an extra scrap piece to test your setups.

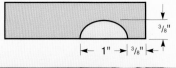

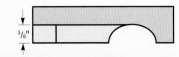

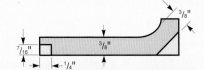

Use your table saw to form coves in the frames. Start by locating an angled fence at two points from the blade as shown above. Measure 1³⁄₈" from the front of the blade and ³⁄₈" from the rear. Test your cut and adjust as needed.

Use a dado head to remove the bulk of the material from the underside of the frames. Then stand the piece on edge to remove the remaining material as shown above.

Flip the piece over and plow the rabbet in the back edge. Then insert a regular saw blade in your saw and slice the angle onto the front edge of the frame.

Chippendale Sofa Table

Good design never really goes of out style. This Chippendale accent table testifies it. Taken from an 18th-century Chippendale catalog, the table remains faithful to his excellent sense of proportion and detail. It is made of common red oak, but you could use mahogany for historical accuracy.

by Carl Spencer

Even posthumously, Thomas Chippendale continues to make sales. When my wife wanted a new sofa table for our family room, we settled on a design from Chippendale's 1762 catalog. The Chippendale Sofa Table certainly proves its timeless appeal. The fanciful leg brackets—typical of Chippendale's later work—are still attractive today.

Chippendale designed almost exclusively in mahogany throughout his long and illustrious career, but we built our reproduction out of red oak to blend with today's more common furniture woods.

Making the Legs and Aprons

The first step in building the table is to cut, the parts to size, according to the dimensions given in the Material List on page 67. With that done, milling can begin with the four legs (pieces 1), which are fashioned from solid stock that is ripped and jointed square to 2¾". Use your table saw to cut a 45° chamfer on the inside corner of each leg (see the Corner Detail Drawing on page 66 for dimensions), then lightly joint the chamfered face to remove any saw kerf marks. Set the legs aside and move on to the aprons (pieces 2 and 3). Machine tenons on both ends of each apron, using a sharp dado set and your table saw's miter gauge.

The mortises that house the tenons also will accommodate the scroll-sawn corner brackets, so it is a good time to make those brackets. Refer to the sidebar on page 64 for complete instructions. When your brackets are completed, turn your attention back to the mortises.

Figure 1: *Mortises in the legs (they house tenons on the brackets and aprons) are cut on a router table using a ¼" spiral-fluted straight bit.*

Begin by installing a ¼" straight bit (spiral fluted works best) in your table-mounted router, and set the fence using the dimensions shown in the Drawings on page 67. To stop the mortises at the correct length, scribe pencil lines on both the router fence and the legs where each cut starts and finishes (see the Drawings for the dimensions).

Remove the stock (see Figure 1, below) in three passes until the mortise is ⅝" deep. When all four legs are mortised, use the same fence setting and bit to make similar mortises in the bottom edges of the aprons. The mortises in the apron will house the tenons on the tops of the brackets, and the dimensions can be found on the Drawings.

Chippendale Designs

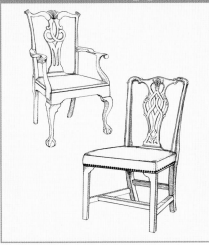

In his earlier work, London furniture builder Thomas Chippendale (1718-1779) made extensive use of cabriole legs and ornate carving.

As his craft matured, he turned increasingly toward straight legs and scrollwork. Chippendale gained lasting fame in 1754 with the publication of his book of furniture designs, *The Gentleman and Cabinet-Maker's Director*.

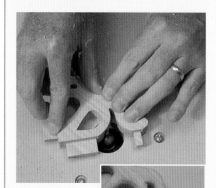

Use your table saw to create tongues on the short sides of the triangular bracket blanks, as shown in the two photos at left. Begin by making a pass to define the tenon (using a sharp blade to combat tearout), then remove the rest of the waste in subsequent passes.

The completed brackets will be attached to the rest of the table with mortise and tenon joints, so stay at your table saw to make tenon shoulders on the two short edges of each triangular blank. Begin by setting your dado blade's height to ³⁄₁₆" and remove enough material from each side of the blank to leave ¼"-thick tongues, as shown in the two photos (at top right). Transform the tongues into tenons (right) by adjusting the dado blade height to ⅝" and removing enough waste to define the tenons. Make photocopies of the design (see the pattern on page 66) and glue them onto the blanks with a low-tack spray. Drill holes through the interior cutout areas and complete the fretwork using a scroll saw or jigsaw. Cutting out the area between the tenons makes final shaping a lot easier. Do the shaping (see the two photos above left) on your router table with a ¼" roundover bit.

Round over the scroll sawn edges of the brackets with a piloted ¼"-radius roundover bit in a table-mounted router.

Start making the brackets (pieces 4) by ripping enough straight-grained ⅝"-thick lumber (see Material List on page 67) into 3½"-wide strips to make eight bracket blanks. Cut the strips into triangles on your table saw using the miter gauge, and make sure the two short sides of each triangle are exactly at 90° to each other or you'll have problems during assembly.

After changing the blade height, use your miter gauge to complete the tenons. The waste between them will be replaced by fillers (pieces 8) during assembly.

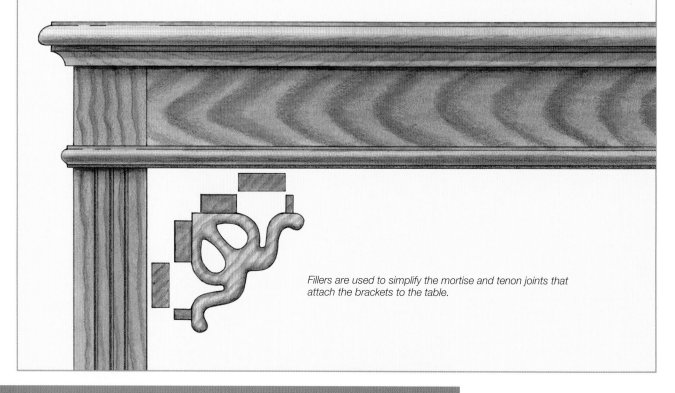

Fillers are used to simplify the mortise and tenon joints that attach the brackets to the table.

Figure 2: *Ease the bottom edges of the legs with a ⅛" roundover bit. At 31¼" long, the legs are short enough to perform this operation while holding each leg vertically on the table.*

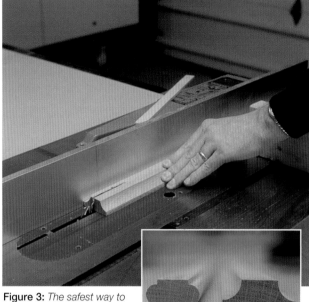

Figure 3: *The safest way to make the narrow moldings that adorn the aprons is to shape both outside edges of wider boards, then rip two lengths of molding from each.*

Adding Decorative Milling

In the Chippendale tradition, the legs on this table are fluted. The flutes are stopped before they reach the top or bottom of each leg (see the Leg Detail Drawing on page 67). To make them, install a ⅛" veining bit in the table router and use the same technique employed to stop the mortises for the brackets: pairs of matching pencil marks on the router table fence and the workpiece.

Stay at the router table to ease the bottom edges of the legs with a ⅛" roundover bit (see Figure 2), then move to the table saw and create ³⁄₃₂" grooves for the tabletop fasteners (pieces 5) on the inside faces of the aprons. They are cut with

a thin-kerf saw blade, and the locations and depths can be found on the Edge Detail Drawing on page 67.

Fashioning the Moldings

True to Chippendale's original 1762 design, decorative moldings are used to dress up the apron. A cove molding (piece 6) runs around the top of each apron, while a wide bead molding (piece 7) adorns the bottom edge. The safest way to make the narrow moldings is to shape both edges of a board (see Figure 3), and then cut off the shaped piece. While routing, make several passes, ending up with a last light pass that both eliminates chatter and minimizes sanding.

*Quick*Tip

Use the Fence to Keep Your Bearings When Routing Some Profiles

You can't mill a bullnose on the edge of a board with a bearing guided bit, at least not if you rely only on the bearing. After making the first cut, you've removed most of the bearing surface for the second cut, so it will be offset (the bit will remove more stock on the second cut than the first). The answer is to make both cuts using the same bearing-guided bit, but you have to rely on your router table's fence, instead of the bearing, to guide the cuts.

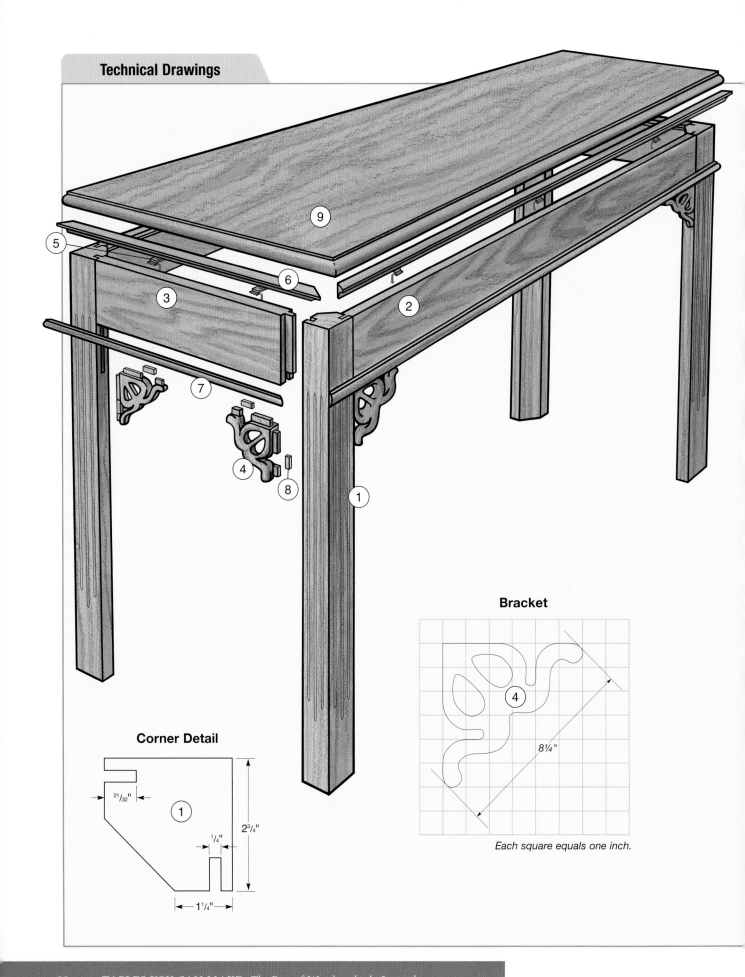

Corner Detail

$^{21}/_{32}$"

①

$^{1}/_{4}$"

$2^{3}/_{4}$"

$1^{1}/_{4}$"

Bracket

④

$8^{1}/_{4}$"

Each square equals one inch.

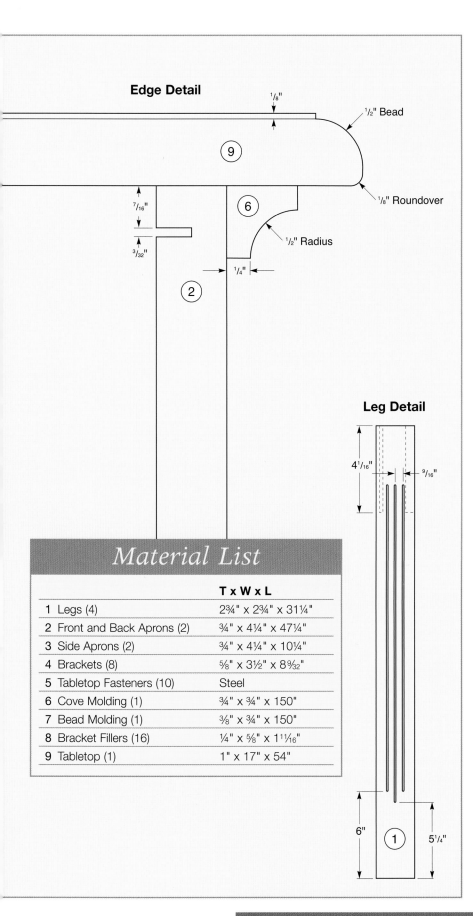

Edge Detail

¹/₈"

¹/₂" Bead

9

¹/₈" Roundover

7/₁₆"

6

³/₃₂"

¹/₂" Radius

¹/₄"

2

Leg Detail

4¹/₁₆"

⁹/₁₆"

6"

1

5¹/₄"

Material List

	T x W x L
1 Legs (4)	2¾" x 2¾" x 31¼"
2 Front and Back Aprons (2)	¾" x 4¼" x 47¼"
3 Side Aprons (2)	¾" x 4¼" x 10¼"
4 Brackets (8)	⅝" x 3½" x 8⁹/₃₂"
5 Tabletop Fasteners (10)	Steel
6 Cove Molding (1)	¾" x ¾" x 150"
7 Bead Molding (1)	⅜" x ¾" x 150"
8 Bracket Fillers (16)	¼" x ⅝" x 1¹¹/₁₆"
9 Tabletop (1)	1" x 17" x 54"

Building the Frame Assembly

The legs, aprons, brackets, fillers (pieces 8), and moldings can be glued up now. Start by gluing the brackets and fillers to the aprons, lining up the brackets with a combination square while the glue is still wet (see Figure 4). When aligned, clamp them in place.

After the glue has dried, fasten the front and back aprons to the legs. To do so, apply glue to their tenons, insert the tenons into the leg mortises and clamp them in place with pipe clamps (see Figure 5). To ensure the legs remain parallel during clamping, insert a spacer between them, down at the bottom. Then, before the glue sets, check the entire assembly for squareness by measuring diagonally.

The two side subassemblies are joined to the shorter apron rail in the same manner, using scrap spacers to ensure parallel joinery. Since the final frame assembly must be checked for squareness on three planes (the top and both ends), you may want to practice the procedure a couple of times until you can do it quickly and accurately, before applying any glue.

After the glue cures, apply masking tape over the legs except where the flutes are, then highlight the flutes with a spray can of flat black lacquer. Remove the masking tape, then sand the entire assembly to 220-grit. You can also give the moldings a final sanding, then trim them to length on your table saw or miter box. Glue the moldings and clamp them in place with spring clamps placed about every five or six inches along their length (see Figure 6 on page 68).

Figure 4: *When gluing the brackets to the aprons, a combination square helps line up everything while the glue is still wet.*

Figure 5: *When attaching the legs to the aprons, two pipe clamps will yield a better joint than one. During this process, a few scraps of paper under the wood will keep glue off the clamps.*

Making the Tabletop

The top (piece 9) is made from 1"-thick boards of various widths, matched for both color and grain pattern. After jointing the edges, arrange the boards so the grain patterns on the ends alternate (one crown up, the next down, etc.). For aesthetic reasons, it's a good idea to never have a joint running right down the center of the top—the glue line and any grain mismatch will be noticeable and distracting. Apply a liberal amount of glue to both edges of each joint, and alternate your clamps (one above the top, the next below) to avoid cupping. Tighten the clamps until the joint is snug, but don't overtighten them or you'll squeeze out too much glue.

When the glue has cured, ask a local cabinet shop owner to run your top through their wide belt sander, taking it down to ¾". Back at the shop, cut the tabletop to final size on your table saw, then sand a ½" radius on the corners with a belt sander. Form the top edges using a ½" beading bit in your router, and create the bottom profile with a ⅛" roundover bit. Sand all of the surfaces to 220-grit.

Finishing and Final Assembly

Stain the leg assembly and top with an oil-based stain. Allow it to dry thoroughly, then apply one coat of sealer. Follow up with three topcoats of brushable semi-gloss lacquer. The

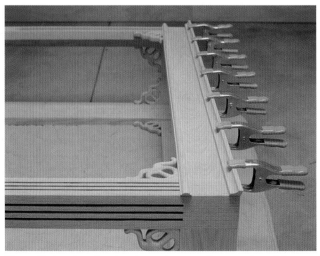

Figure 6: *A series of spring clamps is a sure-fire way of providing equal pressure along the length of molding when attaching it to the apron.*

I was so taken with Chippendale's design I completed the series with an end table and coffee table. Each can be built using the sofa table instructions, with a few dimensional changes. You'll also need 128" of each molding for the end table, and 164" of each for the coffee table.

End Table

Legs	2¾" x 2¾" x 20¼"
Tabletop	¾" x 30" x 30"
Aprons	¾" x 4¼" x 23¼"

Coffee Table

Legs	2¾" x 2¾" x 16¼"
Tabletop	¾" x 30" x 48"
Front & Back Aprons	¾" x 4¼" x 41¼"
Side Aprons	¾" x 4¼" x 23¼"

bottom surface of the tabletop should receive the same treatment to minimize any tendency to cup during humidity changes. Each coat of lacquer must dry completely before you can scuff-sand between coats with 400-grit sandpaper.

After the third coat of lacquer is dry, place the top upside down on a padded workbench. Center the leg assembly on it and mark the locations of the tabletop fasteners. Remove the leg assembly and drill pilot holes for the fasteners. With that done, reposition the legs and install the fasteners.

Finally, place your table behind your sofa and top it off with a hard-bound copy of *The Gentleman and Cabinet-Maker's Director*. After all, you never know when you may need to go shopping for a good project design.

Collector's Coffee Table

A country style Collector's Coffee Table features three interchangeable flocked drawers—a perfect solution for displaying and protecting valued collectibles under a glass top. The topmost drawer becomes the featured display, and you can swap drawers whenever you feel the urge to change the view. The table is made from knotty pine, a traditional choice for country furnishings. A shellac finish—also appropriate for the style—gives the project a warm, amber tone.

by Rick White

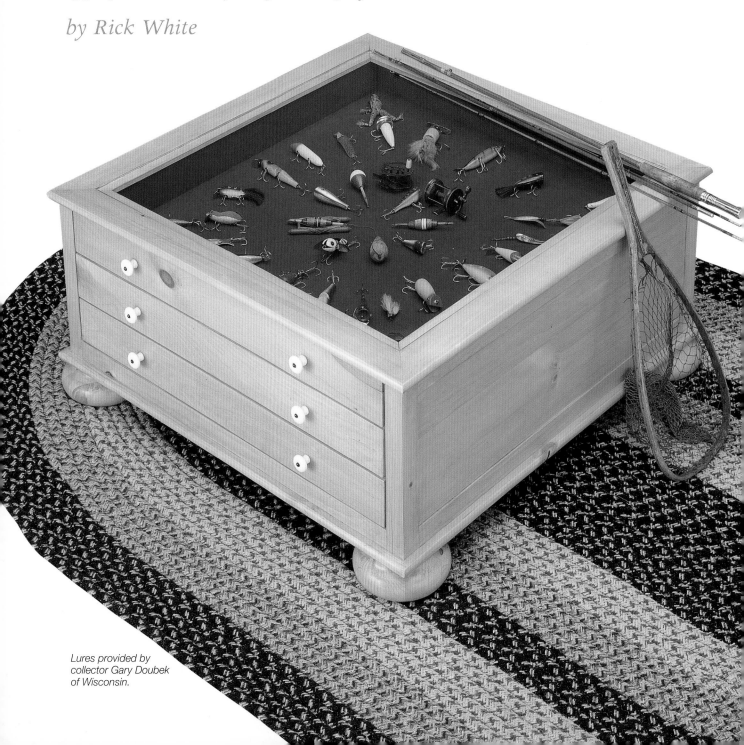

Lures provided by collector Gary Doubek of Wisconsin.

Yesterday's memories have a funny way of becoming today's treasures. Salt and pepper shakers or a handful of fishing lures somehow help us to chart the patterns of our lives. When I designed the Collectors' Coffee Table, knotty pine seemed the perfect complement. Knotty pine was the first choice of generations of American craftsmen. The interchangeable drawers also are made of pine, but I used clear select stock. Each drawer is flocked and you can switch them around to display a different collection any time you choose.

Isabelle Kalway's salt and pepper shaker collection provided by Diane LaVine.

Begin With a Frame

The completed table is essentially a box of drawers with a picture frame top. The top frame sides (pieces 1) are cut to the dimensions given in the Material List on page 73. Now is a good time to get started by cutting all of the parts to the proper size.

A rabbet is cut along the inside top edge of the molding to hold the glass top, as shown in Figure 1. (See the Top Frame Side Detail on page 79 for dimensions). Continue the machining by chucking a ½" roundover bit into your router to shape both the top and bottom edges of the frame pieces to create a bullnose along the outside edge. After mitering the ends of each side, install biscuits at the miters (pieces 2) and glue up the frame. Clamp the subassembly with a web clamp, making sure it's both flat and square as the glue dries.

The bottom subassembly is made of the pine bottom frame (pieces 3) and a plywood bottom panel (piece 4). The outer edges of the pine frame form a skirt for the bun feet. Bullnose the outside edge of the bottom frame as you did with the top frame. Wrap the edges of the plywood with the pine molding, mitering the corners. Glue it in place using three biscuits to a side.

Milling the Carcass

The framework for the box of drawers consists of four stiles (pieces 5) and four corner stiles (pieces 6) glued together to make four corner joints. Rails (pieces 7) run the length of two sides on the top and bottom, while the other two sides have a bottom rail only.

All four of the corner stiles are rabbeted to make the corner joints, as shown in the Exploded View on page 72. Use your table saw to cut the rabbets. Switch to your router table and use a ½" straight bit to cut grooves on the unrabbeted stiles as well as on two of the rabbeted corner stiles. Refer to the Technical Drawings for the locations of all the grooves, mortises, and rabbets. The grooves hold free-floating, ½"-thick side panels (pieces 8) and the back slats (pieces 9).

Next, use the same set up in your router table to rout mortises at the bottoms of the two corner stiles that are not grooved (pieces 6). After you square the ends of the mortises, go ahead and glue the corner joints together. Take care that you match up the parts as shown in the Exploded View and the other Technical Drawings.

As long as you have the router table set up, plow grooves along the length of four of the six rails to accept the side panels. Then form tenons on both ends of all the rails. Make the tenons on your table saw with the help of the saw's miter gauge, following the dimensions shown on the Technical Drawings. Form the tenons on the ends of the back slats (pieces 9) with the same set up. The bottom rail on the front, below the drawers, also receives a notch in each tenon, as shown in the Technical Drawings.

Figure 1: *Keep the waste to the outside of the saw blade to avoid binding when cutting the rabbet in the top molding for the glass top.*

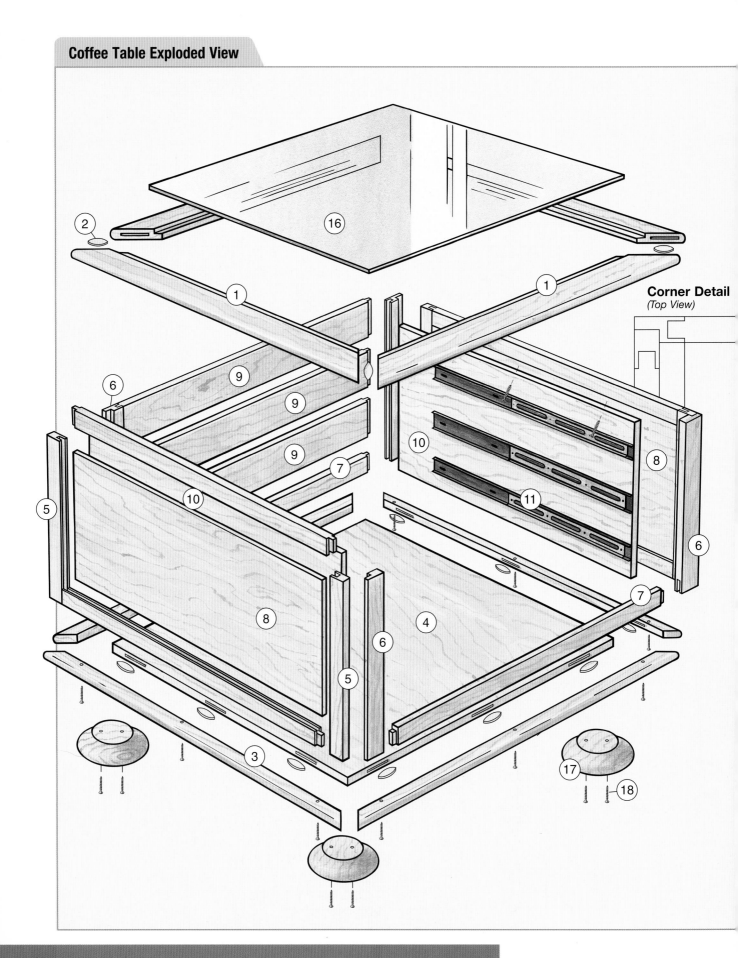

Corner Detail
(Top View)

Material List — Collector's Coffee Table

	T x W x L
1 Top Frame Sides (4)	¾" x 3½" x 35¾"
2 Biscuits (20)	#0
3 Bottom Frame Sides (4)	¾" x 1" x 35¾"
4 Bottom Panel (1)	¾" x 33¾" x 33¾"
5 Side Stiles (4)	¾" x 1⅛" x 12¾"
6 Corner Stiles (4)	¾" x 1½" x 12¾"
7 Rails (6)	¾" x 1½" x 32½"
8 Side Panels (2)	½" x 10½" x 32½"
9 Back Slats (3)	¾" x 3⁹⁄₁₆" x 32½"
10 Panel Backers (2)	¾" x 12¾" x 33"
11 Drawer Slides (3 pairs)	Black, 28" Long
12 Drawer Sides (6)	½" x 3½" x 33"
13 Drawer Fronts and Backs (6)	½" x 3½" x 30⁷⁄₁₆"
14 Drawer Bottoms (3)	¼" x 29¹⁵⁄₁₆" x 32⁷⁄₁₆"
15 Drawer Faces (3)	¾" x 3⁹⁄₁₆" x 31¼"
16 Glass Insert (1)	¼" x 30⅝" x 30⅝"
17 Bun Feet (4)	Pine
18 Bun Feet Screws (8)	#8 x 1⅝"
19 Porcelain Pulls (6)	1¼" Diameter

The three flocked drawers let you change the display from one collection to another at a moment's notice.

Figure 2: *Plywood reinforces the sides and provides a solid base for the drawer slides. The back panel is made up of three separated slats.*

Assemble the Box

Now that the major milling operations are done, move on to assembling the table components. Test-fit the corner joint subassemblies with the floating side panels and the rails. Remember to make a right and left side, taking the drawer opening into consideration. When all of the parts fit correctly, disassemble, then glue and clamp them at the tenon joints until the glue

cures. Don't glue the panels in place, they must float freely. Next, glue and tack the back rail and back slats in place with brads, between the two side subassemblies. Be sure to hold a slight ³⁄₁₆" reveal between each slat (see Technical Drawings) to mimic the look of the drawers on the other side. Now flip the project upside down and glue the last rail in place at the bottom of the drawer opening. Clamp the box securely, measuring diagonally to square the casework while the glue cures. When everything is dry, center the casework on the bottom assembly and trace a light pencil line around its perimeter. Remove the casework and

use your lines to establish the pilot hole locations (see Technical Drawings) for attaching the base to the box. Turn the box on its top edge to glue and screw the bottom in place. There are two plywood panel backers (pieces 10) that fit inside the table compartment (see Figure 2) to accommodate the drawer slides (pieces 11). Drop the panel backers in place now and secure them with glue and brads at the corner joints.

The top frame is secured to the box with screws driven up at an angle from inside the case. A pocket hole jig makes drilling and driving the screws much easier. Attach the top frame with screws and glue, then move on to the drawers.

---

*Quick*Tip

Buying air-dried lumber—Save your "green" when it's too green

Your local sawmill may be a great source for inexpensive lumber, but moisture can be a problem if the mill doesn't kiln-dry its stock. Most small mills pile up logs and store them out in the weather. When they rip them into boards, they usually store these outside in unprotected stickered stacks. The lumber will take a year or more to properly season and dry down to acceptable levels for woodworking. One way to safeguard against buying overly green lumber is to bring a moisture meter with you. Have the sawmill cross-cut a board for you to test it with the meter. Don't test exposed ends, which will dry faster than the rest of the internal area and give you an inaccurate reading. Boards with 6% to 12% moisture content are acceptable for woodworking. Buy wood wetter than that, and you're headed for trouble.

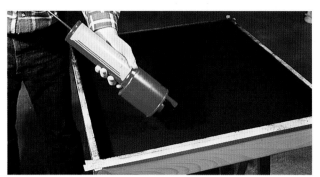

Figure 3: *Flocking the drawers is simply a matter of brushing on colored adhesive, then spraying on the flocking with a special gun.*

Building the Drawers

We used simple box joints to join the drawer sides (pieces 12) to the fronts and backs (pieces 13). As shown in the sidebar at right, they're cut on the table saw with a ½" dado head. A ½" registration key is glued in the miter gauge's auxiliary wooden fence to keep all of the cuts lined up perfectly. Follow the Technical Drawings when making the fingers and gaps so they interlock properly when assembled. After the box joints have been completed, mill a groove in each piece for the drawer bottoms (pieces 14). These dimensions are also shown on the Technical Drawings.

Assemble the drawers with glue and clamps, but don't glue the bottoms in place. Let them float to allow for wood movement. Attach the drawer faces (pieces 15) with predrilled and countersunk screws driven through the drawer fronts. Having them in place will help you install the drawer slides correctly, following the manufacturer's instructions.

Now is a good time to order the tempered glass insert (piece 16) for the top of the cabinet, as the glass shop can make it up while you attend to finishing and a few other details. I chose not to have the glass edges beveled: a polished edge is very attractive and quite a bit less costly.

Finishing Up

Traditional construction deserves a traditional finish, and what better choice than old-fashioned shellac? After giving the entire project its final sanding, follow the instructions on page 76 and 77 to apply this finish. Don't shellac the drawer interiors: they must be sealed with a finish that is compatible with the flocking glue (see the manufacturer's instructions).

Flocking the Drawers

Flocking the drawers is a far simpler operation than one would guess. It involves masking the area to be covered, applying a tinted adhesive, and then shooting colored fibers across the glue before it dries. The most convenient way

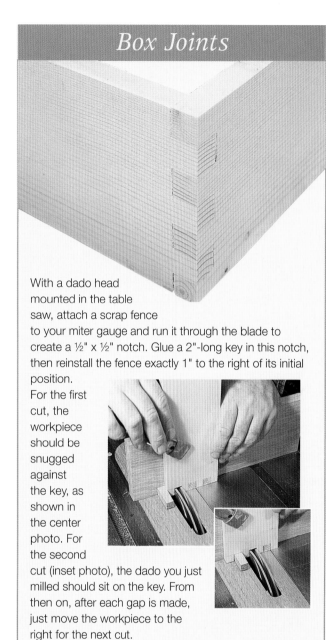

Box Joints

With a dado head mounted in the table saw, attach a scrap fence to your miter gauge and run it through the blade to create a ½" x ½" notch. Glue a 2"-long key in this notch, then reinstall the fence exactly 1" to the right of its initial position. For the first cut, the workpiece should be snugged against the key, as shown in the center photo. For the second cut (inset photo), the dado you just milled should sit on the key. From then on, after each gap is made, just move the workpiece to the right for the next cut.

If the combined total of fingers and gaps is an even number, you repeat the process for the second workpiece. If the number is uneven, clamp a ½" spacer to your auxiliary fence before making the first cut, as shown below. Note that the right edge of this spacer must line up with the left edge of the dado blade.

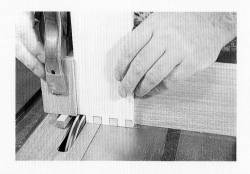

Figure 4: *The bun feet are predrilled and counterbored for screws. Just establish the correct location and screw them in place.*

to apply the adhesive to the drawer interiors is brushing it on with a 2" brush. Load the special application gun with flocking fibers. Depress the handle of the gun to shoot a generous coating of flocking on each drawer (see Figure 3). Don't forget to flock the interior faces of the drawer sides, as they can be seen through the glass top. Let the adhesive and fibers dry for a day, then gently brush or blow off the excess flocking. It's usually available in red, blue, green, brown, and black to suit your color preference.

Final Thoughts

The bun feet (pieces 17) come predrilled, so installing them is a matter of driving screws (pieces 18) at the appropriate locations (see Figure 4). Refer to the Technical Drawings for the correct locations of the feet on the cabinet. We selected old-fashioned porcelain knobs (pieces 19) that attach from the front for a very traditional look. Locate them on the drawers as shown on the Technical Drawings.

Then you'd better start organizing your collections, because it's time to ask your friends over for coffee while displaying your prized collectibles.

How To Apply a Shellac Finish

The ratio between shellac flakes and alcohol is known as a cut. A pound of flakes in a gallon of alcohol is a 1 pound cut—a good place to start. Add shellac to thicken, or denatured alcohol to thin.

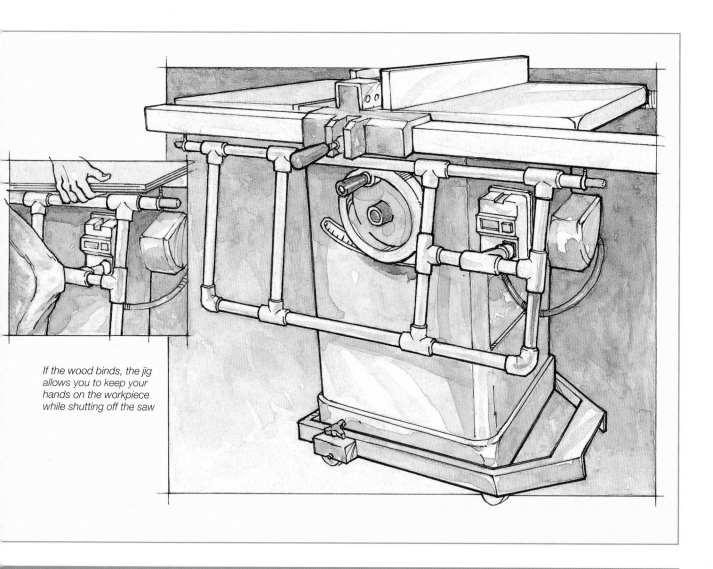

If the wood binds, the jig allows you to keep your hands on the workpiece while shutting off the saw

Shellac is the perfect finish for traditionally styled pine furniture. Its rich amber color provides a beautiful patina that complements knotty pine and continues to warm with age.

It is also surprisingly easy to apply. You can brush it on, but many finishers prefer a hand-rubbed method, dipping a cloth into the shellac and wiping the finish smoothly onto a well-sanded surface. Shellac dries very quickly, so work in small areas, like a side or a drawer front.

As you apply, keep the pad moving smoothly, and don't overwipe. You can add a drop of mineral oil to the bottom of your pad to help it slide more easily. Each coat of shellac is very thin, so build up several coats before smoothing them with an extra-fine abrasive pad. Repeat the process a couple of times and let the finish cure overnight. Then, wipe it down with a cloth dampened with naphtha (not alcohol) to remove the mineral oil residue. Repeat the entire application process one more time and the result will be truly stunning.

Turn a soft, lint-free cloth into an application pad by folding the corners into the center. Repeat the process a couple of times until you have a round, full pad to work with.

Drawer Face Subassembly

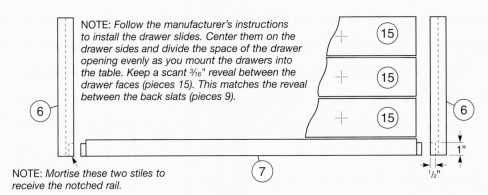

NOTE: *Follow the manufacturer's instructions to install the drawer slides. Center them on the drawer sides and divide the space of the drawer opening evenly as you mount the drawers into the table. Keep a scant ³⁄₁₆" reveal between the drawer faces (pieces 15). This matches the reveal between the back slats (pieces 9).*

NOTE: *Mortise these two stiles to receive the notched rail.*

Side Subassembly

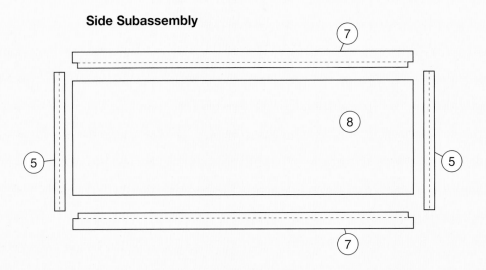

Back Subassembly

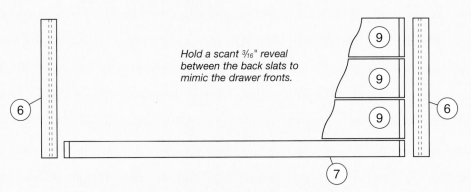

Hold a scant ³⁄₁₆" reveal between the back slats to mimic the drawer fronts.

Stile and Rail Joint
(Top View)

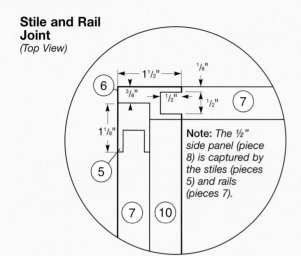

Note: *The ½" side panel (piece 8) is captured by the stiles (pieces 5) and rails (pieces 7).*

Box Joint Detail
(Side View)

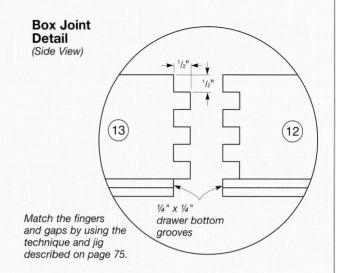

Match the fingers and gaps by using the technique and jig described on page 75.

¼" x ¼" drawer bottom grooves

Rail Detail

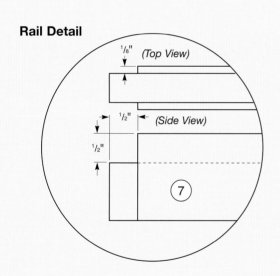

(Top View)

(Side View)

Bun Feet and Screw Locations
(Top View)

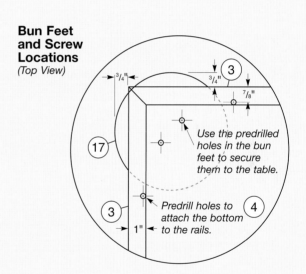

Use the predrilled holes in the bun feet to secure them to the table.

Predrill holes to attach the bottom to the rails.

Drawer Pull Location
(Front View)

Center

7"

Top Frame Side Detail
(End View)

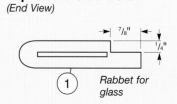

Rabbet for glass

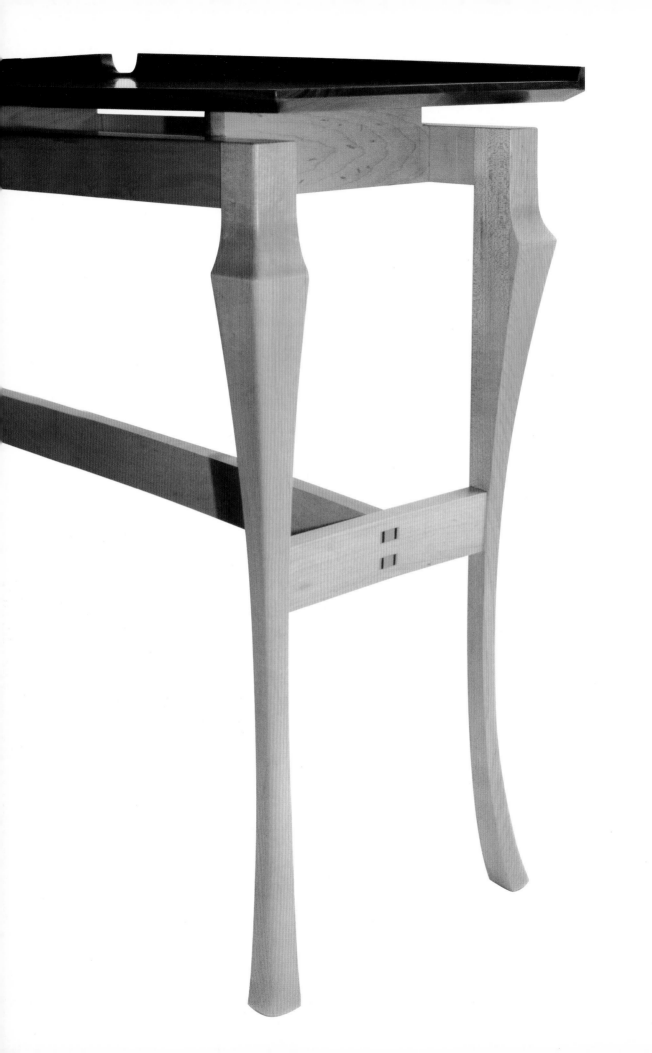

Graceful Hall Table

A harmonious confluence of design, skillful joints, and thoughtful material selection creates a rewarding project for woodworkers with advanced skills. You'll need to sharpen up your spokeshave, hone a scraper or two, and plan on taking your time to carry out the project properly.

by Richard Jones

Like most furniture builders, I like to glean inspiration for my designs from an eclectic range of sources. As a result, my furniture can be contemporary while incorporating both modern and traditional construction. For example, I prefer to cut dovetails by hand: functionally, they're no better than machine cuts, but I believe they are more appropriate in a refined piece. My goal is to create beautiful furniture, not quickly produced utilitarian pieces. That is to say, the concept, design, look, and integrity of my furniture is more important to my clients than how economically it can be produced. That's especially true of this hall table. The concept began with the premise of a tall, elegant table, perhaps located in a large hall or reception area. During the preliminary sketching stage, three elements came quickly to mind. First, it called for cabriole legs. Next, I wanted the top to float above the supporting framework. And finally, a light-colored species in the legset would be offset by a dramatically contrasting darker top.

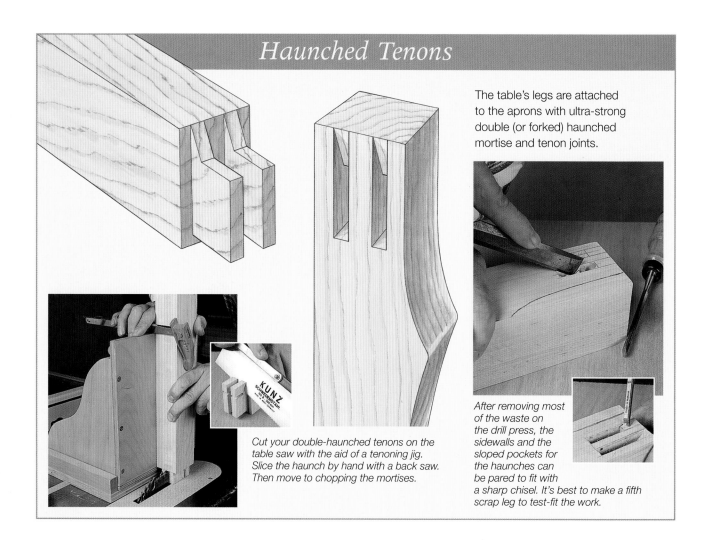

The table's legs are attached to the aprons with ultra-strong double (or forked) haunched mortise and tenon joints.

Cut your double-haunched tenons on the table saw with the aid of a tenoning jig. Slice the haunch by hand with a back saw. Then move to chopping the mortises.

After removing most of the waste on the drill press, the sidewalls and the sloped pockets for the haunches can be pared to fit with a sharp chisel. It's best to make a fifth scrap leg to test-fit the work.

The cabriole curves in the legs further suggested the front of the tabletop, the front rail and the stretcher should all feature gentle curves. In addition, a low, broken pediment (in effect, a decorative raised back edge) also picks up this curve.

Making the Tabletop

A trip to my local lumberyard yielded some nice Santos (Bolivian) rosewood for the top. The rosewood provided the strong visual contrast to the hard maple I selected for the legs. The top's edges feature dramatic chamfers, complementing the table's harmonious gentle curves. The top of this table is essentially a wide assembly made from three narrow, edge-glued boards (pieces 1). Rip, joint, and plane these color-matched boards, after first

selecting them on the basis of the grain orientation. For example, the front board should feature a curved grain pattern, closely matching the chamfered front edge of the top.

After running the boards through your jointer, follow up with a couple of skims with a block plane, forming a spring joint—a barely visible gap that appears at the middle of the long joint between each pair of boards. The technique ensures a tight fit along the whole glue joint.

Use biscuits along the edges for alignment: no need to glue them in, they simply help line up the board edges for gluing. Plane and sand the resulting slab, then put it aside to settle while you build the legset: biscuit locations occasionally telegraph through if insufficient time is left between the

glue-up and the finishing process. Rip, crosscut and joint the rest of the legset elements to the dimensions shown in the Material List on page 84.

Forming a Template for the Legs

Use ¼" hardboard to create the template for the legs. Their profiles, including mortise locations and dimensions, can be found in the Pattern on page 85. Enlarge the pattern pieces by photocopying and attach them to the hardboard (use spray adhesive), then cut the pattern to shape on the band saw. Finesse the edges with files and sandpaper.

Select stock for the legs (pieces 2) so the curvature in their grain follows the template. Orient each leg blank (left front, left back etc.) so the most attractive grain will be most visible from the front.

Use the cabriole template to trace the shape on the two inner faces of each leg, transferring the mortise marks to the relevant faces at the same time. Note all of the joints are kept within the confines of the straight parts of each leg. I suggest you make an extra leg out of scrap stock for experimentation.

You will find it easier to chop the mortises in the legs before you machine their cabriole curves, so set them aside.

An Introduction to the Joinery

With the legs laid out and the tabletop glued up and set aside for the moment, take a minute and preview the rest of the joinery, to help you get oriented. The maple legset for the table is made up of a front and back apron (pieces 3 and 4), a long stretcher (piece 5), two rails (pieces 6) and three short tabletop supports (pieces 7) that suspend and elevate the floating tabletop.

You should know the front and back aprons are slightly narrower than the legs, to create a small decorative offset. The tabletop supports are joined to these aprons with sliding dovetails, and they protrude above them by 1".

The stretcher and rails are joined together with double-wedged (or forked) tenons, to provide additional strength and beauty. The front apron, stretcher and rails are all curved (the rails are actually curved in more than one plane), and a thin veneer of plainsawn lumber (piece 8) will be glued to the front apron later.

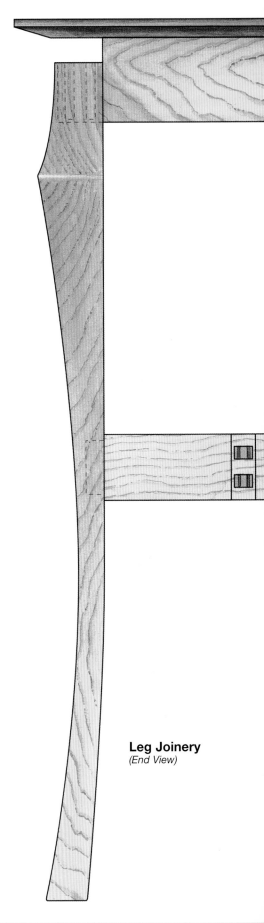

Leg Joinery
(End View)

Shaping Cabriole Legs

The first step in shaping the cabriole legs is to make a hardboard template. Use it to lay out the profile on two adjacent faces of each leg blank. Then band saw each leg to shape, taping the cutoffs back in place after each cut, to keep the blank square and more manageable during the second cut. After sawing, use hand tools and sanders (right) to coax the free-form legs to their final shape.

Use a band saw to form the curves that create these contemporary cabriole legs. Before you cut, evaluate, and orient the legs to best display the figure of the wood's grain.

Use a spokeshave, scraper, compass, and block plane to reduce imperfections to sandable size. Take your time, working with the grain and keeping the mortised areas nice and flat.

Material List – Hall Table

	T x W x L			T x W x L
1 Tabletop (1)	¾" x 17⅜" x 63¾"		7 Tabletop Supports* (3)	1¼" x 3⅜" x 13⁷⁄₃₂"
2 Legs (4)	2¾" x 2¾" x 33⅜"		8 Apron Veneer (1)	⅛" x 2⅜" x 56¾"
3 Front Apron (1)	2⅞" x 2⅜" x 58"		9 Wedges (8)	⅛" x ½" x ¾"
4 Rear Apron (1)	1⅞" x 2⅜" x 58"		10 Screws (9)	#8 x 3" Steel
5 Long Stretcher (1)	1¹⁄₁₆" x 3⅝" x 57⅞"		11 Back Edge (1)	⅞" x 1¹⁵⁄₁₆" x 64"
6 Rails (2)	1" x 2⅝" x 13"			

The center tabletop support is 1⅝" longer than the end ones.

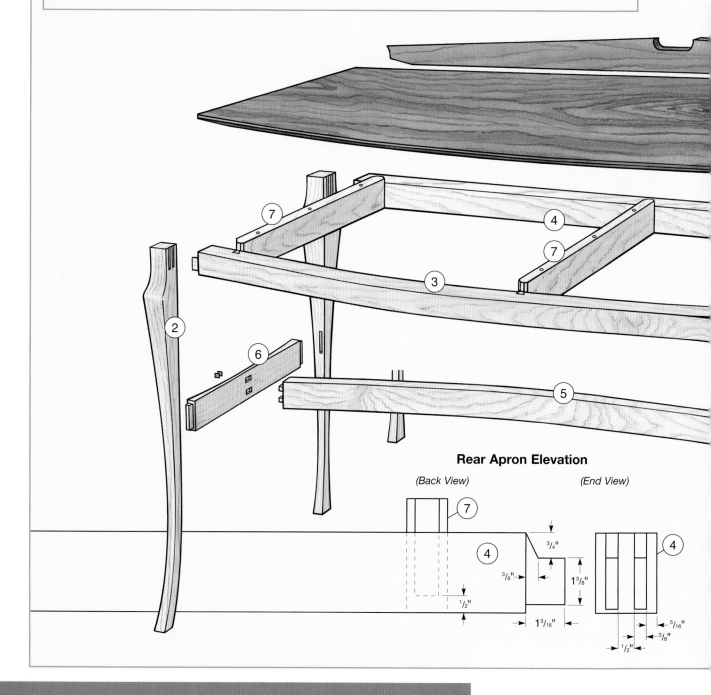

Rear Apron Elevation

(Back View)   (End View)

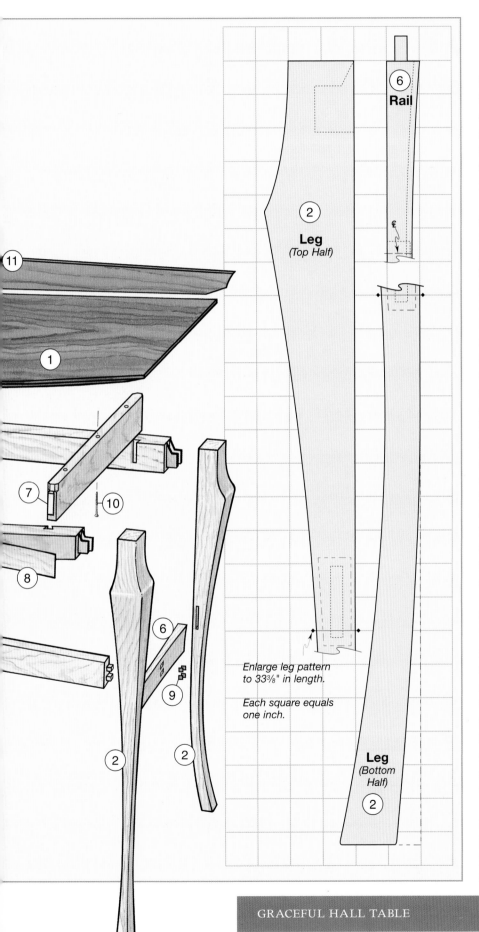

Leg
(Top Half)

②

⑥
Rail

⑪

①

⑦

⑩

⑧

⑥

②

②

⑨

②

Enlarge leg pattern to 33⅜" in length.

Each square equals one inch.

Leg
(Bottom Half)

②

Forming the Haunched Tenons

Haunched tenons have a distinctive sloping aspect that adds to the gluing area…and to their level of difficulty. See page 82 for the proper steps to form the tenons. Practice on scrap before you move to the actual pieces.

With that done, lay out and chop stopped double mortises in the legs, using the extra scrap leg you created for practice. As long as you are working on the legs, lay out and chop the mortises for the rails as well. Then, band saw the legs to shape, taping the cutoff back in place each time to keep the blank square as you work. Remove the saw marks and refine the curves with a variety of tools: I used a compass plane, spokeshaves, a stationary belt sander, a drum sander, scrapers, and a sanding block. With free forms such as these, there is no easy, standardized way to get around the process: you just have to do the work. Round over the sharp front edges and the foot of each leg, making constant comparisons from one leg to the next to maintain their uniformity. For some additional guidelines on the technique, see "Shaping Cabriole Legs" on page 83.

Milling Sliding Dovetails

The aprons have sliding dovetail dadoes machined into their inside faces that match the sliding dovetail tenons on the ends of the tabletop supports. Mill these with a 14° dovetail bit chucked in the router table (see the Technical Drawings for locations and dimensions). Pare away the small decorative chamfers on the top of each tenon—they will be visible after the table is assembled.

Using a two-step process, plow the matching stopped dovetail dadoes into the inside faces of the aprons. Do it on all but the center dado on the front curved apron. Plow the center dado

Sliding Dovetails

Center

4³/₁₆"

3

Sliding dovetails are plowed into both the front and back apron. The dovetails are stopped ½" from the bottom edge. Because of the curvature of the front apron, you'll have to wait to plow the center dovetail groove until after the apron is shaped. All of the others are created while the apron is squared up. The straightedge routing jig is a big help during the process.

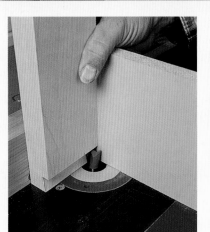
Move to your router table and create the dovetails on both ends of the tabletop supports. Test-fit your joints carefully.

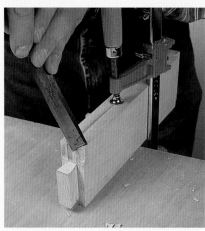
Create a chamfer on the exposed ends of the tabletop supports. These details are visible just under the floating tabletop.

After you plow your stopped dovetail dado onto the apron, square up the end of the dado with a sharp chisel.

later; wait until the curve is created in the front apron. Remove most of the waste with a straight bit, then complete the profile with the same dovetail bit you used on the tenons. (See "Sliding Dovetails," above, for details). Stop the cuts ½" shy of each apron's bottom edge and square the stopped end with a chisel. Dry-fit the tenons until they fit perfectly. Transfer the curves shown on the Technical Drawings to the top edge

of the front apron, and band-saw it to shape. Sand it smooth.

Now that you have the curve established in the front apron, set up and plow the remaining dovetail dado into the center of the front apron.

Forming Forked-and-Wedged Tenons
The long, curved stretcher is joined to the rails with a forked-and-wedged mortise and tenon joint. It is

a time-consuming and persnickety technique, but it's very strong. Lay out the double (forked) tenons on the stretchers, then machine them on the table saw. The kerfs for the wedges are made on the band saw, with small-diameter holes stopping the saw cuts. See Figure 1 on page 89.

The veneer for the front apron (piece 8) is made by squaring up and planing a piece of thicker stock. After

(5)

(6)

(9)

Long Stretcher

(Face View)   *(End View)*

(5)   (5)

$1/2"$

$1/2"$

$1/2"$

$1/2"$

$3/4"$

$1/4"$ $1"$

$2^1/8"$

(6)   (6)

$1/4"$ $1/4"$

$3/8"$

Rail
(Face View)   *(End View)*

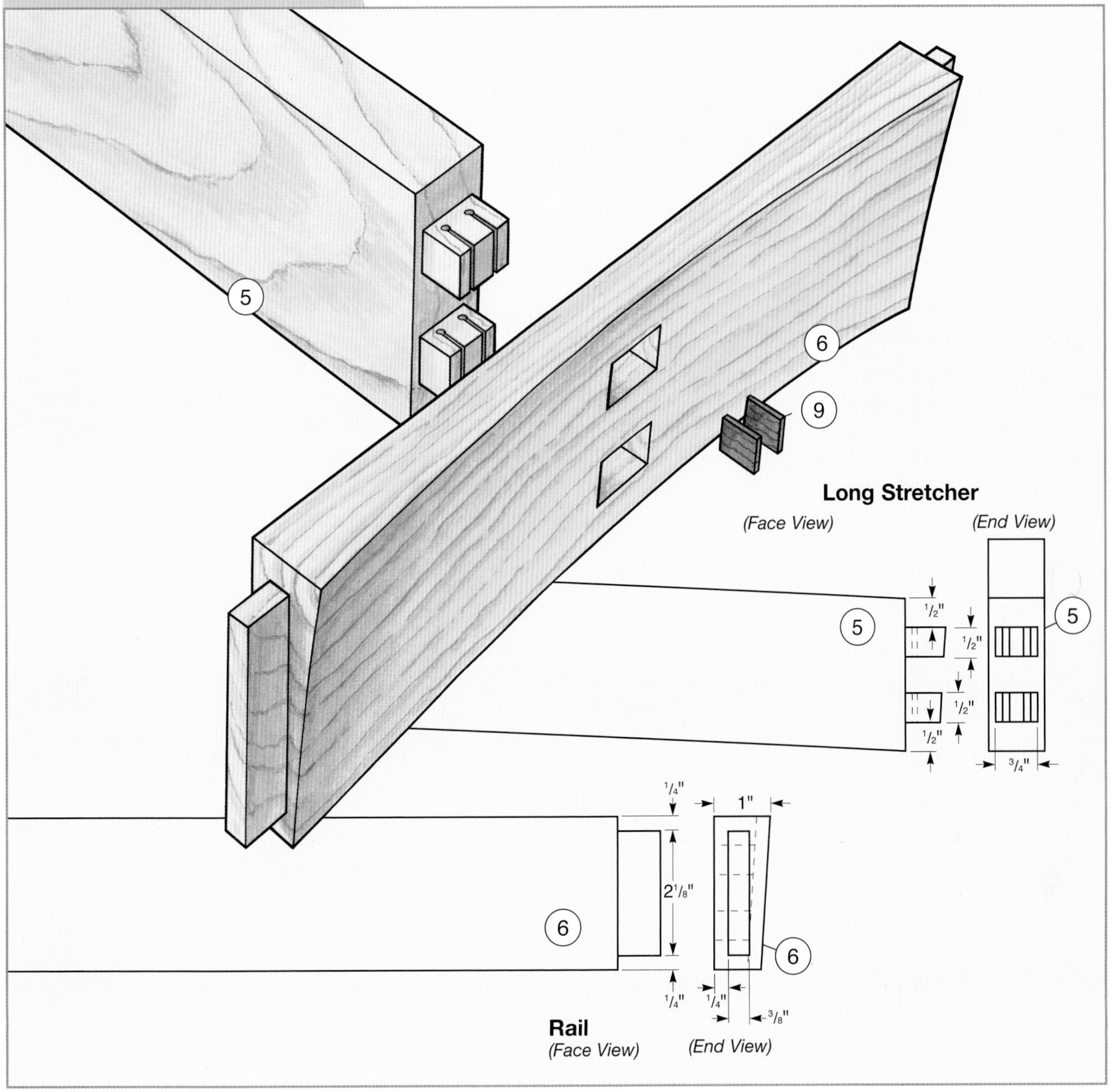

planing, rip a 3/16"-thick strip on your table saw. With a slave board clamped into your planer, plane the cutoff to 1/8" thickness.

Glue and clamp the veneer strip to the front apron using lengths of scrap to spread the clamping pressure. Use polyurethane glue here because it has a long open time. After cleaning up the excess dried glue, re-define the shoulders on the tenons if necessary.

Then rout a bevel on the edges of the front apron so that it runs out right along the glue line (see Technical Drawings). That disguises the joint and the change in the grain pattern.

With all of the tenons completed, the long stretcher can now be band sawn and belt sanded to shape. The inside face of each rail is flat, but the outside face has compound curves that follow the taper of the leg (see

Technical Drawings on pages 90 and 91 and sidebar on page 88). They can be marked freehand during a dry assembly, then cut on the band saw (with the table set at the right bevel) and fine tuned with the compass plane, spokeshave, and other forming tools.

Now band saw the eight wedges (pieces 9, see Technical Drawings) from a piece of dark stock—preferably a cutoff from the tabletop.

The rails on this table have complementary curves carved in two planes. One curve, running along the top edge of the rail, can be found in the Technical Drawings. It's important, however, to note that the curve is deeper on the bottom edge of the rail than on the top edge. It is achieved by setting a slight angle on your band saw's table. The other curve matches the shape of the cabriole leg, yet is held back to create a decorative line where the rail joins the leg.

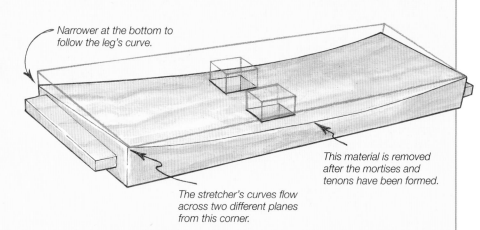

Narrower at the bottom to follow the leg's curve.

This material is removed after the mortises and tenons have been formed.

The stretcher's curves flow across two different planes from this corner.

Looking deceptively simple, the hall table's rails are a very complex bit of woodworking.

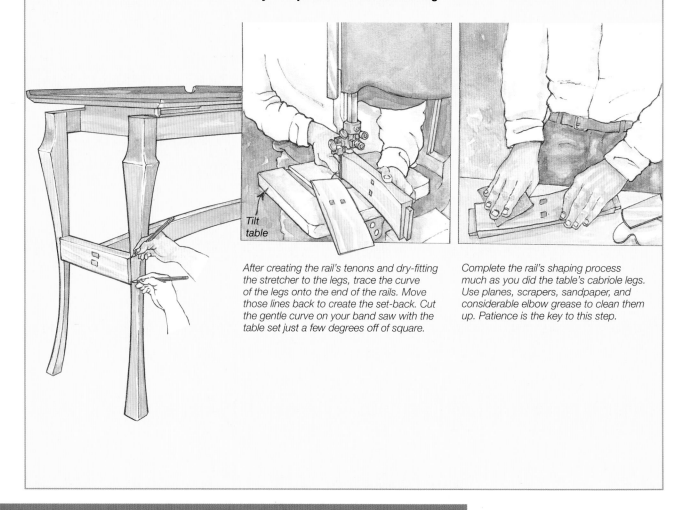

Tilt table

After creating the rail's tenons and dry-fitting the stretcher to the legs, trace the curve of the legs onto the end of the rails. Move those lines back to create the set-back. Cut the gentle curve on your band saw with the table set just a few degrees off of square.

Complete the rail's shaping process much as you did the table's cabriole legs. Use planes, scrapers, sandpaper, and considerable elbow grease to clean them up. Patience is the key to this step.

Figure 1: *The forked tenons are formed on the table saw. The stopped wedge-kerfs are sliced on the band saw.*

Completing the Tabletop

With the legset complete, the tabletop can now be completed. After checking for distortion, perform any minor adjustment on the jointer and planer. Square it up by truing the back edge on the jointer, then trim it to the requisite square size on the table saw. It will require a crosscut sled.

Lay out the front curve according to the Technical Drawings, then bevel the bottom of the front edge with a bearing-guided chamfering bit in the router. The rosewood on the pictured project had a lot of interlocked and twisted grain, so I sanded the top and bottom faces down through the grits from 120- to 220-grit using a stroke sander. Hand-sanding completed the process to 320-grit.

The tabletop's back edge (piece 11), with its small broken arched pediment, is all that remains to be built now. Transfer the profile from the Technical Drawings, then band saw it to shape. Clean up the curves with a drum sander chucked in the drill press, then sand it down to 320-grit. Glue and clamp the piece to the tabletop, then dry-fit the completed top to the legset.

Assembling and Finishing the Legset

Prior to assembly, all parts should be scraped and then sanded to 320-grit. Then you must counterbore the three tabletop supports for their screws (pieces 10), as shown on the Technical Drawings. After that, the table's legset can be assembled in four distinct stages.

First, glue the long stretcher to the two rails and drive in the wedges. After drying, clean the wedges flush to the curved shape of the rails with a chisel and sandpaper.

Next, glue each pair of legs (the front and then the back) to their respective aprons. Make sure the haunched tenons are seated properly and each subassembly is square and true as you apply clamping pressure.

The third step is to glue and clamp the tenons on the H-shaped stretcher/rail subassembly into their relative leg mortises.

And the final legset assembly step is to glue the sliding dovetails on the tabletop supports into place by sliding each one down individually, thus revealing one reason for selecting the joint in the first place: it allows for a less stressful glue-up procedure.

Minor trimming and sanding may be required after each stage of the glue-up. Once completed, apply at least five coats of Tung oil: it's fairly easy to damage but simple to repair, has a nice feel to the touch, and darkens maple satisfactorily.

Finishing the Tabletop

I sprayed three coats of satin pre-catalyzed lacquer on all faces, rubbing down the dust nibs in between. Pre-catalyzed lacquer was chosen for its ability to resist spills and other damage. The top coat was finished with #0000 steel wool and liquid wax to leave a slippery smooth finish that's a delight to touch. Should there be a need to refinish in the future, the top can easily be removed to facilitate this.

Once the finish has cured, attach the legset to the upturned top by driving the nine screws through the supports into countersunk pilot holes in the underside of the top. Turn your hall table upright and place it on exhibition in a nice, conspicuous place.

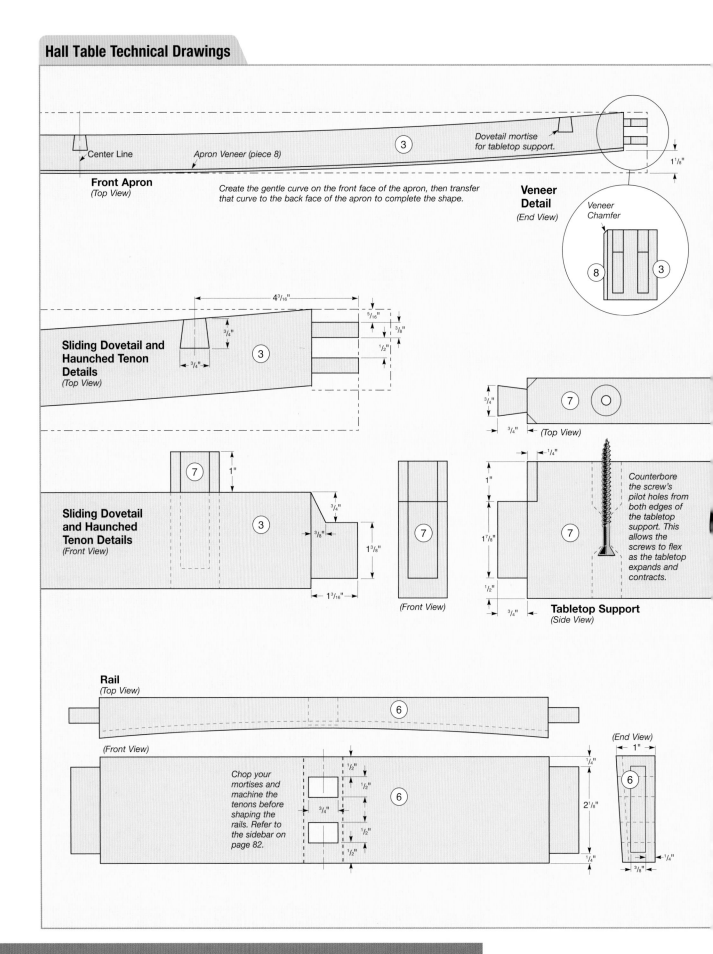

Front Apron
(Top View)

Center Line

Apron Veneer (piece 8)

③

Dovetail mortise
for tabletop support.

1 1/8"

Create the gentle curve on the front face of the apron, then transfer
that curve to the back face of the apron to complete the shape.

**Veneer
Detail**
(End View)

Veneer
Chamfer

8   3

**Sliding Dovetail and
Haunched Tenon
Details**
(Top View)

4 3/16"

5/16"

3/8"

3/4"

1/2"

3/4"

③

**Sliding Dovetail
and Haunched
Tenon Details**
(Front View)

7

1"

3/4"

3/8"

③

1 3/8"

1 3/16"

⑦

(Front View)

3/4"

3/4"

(Top View)

1/4"

1"

1 7/8"

1/2"

3/4"

⑦

Counterbore
the screw's
pilot holes from
both edges of
the tabletop
support. This
allows the
screws to flex
as the tabletop
expands and
contracts.

Tabletop Support
(Side View)

Rail
(Top View)

⑥

(Front View)

Chop your
mortises and
machine the
tenons before
shaping the
rails. Refer to
the sidebar on
page 82.

1/2"

1/2"

3/4"

1/2"

1/2"

⑥

(End View)

1"

1/4"

2 1/8"

⑥

1/4"

1/4"

3/8"

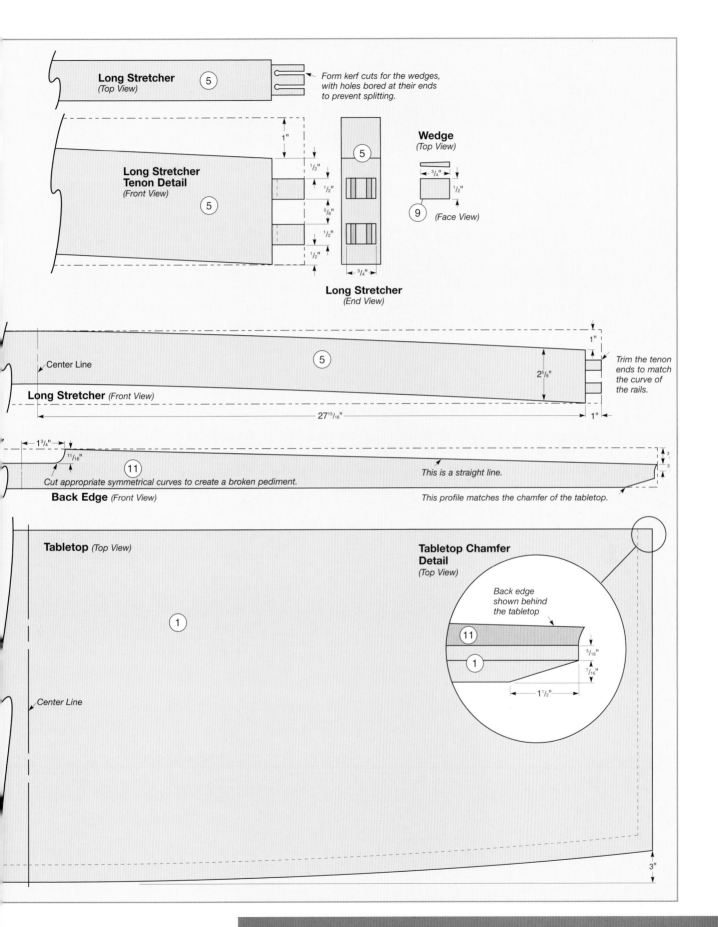

Long Stretcher
(Top View)
⑤

Form kerf cuts for the wedges, with holes bored at their ends to prevent splitting.

1"

Long Stretcher Tenon Detail
(Front View)
⑤

1/2"

1/2"

5/8"

1/2"

1/2"

⑤

3/4"

Long Stretcher
(End View)

Wedge
(Top View)

3/4"

1/2"

⑨

(Face View)

Center Line

⑤

1"

2 5/8"

Long Stretcher *(Front View)*

Trim the tenon ends to match the curve of the rails.

27 15/16"

1"

1 3/4"

11/16"

⑪

Cut appropriate symmetrical curves to create a broken pediment.

This is a straight line.

3/8"
3/8"

Back Edge *(Front View)*

This profile matches the chamfer of the tabletop.

Tabletop *(Top View)*

①

Center Line

Tabletop Chamfer Detail
(Top View)

Back edge shown behind the tabletop

⑪

①

5/16"

7/16"

1 1/2"

3"

Shaker Hall Table

An adaptation of a table originally built in the mid-1800s stays true to the
Shaker tradition of simple, functional furniture that is built to last.

by Jack Danielson

When woodworkers think of the Shakers, one thing springs quickly to mind: The exquisite simplicity of their furniture designs.

Shaker woodworking is truly a marriage of form and function, and the Shaker Hall Table is no exception. The original version of the piece was used by the North family in the Shaker village at New Lebanon, New York, around 1840. That piece was slightly deeper than this one, and featured three drawers across the front apron. The original craftsman's material choices are hard to improve on. He used cherry for all the visible parts and clear pine for the hidden drawer components and web frame pieces. I used the same materials in my version.

Start with the Top

Because it will be the focal point of the table, choose your best stock for the top (piece 1). Always select an uneven number of boards to form a panel like this so a board ends up defining the center of the top instead of a joint line. Be sure to spend time arranging the pieces before you joint the edges, but with a small top, don't worry too much about alternating the crowns. Instead, concentrate on the final appearance of the top and let that guide you in your selection process.

After jointing, glue the edges and, using a piece of scrap to protect the cherry, lightly tap the boards with a mallet until they're aligned perfectly. Tighten the clamps until slight beads of glue begin to emerge from the joints. Wait about 15 minutes, and scrape off the rubbery glue beads. When the glue is thoroughly dry, lay a straightedge across the tabletop and scribble pencil lines on the high spots. Now use a belt sander to sand the top flat, concentrating on these high areas first, then the full panel.

Cut the tabletop to length next, making sure your cuts are perfectly square. (See the tip at right for a technique on squaring panels.) With the top milled to final size, go ahead and cut the rest of the pieces to overall size, following the Material List, page 95.

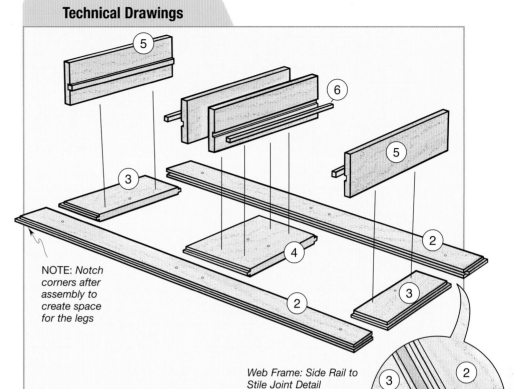

Technical Drawings

NOTE: *Notch corners after assembly to create space for the legs*

Web Frame: Side Rail to Stile Joint Detail

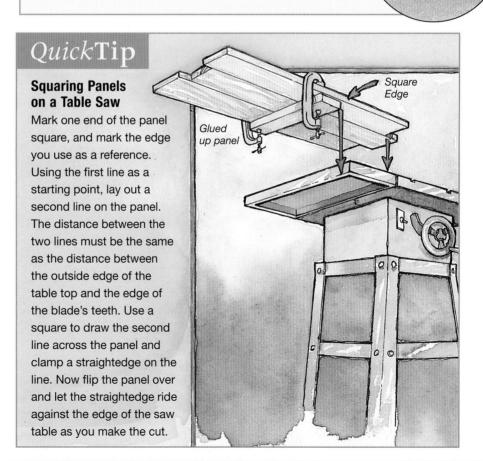

QuickTip

Squaring Panels on a Table Saw

Mark one end of the panel square, and mark the edge you use as a reference. Using the first line as a starting point, lay out a second line on the panel. The distance between the two lines must be the same as the distance between the outside edge of the table top and the edge of the blade's teeth. Use a square to draw the second line across the panel and clamp a straightedge on the line. Now flip the panel over and let the straightedge ride against the edge of the saw table as you make the cut.

Square Edge

Glued up panel

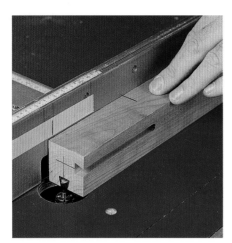

Figure 1: *A ³⁄₁₆" straight bit removes most of the waste in the sliding dovetail grooves, then a ½" dovetail bit finishes the job. To limit the length of the cut, visual stops are marked on both the fence and the workpiece.*

Making the Web Frame

The drawer support subassembly is a simple web frame, (see Exploded View, this page) composed of two stiles (pieces 2) and three rails (pieces 3 and 4). With all five pieces cut to size, create tongues on the ends of the three rails, and grooves on the inside of each stile. Refer to the Technical Drawings on pages 98 and 99 for dimensions, and make these joint cuts on your router table.

Glue and clamp the web frame together (checking for squareness by

Figure 2: *Use scrap cutoffs from the apron stock, because they're the exact thickness of your workpieces, to set the fence for the dovetail cuts on the aprons.*

measuring diagonally), then set it aside. Once the glue cures, go back to the Technical Drawings for the location of the notches where the frame will meet the legs. Cut these out with your jigsaw.

The next bit of machining is to form a tongue all the way around the outside edge of the web frame. When the table is assembled, this tongue will fit into grooves on the inside faces of the aprons. Form the tongue on the router table (see Technical Drawings for dimensions), using a rabbeting bit with a guide bearing or a straight bit in combination with the router table fence.

Before moving on to the aprons, machine and install the drawer runners and slides (pieces 5 and 6). Cut the runners to size and rout a groove on one face of each to accept the slides (see Technical Drawings for locations). Glue the slides in the runner grooves and, when the four subassemblies are dry, screw and glue them to the web frame from the bottom up—just be sure the slides are oriented correctly to accept the drawers.

Cutting the Leg Dovetails

The legs (pieces 7) are tapered. However, there is another machining step to complete on the legs while they're still square. The aprons are attached to the legs with sliding dovetail joints, and the tails of each joint are cut into the legs. The pins will be formed on the ends of each apron in the next step.

The easiest way to cut the stopped grooves in the legs is on your router table. Use the Technical Drawings (pages 98 and 99) and the Leg Elevations on this page to set your fence and bit height, then mark stops on your fence and workpiece to keep the length of the cut to 4". Install a ³⁄₁₆" straight bit in the router to remove most of the waste, and then run a piece of scrap to check your setup. Now mill two grooves on each leg — one on each of the inside faces that will be tapered.

Cutting the Apron Openings

STEP 1: *Extend your saw's blade to full height to mark the start and end of its cut on the fence. Now lay out the drawer openings on the apron and line one up so the blade, when raised fully, will emerge at the leading edge of a cut. Push the workpiece to the end of the cut, as shown above, then hold the piece firmly in place until the blade stops spinning.*

Leg Elevations
Top View

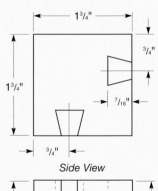

Side View

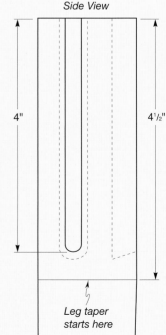

Leg taper starts here

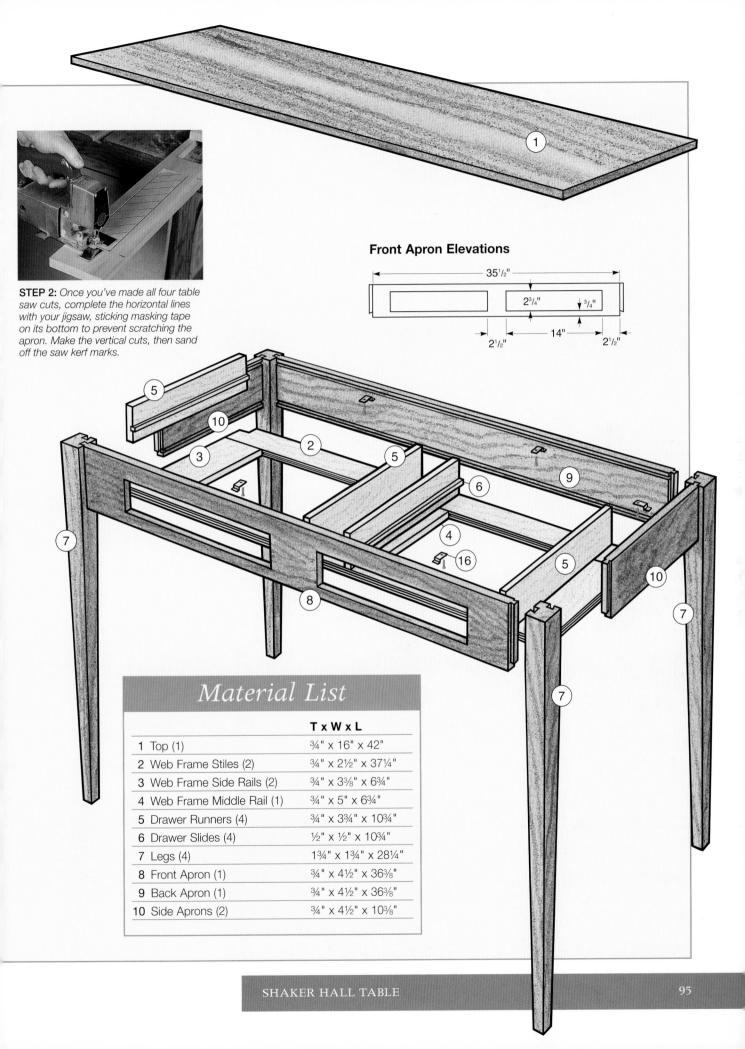

STEP 2: *Once you've made all four table saw cuts, complete the horizontal lines with your jigsaw, sticking masking tape on its bottom to prevent scratching the apron. Make the vertical cuts, then sand off the saw kerf marks.*

Front Apron Elevations

35½"
2¾"
¾"
14"
2½"
2½"

Material List

	T x W x L
1 Top (1)	¾" x 16" x 42"
2 Web Frame Stiles (2)	¾" x 2½" x 37¼"
3 Web Frame Side Rails (2)	¾" x 3⅜" x 6¾"
4 Web Frame Middle Rail (1)	¾" x 5" x 6¾"
5 Drawer Runners (4)	¾" x 3¾" x 10¾"
6 Drawer Slides (4)	½" x ½" x 10¾"
7 Legs (4)	1¾" x 1¾" x 28¼"
8 Front Apron (1)	¾" x 4½" x 36⅜"
9 Back Apron (1)	¾" x 4½" x 36⅜"
10 Side Aprons (2)	¾" x 4½" x 10⅜"

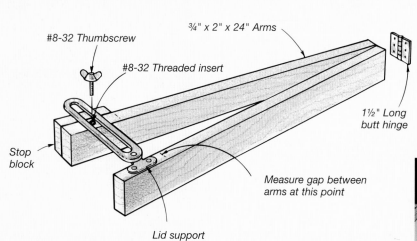

#8-32 Thumbscrew

#8-32 Threaded insert

¾" x 2" x 24" Arms

1½" Long butt hinge

Stop block

Measure gap between arms at this point

Lid support

Shaker Table Leg Dimensions

28¼"

4½"

¾"

Tapered legs are elegant, and cutting them is easy, especially with a tapering jig on a table saw. Here's a classic design that features two straight pieces of wood hinged together at one end. A lid support near the other end lets you change the angle. A small block of wood screwed to the side of one arm acts as a stop. To use the jig, make the gap between the arms at the stop block equal the amount you want removed from the bottom of the legs. For the hall table, the distance is ¾". Align the saw blade with the top of the taper (on this table, the distance is 4½" from the top of the leg, because the taper begins at the bottom of the 4½"-wide apron). Start the cuts near the top of the legs and work down to the narrow ends.

If you don't want to build a tapering jig from scratch, the aluminum one shown in the photo above is an inexpensive alternative.

Switch to a ½" dovetail bit with a 14° bevel. Again, start with your piece of scrap to check the setup, then cut the tails, as shown in Figure 1.

The Aprons

As long as you're set up on the router table, switch your attention to the aprons (pieces 8, 9 and 10) to complete the other half of your dovetail joints. Make these cuts with the same 14° dovetail bit.

To complete the cuts, the workpieces are held vertically as they're moved across the table (see Figure 2). Make sure your fence is high enough to keep the piece truly vertical, and use an auxiliary fence if necessary. Set the fence so only part of the bit is exposed, and cut one side at a time. Test the scrap piece

in the leg until your setup is perfect, then mill the cherry workpieces. Finally, trim the bottom end of the pins so they seat perfectly in the rounded end of the groove in the legs.

The front apron (piece 8) has two holes cut into it for the drawers. Use the Technical Drawings to lay out these openings, then follow "Cutting the Apron Openings" on pages 94 and 95 to complete the cuts.

The last milling operation on the aprons is to cut grooves along the insides of each of the four pieces. These grooves are cut on the table saw with a dado head, and they will house the web frame you assembled earlier. See the Technical Drawings for dimensions and location.

Figure 3: *Use a high auxiliary fence on the miter gauge to cut the dovetail pins on the drawer sides. A dovetail saw can be used to cut the tails (right) on the drawer fronts.*

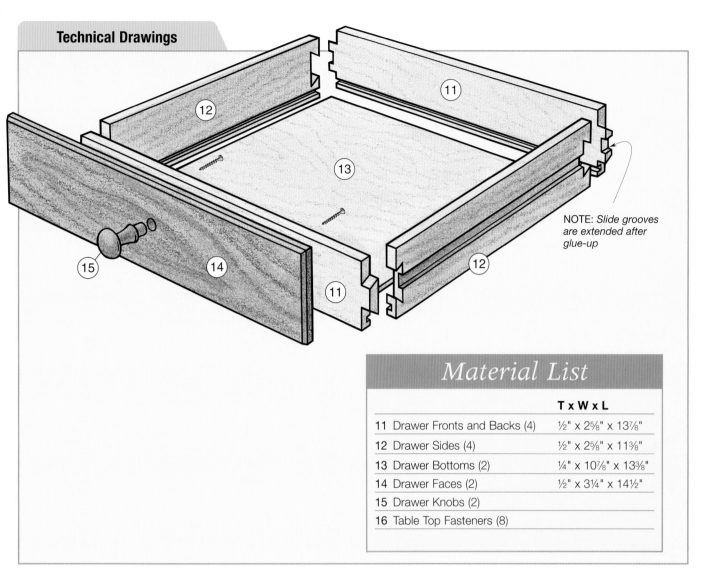

NOTE: *Slide grooves are extended after glue-up*

(15) (14) (11) (12) (13) (12) (11)

Material List

		T x W x L
11	Drawer Fronts and Backs (4)	½" x 2⅝" x 13⅞"
12	Drawer Sides (4)	½" x 2⅝" x 11⅜"
13	Drawer Bottoms (2)	¼" x 10⅞" x 13⅜"
14	Drawer Faces (2)	½" x 3¼" x 14½"
15	Drawer Knobs (2)	
16	Table Top Fasteners (8)	

Tapering the Legs

Traditionally, a table saw has been the tool of choice for tapering legs, although a jointer will also work well. To cut tapered legs on a table saw, you'll need to purchase or build a version of the tapering jig described on page 96. With the jig in hand, note that the tapers don't run the full length of each piece. The top 4½" of each leg remains square (where it meets the apron), so each taper is actually only 23¾" long.

Draw the leg pattern (see the Technical Drawings for dimensions) onto some scrap, then rip a sample taper on some ¼" plywood. Make adjustments as necessary until you're satisfied with the setup, then rip two tapers on each leg. The tapers are on

the same sides as the sliding dovetail grooves you machined earlier.

Now you're ready to dry-assemble your table to make sure everything fits just right.

Building the Drawers and Drawer Slides

The most interesting aspect of the drawers is the large dovetail joint that holds the drawer fronts and backs (pieces 11) to the sides (pieces 12). Typical of Shaker craftsmanship, the joints are simple in design and exceptionally strong.

Before creating these dovetails, cut all the parts to size and set up to mill the grooves for the slides in the drawer sides (see Technical Drawings). But first double-check your layout lines by testing

a side against the piece it will match. To do it, lay a penny or washer on the web frame and hold the drawer sides against the drawer slides. The spacer ensures the drawers will move easily, even when the wood expands and contracts. While you're at the saw, use the dado setup to mill the ¼"-wide grooves in each side, front and back that will house the drawer bottoms (pieces 13).

With all of the square cuts done, you're ready to make the dovetail pins on the ends of each drawer side (see Technical Drawings for the layout). Accomplish that by using a 14° dovetail bit in your router table and a high auxiliary fence on your miter gauge (see Figure 3). Make several passes to clean out the waste, then transfer the resulting pattern

Front Apron
(Front view)

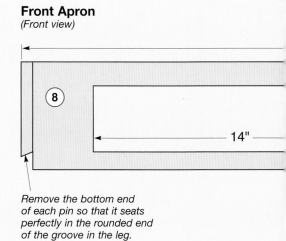

⑧

14"

Remove the bottom end of each pin so that it seats perfectly in the rounded end of the groove in the leg.

Drawer Front
(Front view)

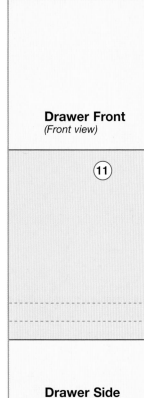

⑪

1/2"

(End view)

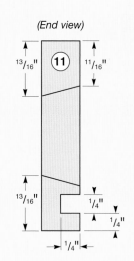

⑪

13/16" 11/16"

13/16" 1/4"

1/4"

1/4"

Drawer Side
(Side view)

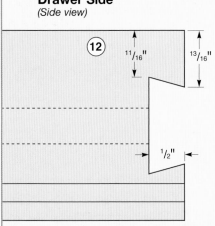

⑫

11/16" 13/16"

1/2"

(End view)

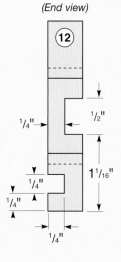

⑫

1/4" 1/2"

1/4"

1/4" 1 1/16"

1/4"

NOTE: Cut the pins on the ends of the drawer sides first, then use them to help lay out the tails on the drawer fronts.

Corner Notch Detail

7/8"

7/8"

②

NOTE: Corners are notched after the web frame is assembled to create space for the leg.

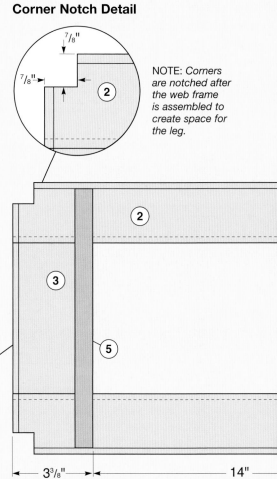

②

③

⑤

3 3/8" 14"

Tongue Detail

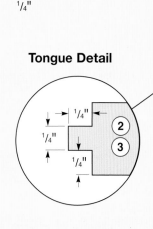

1/4"

1/4"

②

③

1/4"

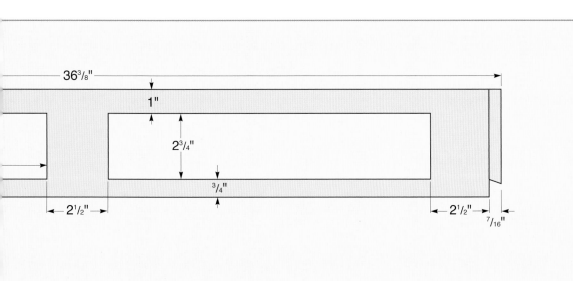

36³/₈"

1"

2³/₄"

³/₄"

2¹/₂"

2¹/₂"

⁷/₁₆"

Drawer Runner
(Side view)

(End view)

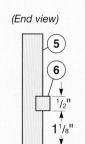

⑤

⑥

¹/₂"

1¹/₈"

⑤

Leg
(Top view)

1³/₄"

⑦

³/₄

1³/₄"

⁷/₁₆"

³/₄"

1"

Web Frame
(Top view)

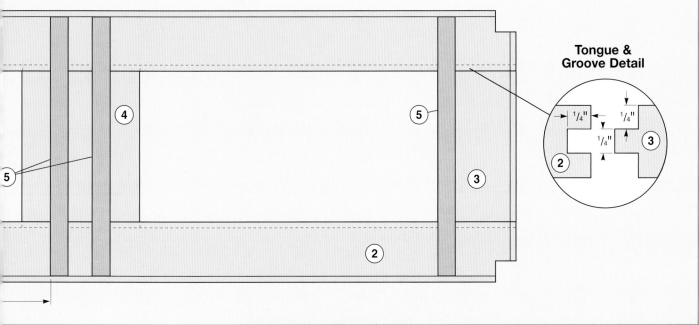

④

⑤

⑤

③

②

**Tongue &
Groove Detail**

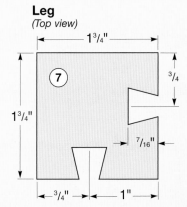

¹/₄"

¹/₄"

¹/₄"

③

②

Shaker Hall Table
(Front view)

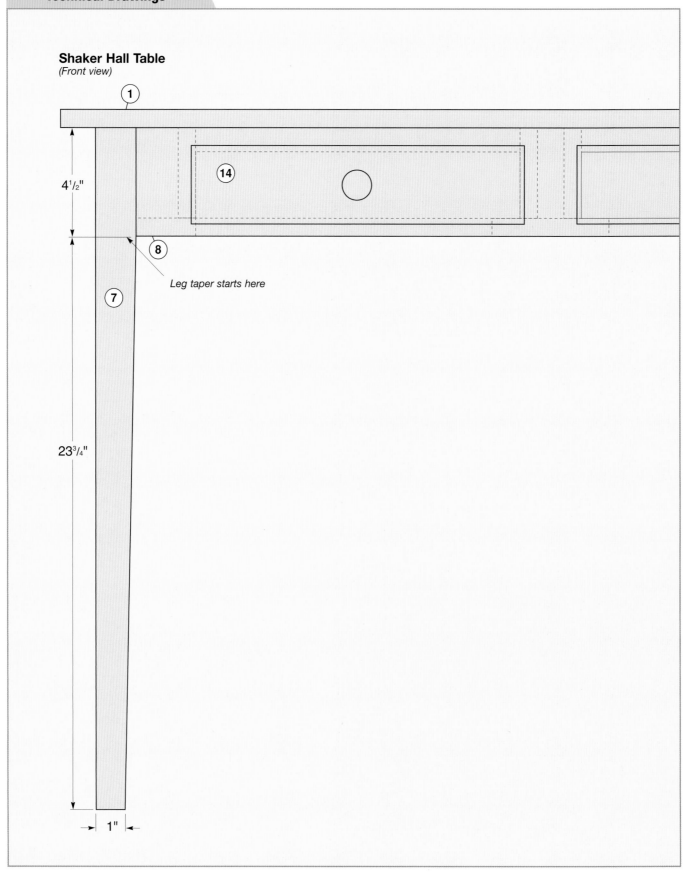

①

⑭

4¹/₂"

⑧

Leg taper starts here

⑦

23³/₄"

1"

to the edges of the drawer fronts. A dovetail saw is the best tool to cut the tails on the ends of the drawer fronts (see Figure 3 inset).

Dry-fit all of the parts, and once you're satisfied with the fit, glue everything together except the drawer bottoms, which float freely to allow for shrinkage and expansion. Before tightening your clamps, measure diagonally in both directions to verify the drawers are square. When the glue is dry, use a sharp chisel to extend the slide grooves through the drawer's back.

The drawer faces (pieces 14) receive a ¼" wide 45° chamfer that extends halfway across the edge. Use your router table for this cut.

The easiest way to line up the drawer faces properly is to use hot melt glue. Insert one of the drawers in the table and clamp it in place so the front is flush with the face of the front apron. A straightedge clamped across the apron will align the bottoms of the two drawer faces. Put a small dab of hot melt glue on the inside of each face and press it in place. When the glue sets, remove the drawer and install screws from the inside of the front to hold the face permanently.

Predrill for the screws, using an oversize bit in the drawer front to allow for movement and a slightly undersized bit in the drawer face to ensure a good hold. Install the drawer knobs (pieces 15), test the operation, and move on to the finishing phase.

Finishing Up

It's a good idea to seal both sides of the tabletop so that warping doesn't occur. This is because the unfinished surface will absorb moisture from the air at a different rate than the top side, which can cause the wood to move unevenly and warp. Sand the entire table and finish everything before installing the top. Use three coats of natural Danish oil or orange shellac to bring out the luster in the cherry, followed by a coat of wax. Rub some paraffin wax on the drawer slides to make the drawers slide smoothly. In the proper Shaker mindset for this project, tradition says our workmanship must not only look fine but also work well.

Finally, fasten the top to the aprons with eight desk top fasteners (pieces 16). They simply screw in place.

In the Shaker tradition, the front apron is made from a single piece of cherry with openings cut out for the two drawers. These drawers are held together with large dovetail joints.

Historical Fact

Mother Ann Lee, founder of the Shakers in America, arrived in New York on August 6, 1774. Her followers established a Gospel Order settlement at New Lebanon, New York, that became the first of 19 Shaker villages throughout New England, Ohio, Kentucky and Indiana. The Tree of Life (illustrated below) was first painted by Sister Hannah Cohoon In 1854, and it is often regarded as the symbolic emblem of the Shaker religion.

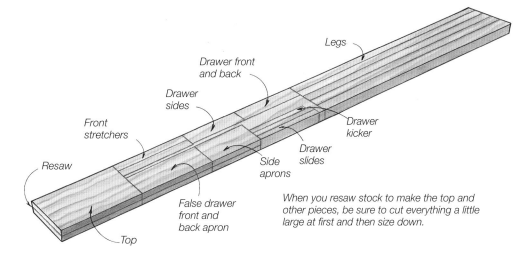

Legs

Drawer front
and back

Drawer
sides

Front
stretchers

Resaw

Drawer
kicker

Side
aprons

Drawer
slides

Top

False drawer
front and
back apron

When you resaw stock to make the top and other pieces, be sure to cut everything a little large at first and then size down.

One Board Hall Table

One board doesn't actually describe the style or look of this table, but it is a pretty complete description of the material that goes into it. If you haven't been hoarding special pieces of stock (maybe you're just getting started with this hobby or haven't yet become a wood-aholic) then shopping is really simple. A seven-inch-wide, eight-foot-long piece of 8/4 stock is all you will need. A one board approach creates a beautiful table with consistent figure and color. My version of the project came from a wonderful piece of Lake Superior flame birch.

by Dick Coers

Dividing and Cutting

Take a look at the one board diagram, above, and begin cutting the longer pieces of stock to their rough lengths, but a little oversized to start. Cut the legs (pieces 1) into squared-up full leg blanks for tapering later and, using the Material List on page 105 as a guide, cut the rest of the pieces to size. Some pieces will need to be resawn and planed to the proper dimensions.

Arrange the leg pieces so the best faces will be viewed on the table. Mark the tops of the legs to keep the orientation. Lay out and cut the mortises in the aprons and stretchers (pieces 2 through 4) and matching mortises in the legs (check the Exploded View on page 104 for locations and placement details). Use your drill press to remove most of the waste and clean up the mortises with a sharp chisel. On your dry fit, you'll notice the legs are offset from the aprons just a bit. Size and cut the large and small floating tenons (pieces 5 and 6) to fit the mortises you just made.

Quick Tapering Jig

Fence

Toggle Clamp and
Mounting Block

Stop

Bed

Use this safe, simple jig to cut accurate tapers on your table saw.

Make the bed from ¾" plywood 10" longer than your workpiece and wide enough to accommodate a toggle clamp. Next, rip a 4"-wide piece of ¾" ply for the jig's fence. Slice a couple of small pieces from the stock to make a stop for the jig bed and a mounting block for the toggle clamp. Lay a leg blank onto the jig bed with the side you wish to taper overhanging the edge; attach the fence and stop to position the leg blank. Position and attach the mounting block and toggle clamp so you can secure the leg stock without contacting the area to be sawn.

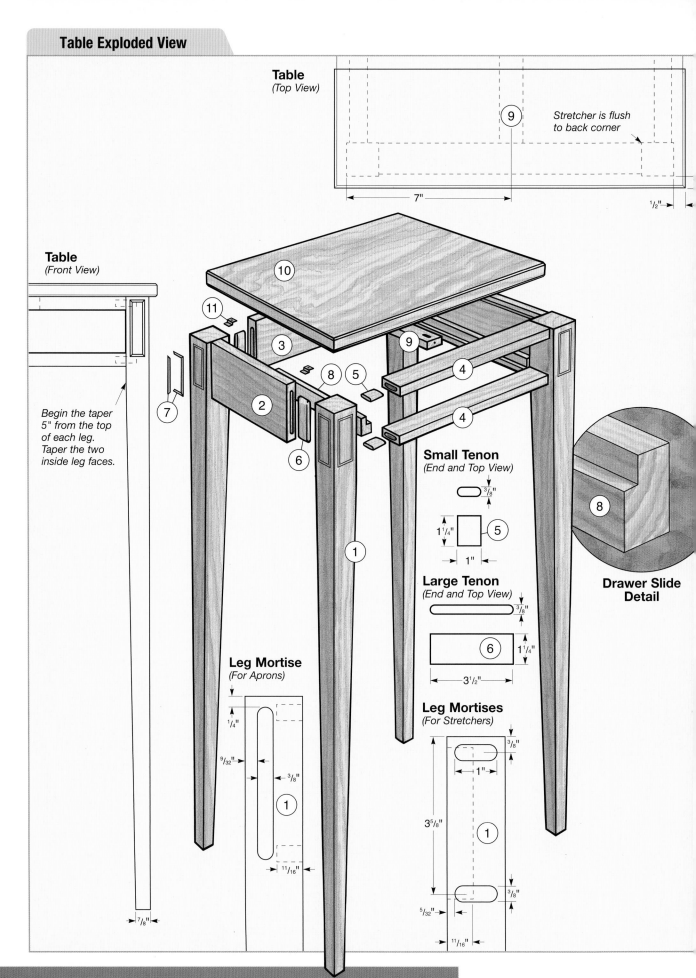

Table
(Top View)

⑨ Stretcher is flush to back corner

7"

1/2"

Table
(Front View)

⑪

③

⑩

⑨

④

④

Begin the taper 5" from the top of each leg. Taper the two inside leg faces.

⑦

②

⑧

⑤

⑥

①

7/8"

Small Tenon
(End and Top View)

3/8"

1 1/4"   ⑤

1"

Large Tenon
(End and Top View)

3/8"

⑥   1 1/4"

3 1/2"

Drawer Slide Detail

⑧

Leg Mortise
(For Aprons)

1/4"

9/32"   3/8"

①

11/16"

Leg Mortises
(For Stretchers)

3/8"

1"

3 5/8"   ①

3/8"

5/32"

11/16"

Stretcher
(End and Side View)

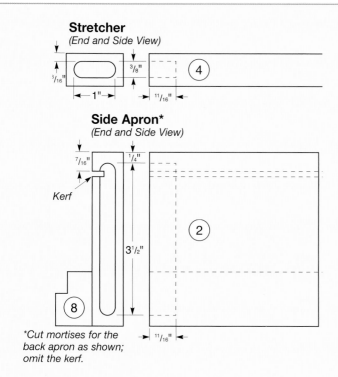

Side Apron*
(End and Side View)

Kerf

*Cut mortises for the
back apron as shown;
omit the kerf.

Drawer Slide
(End View)

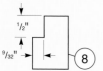

Material List – Table

	T x W x L
1 Legs (4)	1⅜" x 1⅜" x 35¼"
2 Side Aprons (2)	¾" x 4" x 8¼"
3 Back Apron (1)	¾" x 4" x 11¼"
4 Front Stretchers (2)	⅜" x 1⁹⁄₃₂" x 11¼"
5 Small Floating Tenons (4)	⅜" x 1" x 1¼"
6 Large Floating Tenons (6)	⅜" x 3½" x 1¼"
7 Inlay (1)	⅛" x ⅛" x 72"
8 Drawer Slides (2)	⅞" x 1¼" x 8¼"
9 Drawer Kicker (1)	¾" x 1" x 8²⁵⁄₃₂"
10 Top (1)	¾" x 12" x 15"
11 Tabletop Fasteners (4)	Steel

Low-risk Inlay Jig

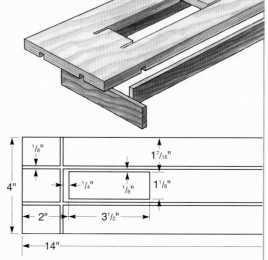

Build the jig from ½" plywood to the
dimensions shown above. The opening is kept
close to one end of the jig to provide room to
clamp the fixture onto the leg blanks without
interfering with your router movement. Cut
a dado and two grooves on the underside
to locate the three cleats, as shown in the
elevation and exploded views above.

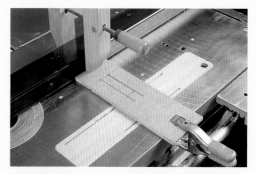

*To cut the jig opening, position the jig blank against
the rip fence on the table saw with the blade lowered
below the table. Then carefully elevate the blade to
form the opening.*

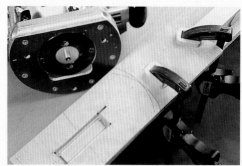

*Use a homemade jig, a ⅜" O.D. rub collar and a ⅛"
veining bit to cut the inlay slots. Plunge your router
and take a single lap around the jig opening. Make
sure the rub collar hugs the jig constantly.*

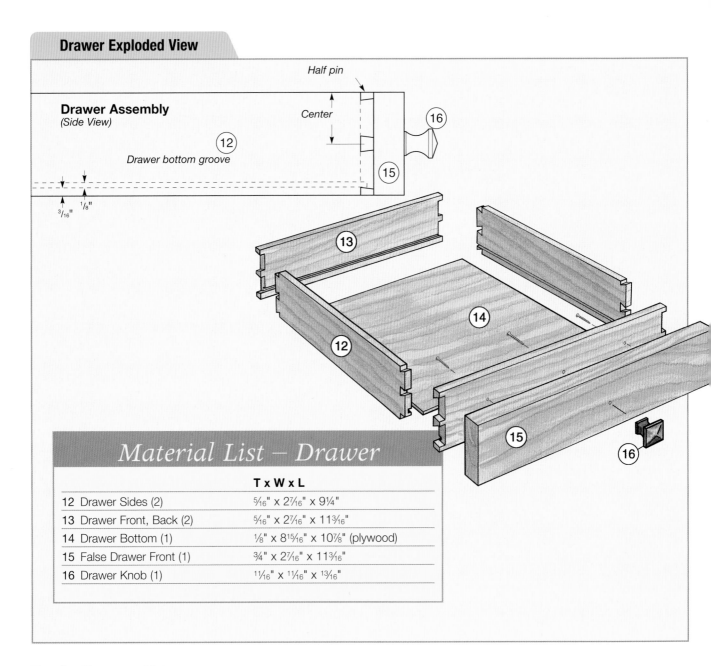

Drawer Exploded View

Drawer Assembly
(Side View)

Half pin

Center

(16)

(15)

(12)

Drawer bottom groove

³/₁₆" ¹/₈"

(13)

(14)

(12)

(15)

(16)

Material List – Drawer

	T x W x L
12 Drawer Sides (2)	⁵/₁₆" x 2⁷/₁₆" x 9¼"
13 Drawer Front, Back (2)	⁵/₁₆" x 2⁷/₁₆" x 11³/₁₆"
14 Drawer Bottom (1)	⅛" x 8¹⁵/₁₆" x 10⅞" (plywood)
15 False Drawer Front (1)	¾" x 2⁷/₁₆" x 11³/₁₆"
16 Drawer Knob (1)	1¹/₁₆" x 1¹/₁₆" x 1³/₁₆"

Forming Tapers and Inlays

Lay out the taper on one of the legs. The outside two faces are straight and the insides have the taper. Start the taper 5" from the top and reduce the leg to ⅞" square on the bottom. Use the jig described on page 103 to slice tapers on the inside faces of each leg. Once all the tapers have been cut, move on to the decorative inlay (piece 7) on the outside faces at the top of each leg. Again, as with the tapers, the key to success with this task is to build the simple jig described on page 105. The jig is designed to work with a ⅜" O.D.

guide bushing set in a plunge router base. Install a ⅛" router bit and set the bit height to cut just shy of ⅛" deep with the router sitting on the inlay jig. Make several test cuts in scrap cut to the size of the leg stock in order to get the feel of the procedure. Position the jig on the end of a leg with the blank held tight against the jig's cleats, using two clamps to secure it properly. Start in one corner, plunge the bit, and continue around the opening in a clockwise direction. Lift the router when you get back to the starting point. Recutting may enlarge the groove and cause problems as you are fitting

the inlay pieces. Repeat the process on all the faces where the inlay appears. Use a wide chisel to square up the corners. Hold the flat back of the chisel on the wall of the groove and rock it down into the uncut area to create perfectly square corners.

With the grooves cut, prepare some mahogany for the inlay. (You also can buy commercially available ⅛" inlay strips, as well as more elaborate inlays with patterns.) Resaw your mahogany and plane it to ⅛"-thick. Put a zero-clearance insert in your table saw and use a sharp blade to rip ⅛"-wide inlay strips. Dry-fit

Some folks shy away from dovetail joints, thinking them too difficult and time-consuming. If your only option was to cut them by hand with a backsaw we'd probably agree, but with modern jigs and routers, this joint is within the scope of most woodworkers. We used the Keller Jig to cut dovetails in the drawer sides, front and back for this project. Always test your setup on scrap lumber dimensioned to the exact size of the stock used in your project. We find it useful to run the tails 1/32" long and sand them smooth.

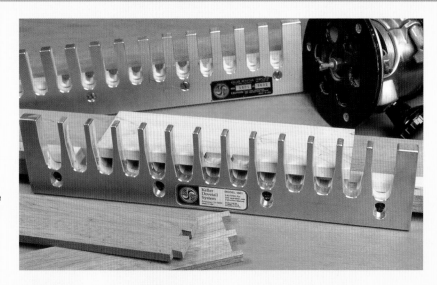

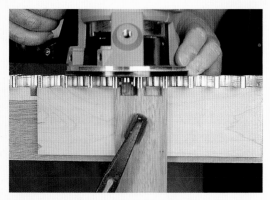

Use the Keller Jig to machine the drawer front and back first, forming the half pins at each end and then centering a pin in the middle.

Next, machine the tails on the drawer sides. Check each side for cupping, orienting any bow to the inside to prevent separation as the drawer ages.

the first strip you cut to ensure the rest will fit properly. Make the inlay pieces snug enough to just barely fit into the groove. If just the slightest tap with a hammer is needed to persuade them into place, you've got a perfect fit. Mitering the inlay to length is something of a challenge. The short pieces cause you to work close to the saw blade. A small extension on your miter gauge with a stop will safely cut the parts to their exact length. To be extra safe, use a piece of scrap or length of dowel to hold the small parts during cutting.

Wrapping Up the Legs and Aprons

Grab a knife or scraper to pare a slight chamfer on the back edges of the inlays. Run a small bead of glue in the bottom of the slot and tap them home. Or press the inlays into place using a wallpaper seam roller to help reduce the chance of breaking a delicate piece. When the glue securing the inlays has cured, you may have to carefully scrape the inlay flush.

Now use a 1/8" roundover bit in a trim router or medium-grit sandpaper to break all the edges of the legs fairly heavily, then finish-sand the legs to 220-grit. Run the tapered faces of the legs over the

jointer, set to a light pass, to remove the saw marks. A scraper also works for this clean-up if you don't have a jointer. Avoid using a power sander on the legs near the mortises. It can round over the surface and spoil the joint. It's better to use a scraper or hand-sanding block here.

Sand the apron and stretchers as well, and break just the bottom edges of these pieces. The ends and tops need to remain square—they butt against other parts. Now cut a kerf in the side aprons for tabletop fasteners. See the Drawings on page 105 for the proper kerf locations.

Starting the Assembly

Glue up the legs and aprons in two sub-assemblies: First, join the legs to the side aprons and then, when the glue has cured, attach those sub-assemblies to the back apron and stretchers. Be prudent with the amount of glue you use. It is important to avoid excess glue squeeze-out on the visible surfaces.

Machine the drawer slides (pieces 8) on your table saw by plowing rabbets as shown in the Drawer Slide Detail on page 105. Turn to your drawer kicker (piece 9) and drill a pocket hole at each end of the piece.

Move to the table sub-assembly and glue and clamp the drawer guides in place against the side aprons (flush with the bottom stretcher). Install the drawer kicker (see the Drawing on page 104 for placement), using clamps to steady it as you drive the attachment screws home.

Topping It All Off

Glue up the top (piece 10) from the resawn pieces you cut earlier. Take care when you align the pieces to get a book-matched grain orientation. It is a great way to really show off the figure of the wood. After the glue has dried, size the top and use a belt sander to smooth the surfaces. Switch to a router and form ³⁄₃₂" chamfers on the top and bottom edges. After sanding the top to 220-grit, attach it to the legs. To do this, place the top face down on a solid-padded work surface and set the leg sub-assembly in position. Fit tabletop fasteners (pieces 11) into the apron kerfs and drive the screws through the holes into the tabletop. With everything lined up, remove the top and set it aside until you've applied the finish.

Making the Drawer

Cut grooves in the drawer sides, front and back (pieces 12 and 13) to accept the drawer bottom (piece 14). I used a Keller Jig to cut through dovetails on the drawer

Shaping a Knob in Two Steps

You could use a nice brass pull on this project, but I made a simple yet striking hardwood knob out of walnut. It's easy to make in just two steps and a perfect accent to a stylish table like this one.

Drawer Knob
(Side View)

Disc-sand the top bevel angles holding the workpiece against a miter gauge.

Spindle-sand the inner contours to shape, then band saw the knob free.

pieces, as shown on page 107. Dry-fit the drawer components and, once they all fit well, glue and clamp them together. Don't glue the drawer bottom in place: it must float freely. Size the false front (piece 15) to allow a ¹⁄₁₆" clearance all around the drawer opening. Break all its edges with

sandpaper and final-sand to 220-grit.

While a solid-brass knob would look good on this piece, I departed from the one board concept and designed an end grain knob from walnut (piece 16), as shown in the sidebar above.

Finishing and Final Assembly

Fit the drawer in the table. Finish sand all the parts and make a final check for glue squeeze-out by wiping with mineral spirits.

Apply three coats of polyurethane varnish, sanding after the second coat with 320-grit paper. Lay down the last coat, then final-sand with 600-grit. Buff with 0000 steel wool to create a soft, satiny sheen.

Predrill the false drawer front to center the knob. With the drawer in the table, position the false front in the opening, using shims to keep it centered. Temporarily drive a single screw through the predrilled hole in the false front and into the drawer. Open the drawer and make sure the alignment is correct. Then drive two #6 screws from inside to attach the false front. Remove the temporary screw and drive a #8 screw from the inside to attach the knob. (Be sure to predrill the knob first!) Reinstall the top and wax the drawer slides to complete the project.

The One Board Hall Table is not a normal hall table, but tucked discreetly beside a door, it makes an elegant place to set the mail or a purse while removing a coat.

QuickTip

A Simple Scraper Holder

The sharp ends of scraper blades can be hard on your hands, but you can get some relief by mounting your scraper in a holder. This simple scraper holder design consists of two 4" lengths of ¾"-diameter dowel joined by a flexible piece of ⅛" plywood. Rout a ¼" slot into each dowel and glue the plywood into these slots. To achieve maximum flexibility, orient the plywood so the exterior grain runs parallel to the dowels. Slip the blade into place in the slots and secure it with a binder clip.

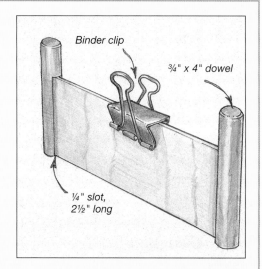

Binder clip

¾" x 4" dowel

¼" slot, 2½" long

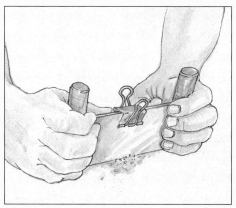

Keep in mind the time of year when making drawers. If you make a snug-fitting drawer during a Midwestern winter, don't expect to get it open on a humid day in August.

Cabriole Leg Side Table

Template routing and a bit of hand tool shaping render
lovely legs on a cherry nouveau cabriole table.

by Paul Anthony

When it comes to furniture projects, side tables are a perennial favorite. They dress up any room and offer a great opportunity to showcase your woodworking skills to family and friends.

One of the primary features of any table is its leg design. With the Cabriole Leg Side Table, I wanted to step away from typical tapered or turned legs to something more elegant. The legs are designed to be sort of nouveau cabriole—conveying the grace of a traditional cabriole leg without the visual weight. They are surprisingly easy to make. I devised a system of template routing that ensures the profiles match very closely. After routing, a bit of planing, shaving, and filing refines the legs to their final form. You'll probably find the task to be quite rewarding without being too difficult.

Cutting the Pieces to Rough Size

Begin by cutting all the pieces roughly to size. Use roughsawn lumber if possible because it allows more stock control. A light pass through your planer will reveal the general grain and figure of your roughsawn lumber. Select the most attractive boards for the top (piece 1). Lay out your pieces several inches oversized in length and at least ¼" oversized in width. After ripping and crosscutting to the rough sizes, sticker the pieces and let them sit for a day or so in the shop. Doing so allows the gross wood movement to occur before final machining.

Making Leg Blanks

While waiting for the top and apron stock to relax (pieces 2 and 3), you can work on the legs (pieces 4). We'll use templates to rout the front and side profiles before doing the final shaping.

Start by making the front and side templates using ½" hardwood plywood, cutting them to the shapes shown in the Exploded View on page 112. Note the horn at the top and bottom of each leg. The material is used for clamping and will be cut off after the leg has been shaped. Cut close to the lines using a jigsaw, then hand plane and sand the edges to ensure

straight lines and fair curves. Mark the centerlines and horn lines on the template and extend the centerlines down the ends of the templates. In order to stiffen the side template, glue on a piece of ¾"-thick plywood that is trimmed to match the template using a flush-trim router bit. Mark the front profile template to identify its front and back.

Given all of the shaping that will happen on the legs, and how prominently the shapes will show on the finished table, choose straight-grained stock for the leg blanks, laying out a centerline on each end. Mark the horn lines onto the blanks and lay out the front and side profiles, aligning the side template centerlines with those on your blank. Lay out the front profile on the back edge of each leg, too.

It's best to rout the mortises in the legs before shaping them because the square blanks provide a longer surface for your router edge guide. Fully lay out one ¼" x 2½" mortise, as shown in the elevation drawings. You'll use this to set up your router edge guide. The rest of the mortises need only start and stop lines, which you should lay out now, too. Then cut the mortises to ⅝" deep, as shown in Figure 1.

① 45°

Tabletop Chamfer
(Edge View)

1/4"

Apron
(Inside and End Views)

1/4"

5/16"

3/8"

1/16"

②
③

3/8" Deep

1/4"

3/8"

2 1/2"

②
③

1/4"

15/16"

1/2"

15°

Leg Mortise
(Side Views)

1/4"

2 1/2"

5/8" deep

9/16"

④

Loose Tenons
(Front and Side Views)

2 3/8"

⑤

1/4"

15/16"

1/8" R.

Tabletop Fasteners
(Top and Side Views)

⑥

1/2"

5/16"

NOTE: *The three leg profile sections should be transferred to stiff cardboard and carefully cut out. As you shape the contour of the legs, use the cardboard gauges to help provide uniformity on all four legs.*

Leg: Front Template

Leg: Side Template

Horn

Horn

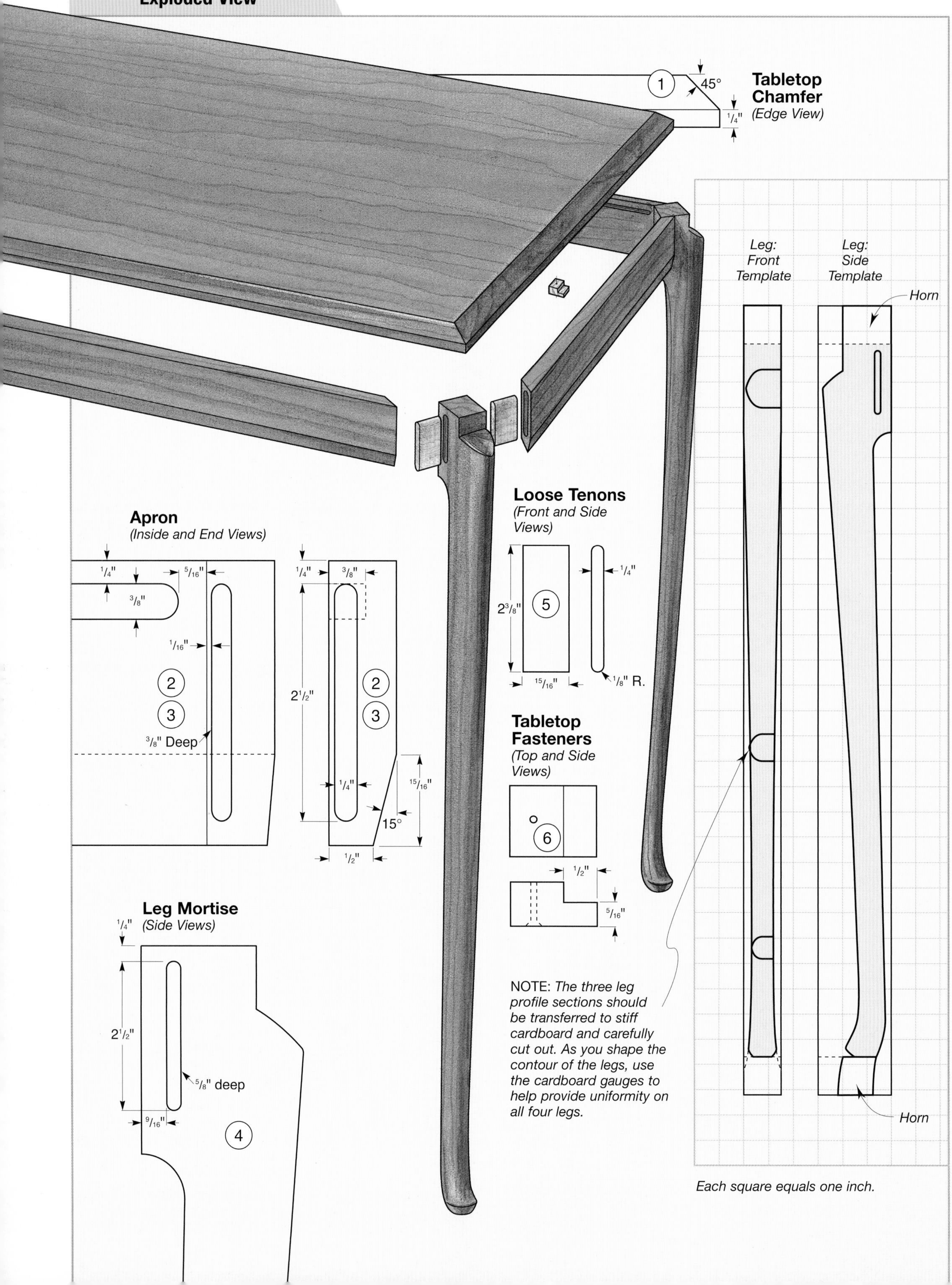

Each square equals one inch.

Material List

		T x W x L
1	Top (1)	1³⁄₁₆" x 20" x 50"
2	Short Aprons (2)	¾" x 3" x 16"
3	Long Aprons (2)	¾" x 3" x 46"
4	Leg Blanks* (4)	1½" x 3" x 31¼"
5	Loose Tenons (8)	¼" x 2⅜" x 1⁵⁄₁₆"
6	Tabletop Fasteners (6)	½" x 1" x 1¼"

*Leg blanks are longer than the finished legs.

Figure 1: *To rout the mortises in the legs, plunge to full depth at the beginning and end of each mortise. Then remove the waste in between by making successive shallow cuts until you reach the mortise depth.*

Cutting the Profiles

Next, cut the side profile on each leg. Begin by bandsawing to within ¹⁄₁₆" of your cutline. You'll need to attach full-length offcuts later for template routing, so make each cut in one continuous pass. For the front of the legs, begin at the top, saw along the horn line, swoop up around the tip of the knee, then down to the toe. Finish up the cuts above the knee and make the V-cut where the foot meets its horn.

Screw the side profile template to the leg horns, aligning the centerlines on each. Mount the template to the right side of the leg to prevent routing against the grain at the knee and toe. Use hot-melt glue or double-sided tape halfway down the leg to prevent template flex. Rout to the profile using a flush trim bit on a router table, as shown in Figure 2.

Use hot-melt glue to reattach the offcuts to the leg, carefully aligning the edges. To prevent workpiece tearout when removing the offcuts, first apply thick cellophane tape to the leg at the hot-melt glue locations. Now band saw the front profile. Feed the workpiece knee-down Figure 3 to present an uninterrupted bearing surface to the saw table.

The 3" width of the leg is too wide to template rout with most bits, so you should rout it in two steps. Begin by attaching the front profile template to the front of the leg blank using enough hot-melt glue or double-sided tape to prevent flexing. Outfit your table router with a

flush-trim bit that has a bearing at the shank end and a cutting flute at least 1¼" long. Then rout flush to the template as shown in Figure 4, next page. Finish up by switching over to a flush-trim router bit with a 2" cutting flute and a tip-mounted bearing for riding along the previously routed surface, as shown in the inset for Figure 4.

Shaping the Legs

Smooth all the faces and fair the profile curves using a block plane, spokeshaves, and a scraper. A block plane held sharply skewed will plane the surfaces most of the way down from the knee, as shown in Figure 5, next page. If you're not handy with a plane and spokeshaves, you can use rasps and files instead.

After smoothing the curves, draw a centerline down the front of the leg. Measure across the width at several points, making tick marks, then use a flexible strip of wood or plastic to connect the marks and establish the line.

Use some stiff cardboard to make cross section templates (see the pattern on page 112). Then set a block plane for a heavy cut and begin planing the curves at the front of the leg, working from the knee downward (see Figure 6). Work as symmetrically as possible, removing the same amount of material from each side of the centerline. Use the templates to gauge your progress as you go, working the curves to within about 2" from the foot.

Figure 2: *After bandsawing the front and back profiles to within ¹⁄₁₆" of the cutting line, attach the side template and rout to the line using a flush-trim bit.*

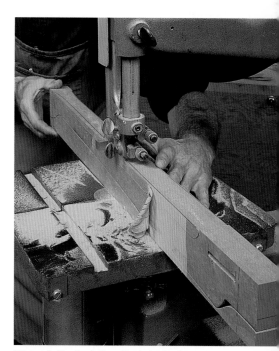

Figure 3: *Reattach the offcuts to the front and back of the leg with hot-melt glue, then bandsaw the side profiles to within ¹⁄₁₆" of the cut lines.*

Figure 4: *The first step in routing the side profile is to use a flush-trim bit with a bearing at the shank. The bit translates the shape of the front template to the stock. Then switch to a bit with a tip-mounted bearing (inset), to finish the profile. This bearing rides along the routed surface you just created.*

Figure 5: *A block plane held sharply skewed will smooth away most of the router marks. Use spokeshaves, scrapers, or files on tighter curves near the foot.*

Figure 6: *Use cardboard cross-section templates (see the Drawings) to gauge your progress when shaping the curves on the front of the leg.*

Figure 7: *Turn to your chisels to complete the shaping of the legs. After undercutting the toe, carve from the foot toward the ankle to shape what your block plane couldn't reach. Then move up to the knee and use a straight chisel (inset) to pare opposing facets, starting 3/16" from its centerline.*

When you're close to the desired profile, set your block plane and spokeshaves for a fine cut, then go over the surfaces again. After taking each pass, roll the tool over on the curve just a bit to take each subsequent pass. You'll end up with a surface made up of a series of close, small facets that can be sanded smooth. When you are done shaping the front, round over the rear of the legs to a radius of about ⅛".

You're ready to begin carving the foot. First, undercut the area below the toe, carving away the top section of the horn at the same time (see Figure 7). Use your spokeshaves, chisels or files to generally round the shin. Smooth the entire leg with 100- and 150-grit sandpaper.

With the sanding completed, start on the final shaping of the foot and knee. Brush the workpiece to rid it of sanding grit, then carve two opposing facets,

about 2" long on either side of the foot, as shown in the inset to Figure 7. Each facet is about ½" wide at its low end. The upper end blends into the curve at the front of the leg.

Use a wide chisel to create a sharp junction where the top of the knee meets the top of the leg. Pare the tapered facets on each side of the knee. Cut each taper about ¼" at its widest point. Don't fret if the cuts aren't perfect. You can fair them afterward using a fine-grit emery board like

Figure 8: *When it's time to rout the mortises in the mitered aprons, clamp them back-to-back. The resulting peak creates a shoulder for the edge guide and provides bearing for the router base.*

of a case or deep frame, with a spline or loose tenon spanning two mating slots or mortises—it provides increased joint strength. The trickiest part of making a blind spline-miter joint (where the edges of the spline don't reach the edge) is cutting the mortises. Here's how to approach it.

First, lay out a ¼" x 2½" mortise on the face of one miter, locating it ¹⁄₁₆" in from the inside edge. Clamp all four workpieces back-to-back to form a peak, as shown in Figure 8. It creates a square edge for registering a router edge guide and at the same time provides more surface for the router base to ride on. Align the workpiece ends and locate a clamp as close as possible to the end without obstructing router travel. Mount the whole assembly in a bench vise or clamp it against the edge of a thick benchtop with a couple of pipe or bar clamps. Before cutting, extend the mortise end lines across all of the faces.

Set up your router with an edge guide and adjust the fence so the cut favors the inside edge of the miter. You can make your fence out of a short, straight length of wood clamped to the router base. Rout the ⅜"-deep mortises. Make sure the rotation of your bit is pulling the fence tight to the stock as you cut to prevent climb-cutting. Rout the mortises in the two center pieces first, then unclamp the assembly and slide the outer pieces to the other end, aligning everything for routing the opposite ends of the inner pieces. Afterward, reverse the sandwich and rout the remaining mortises similarly.

those used for nail manicures. Round the edges above the knee to match the width of the facet at its top end.

Finish up by cutting the leg to final length. First, cut the top horn off each leg. Then cut all of the legs to 28¼" using a stop block on your saw to ensure consistent length. Shim at the rear of the leg to prevent it from collapsing against your chop saw fence or table saw sled fence as you trim off the lower horn. Finish up by doing any necessary shaping and sanding near the sole of the foot after removing the horn.

Blind Spline-miter Joinery

Joint, plane, rip, and crosscut the aprons to size and mark them for orientation, placing the nicest grain facing outward. Saw a miter on each end.

The apron-to-leg joints on the table are unusual. I basically sandwiched a leg in between a splined-miter, or loose tenon, joint. A typical splined-miter joint is often used to connect the corners

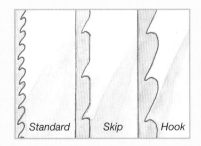

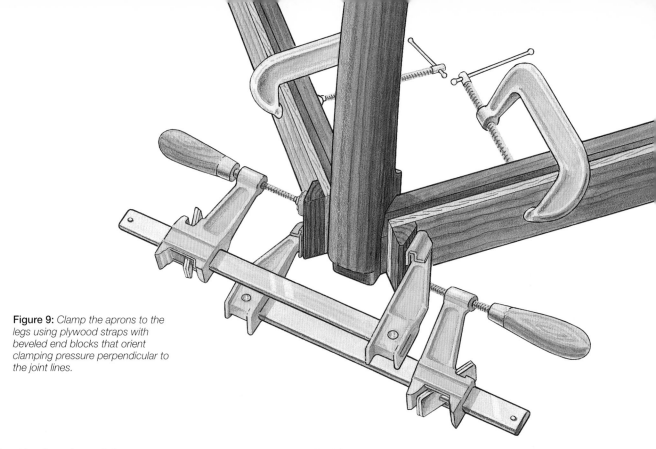

Figure 9: *Clamp the aprons to the legs using plywood straps with beveled end blocks that orient clamping pressure perpendicular to the joint lines.*

Forming the Bevels and Grooves

Set your table saw blade to a 15° angle and saw the bevels on the aprons as indicated in the Exploded View. Clean up the saw marks with a hand plane afterward. Saw or rout a groove near the top inside edge of each apron to accept the tabletop fasteners, as shown in the Drawings. Stop the grooves short of the apron ends so you do not compromise joint strength. Alternatively, you could cut a series of short grooves at the fastener locations using a biscuit jointer.

In preparation for assembly, sand the aprons and legs through 220-grit, and make the loose tenons for the joints. To make the tenons (pieces 5), first mill a strip of ¼" x 2⅜" stock about a foot long. Plane the stock for a snug fit into your mortises. Rout, plane or sand a bullnose profile on the edges of the strip, then crosscut eight ¹⁵⁄₁₆" long sections to create the individual tenons.

Dry-assemble the base to make sure everything fits well and to rehearse your clamping procedures. The best way to clamp these joints is to make up some plywood clamping straps that include beveled blocks on the ends for applying clamping pressure directly across the joint, as shown in Figure 9. To make the clamping straps, glue the blocks in square form to the ends, then saw the bevels after the glue dries.

When gluing up, apply glue to the faces of the miters as well as to the mortises and tenons. Make sure to carefully align the aprons with the tops of the legs. Wipe away any excess glue immediately with a damp rag. You could instead wait until the glue turns rubbery, then cut it away with a sharp chisel.

Making the Tabletop

To make the top from several boards, joint one face of each board, then plane it to 1³⁄₁₆" thick. Try to plane equal amounts off both faces to equalize any inherent stresses in the lumber. Then comes the fun part — laying out the individual boards for position. Consider any tabletop you make to be a canvas of sorts, and compose the grain for nice flow and a good color match along the joint lines.

As with any edge-joined panel, it's usually more attractive to arrange the boards so their widths are approximately symmetrical. It also helps to match straight grain to straight grain at the edges of boards, or at least aim for grain that continues the same slope on an adjacent board. In any case, try to avoid crashing wild grain into straight grain along a joint line. When you are happy with the arrangement, draw a large triangle that spans all the boards in the top for reference when you do your glue-up.

Glue up the top, carefully aligning the edges to be as flush as possible. If you've dressed your stock flat, you won't need biscuits or splines to help alignment. It may help to use a rubber mallet to smack any proud boards into line. After glue-up, wait several days before planing or sanding the top. Glue introduces moisture into the wood, swelling it at the joints. If you flatten the top before the moisture has had a chance to thoroughly evaporate, you invite depressions at the joint lines later.

After the glue cures, rip and crosscut the top to final size. Flatten it using a belt sander or hand plane, then sand the top through 220-grit. I routed a chamfer on the edge, but you could leave the edges square if you like, slightly easing them with sandpaper.

If you dread sanding out router and saw burn marks, there's an easy solution to take some of the hassle out of the process. Brush on a solvent (naphtha, alcohol, mineral spirits or even water), let it soak for a minute, and sand. Mineral spirits work best, but any solvent will help loosen the carbon on the wood surface. For even quicker sanding, use a flexible-shaft tool outfitted with a diamond burr, and apply the burr using light passes to remove the blemish.

Fasten the top to the base using tabletop fasteners (pieces 6). You can make your own from wood, but commercial metal clips also work fine. When screwing the clips to the top, set the shoulders of the clips back a bit from the side aprons to allow expansion of the top when it's humid.

Finishing Up

After an industrious and careful final sanding up through 180-grit, apply a clear finish of your choice. A low-gloss varnish or matte lacquer would both be good options for this table style. If the cherry you've chosen for the project is too light for your tastes, you can age it with sodium hydroxide using the technique offered by contributing editor Michael Dresdner, at right, before applying a topcoat.

Now, with such a lovely table on hand, the biggest challenge you'll have is deciding where to put it.

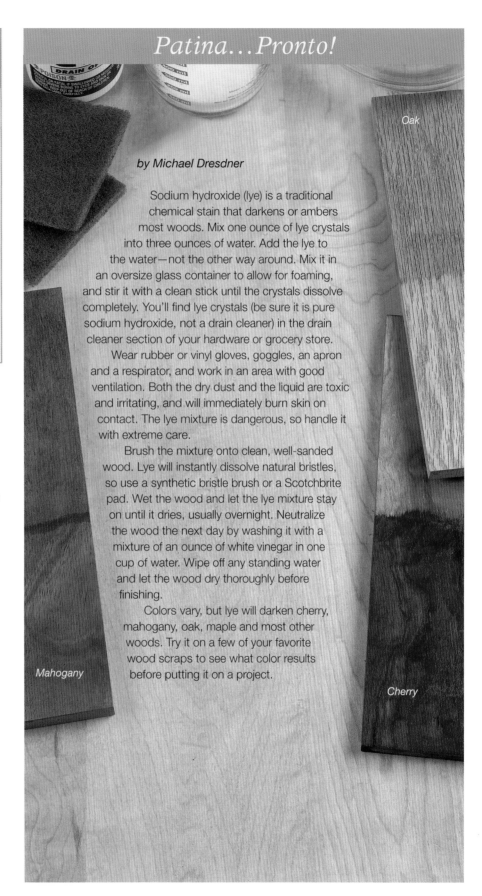

Patina...Pronto!

by Michael Dresdner

Sodium hydroxide (lye) is a traditional chemical stain that darkens or ambers most woods. Mix one ounce of lye crystals into three ounces of water. Add the lye to the water—not the other way around. Mix it in an oversize glass container to allow for foaming, and stir it with a clean stick until the crystals dissolve completely. You'll find lye crystals (be sure it is pure sodium hydroxide, not a drain cleaner) in the drain cleaner section of your hardware or grocery store.

Wear rubber or vinyl gloves, goggles, an apron and a respirator, and work in an area with good ventilation. Both the dry dust and the liquid are toxic and irritating, and will immediately burn skin on contact. The lye mixture is dangerous, so handle it with extreme care.

Brush the mixture onto clean, well-sanded wood. Lye will instantly dissolve natural bristles, so use a synthetic bristle brush or a Scotchbrite pad. Wet the wood and let the lye mixture stay on until it dries, usually overnight. Neutralize the wood the next day by washing it with a mixture of an ounce of white vinegar in one cup of water. Wipe off any standing water and let the wood dry thoroughly before finishing.

Colors vary, but lye will darken cherry, mahogany, oak, maple and most other woods. Try it on a few of your favorite wood scraps to see what color results before putting it on a project.

Oak

Mahogany

Cherry

Arts and Crafts—Style Side Table

Whether nestled next to a living room chair or alongside a bed, an elegant side table is both practical and beautiful. Open and sturdy, simple and stylish ... this Arts and Crafts–inspired design makes for a great project.

by Mike McGlynn

ng a Christmas
der every year.
way with giving
ern Living. This
should have
hem a piece of
e ago—I gave
shop as a

s and
o a chair in
e out of the
edium-dark
hat makes

unt of wood
), it was a pleasure
y selection
boards that were
wood for the top,
n that could be
ompose a pleasing
e a couple of
but a more subtle
oards, I envisioned
and how much
s a sorry day when,
ue-up, the panel
es.
s adjust for a few
efore milling them.
d Minnesota winter.

Begin Milling the Lumber

My first milling step was to cut the boards into pieces that were an inch or two oversized in length, making sure I had the best orientation before I rough cut them. Next, I face-jointed each of the boards to create one perfectly flat face. I then ran all of the pieces through the planer and took them down to their proper thicknesses. At that point, I compared the widths of my pieces to the widths of my finished panels. To achieve a balanced looking panel, it is often necessary to adjust the board so the grain pattern is centered. I don't just joint one edge and cut it to width. I cut and joint my pieces so that my glued-up panels are ¼" wider than finished. That allows me to clamp them up without using any kind of pads.

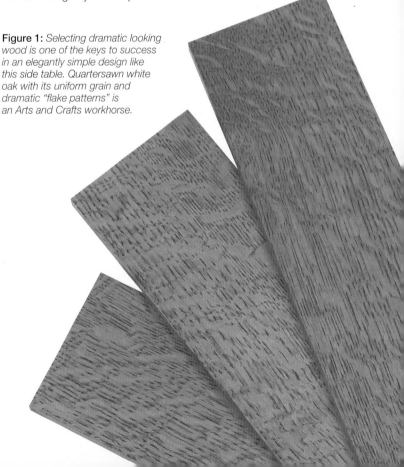

Figure 1: *Selecting dramatic looking wood is one of the keys to success in an elegantly simple design like this side table. Quartersawn white oak with its uniform grain and dramatic "flake patterns" is an Arts and Crafts workhorse.*

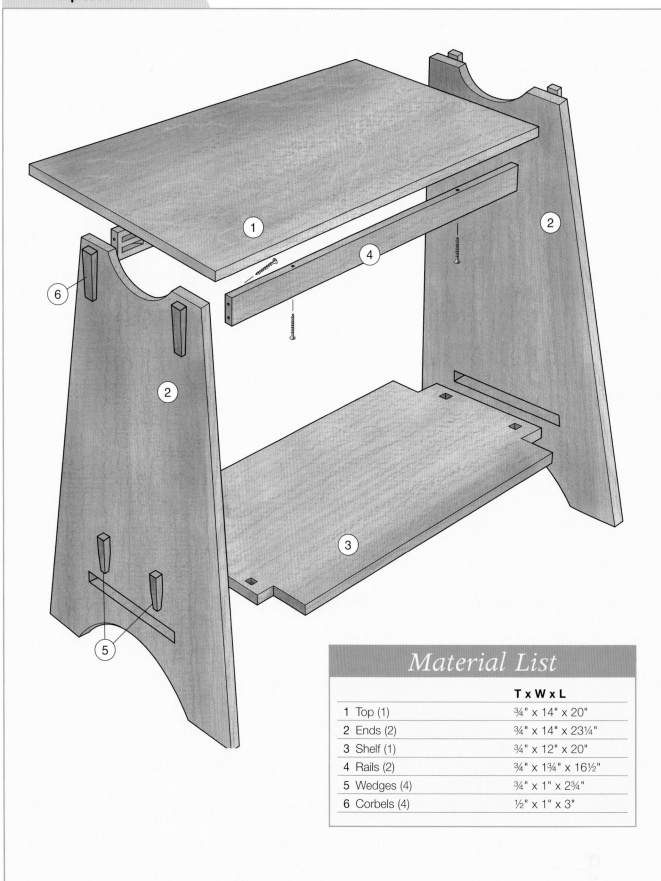

Material List

		T x W x L
1	Top (1)	¾" x 14" x 20"
2	Ends (2)	¾" x 14" x 23¼"
3	Shelf (1)	¾" x 12" x 20"
4	Rails (2)	¾" x 1¾" x 16½"
5	Wedges (4)	¾" x 1" x 2¾"
6	Corbels (4)	½" x 1" x 3"

Marking Out the Joints

When I was finished milling the boards, I selected pieces for the top, sides, and the shelf (pieces 1 through 3), laid them out and marked them for biscuit joints. I made sure while placing the biscuit joints that the biscuits would not be exposed when the panels were cut to length, or when the cutouts on the ends were revealed. I then cut all of the biscuit joints. Because I was planning on using a water-based stain, I was already thinking about my glue choice. It makes a difference.

If a panel is glued up with regular white or yellow glue and then stained with a water-based stain, the glue line often picks up the stain and sticks out like a sore thumb. Believe me, I speak from hard-earned, and expensive, experience. To avoid the problem, I always use Titebond® II when I know I'll be using a water-based stain.

I glued up the four panels using three bar clamps on each, while making sure they were as flat as possible—even the best biscuit joints have a bit of slop that can usually be flatted out with some judicious mallet taps—before I cranked the clamps down. I always make it a point to scrape off all of the squeezed-out glue when it is at a nice rubbery stage. That prevents the inevitable tearout that happens if the glue is left to harden and then scraped off.

The following day, I took the panels out of the clamps and prepared to cut them to size. But first, I used a sharp scraper to carefully remove any bit of glue that was left, and feathered out any small irregularities. I have found this is the perfect time to give panels their initial sanding: the panels are still oversize so I don't have to worry about accidentally rounding over any edges. I always raise the grain before I sand as it makes the sanding go much faster. I sanded to 120-grit.

Once I had sanded all of the panels, I cut them to size. When cutting panels to size, it is important to cut the ends first and then the sides. That helps prevent chipout on the corners. I cut the end panels to length and then width. While they were still in a rectangular shape, I laid out the top and bottom cutouts, the side tapers, and the through mortises. Using the shelf as a guide, I very carefully marked the through mortises on both sides of the panels. It is very important the layout lines are in exact alignment with each other, or the mortise will end up slanted one way or the other. After doing

Figure 2: *Pocket-hole joinery (right) secures the rails and is hidden by the top. Since no mortises or machined means align the rails, take extra care that all the parts are in their proper relationships before driving the screws home.*

the entire layout I cut the side tapers on the bandsaw and finished them up with a sharp plane. I cut the top and bottom cutouts on the bandsaw and finished them off with a curved sanding block.

The shelf took a bit of thinking and layout to get right. After cutting the shelf to length and width, I laid out the wedge mortises and the notches to make the through tenons. I used my table saw to cut most of the notches and finished them off with a hand saw and chisel. The top and rails (pieces 4) are the easy pieces to size, as they are simple rectilinear parts.

Two last sets of parts needed to be built before the part set would be complete: the wedges and the corbels (pieces 5 and 6). I made a cardboard template for both parts and laid them out on the wood I had selected earlier. The pieces are so small I found it easiest to cut them out on the band saw and then hand plane and sand them to size. I left the wedges a little bit thick so I would be able to size them as I did the assembly.

Chopping the Mortises

Cutting the six through mortises was the most time-consuming part of this project. Through mortise and tenons are an exercise in subtle touch. If the mortise is over-tight, the tenon will drive very hard and chip out the outside face; if the mortise is too large, there will be a loose fit that will

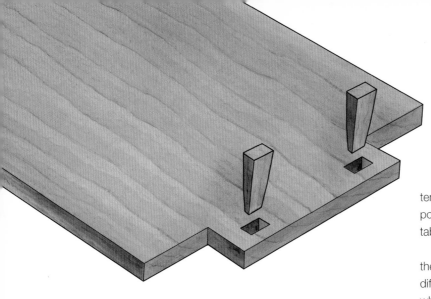

Figure 3: *Fitting the wedges into their mortises is a trial and error process. While the wedges are functional, they also add a lot of aesthetic value.*

substantially weaken the overall structure of the piece. My process is the same for all through mortises: I chisel from both sides and take great care to establish the outer borders of the mortise. I usually undercut the mortise slightly so that I have a tight fit on both faces. I find that it is very important to not make my first cut right on the layout line. Instead,

I first chisel away some waste about ¹⁄₁₆" inside the line, then cut on the line, which prevents the taper of the chisel from forcing the chisel outside the line or crumpling the edge of the mortise. When I'm approaching the final size, I constantly check the fit with the shelf and the wedges. I look for a fit that takes a light tap with a rubber mallet to drive home. I am very careful to not chip the outside face of the parts as I drive the parts together.

To facilitate it, I put a very subtle break on the outside corners—not anything more than 220-grit paper. The mortises for the wedges are undercut ¹⁄₁₆" so there is a tight fit no matter how much the wood shrinks or swells.

I used pocket holes to attach the rails to the ends, but tenons or biscuit joints also could be used. After putting two pocket holes per end, I drilled the two holes to attach the tabletop through the rails.

At that point, I dry assembled the table and fitted the wedges. It is almost inevitable there will be some tiny differences in the wedge mortises. I fit the wedges so that, when driven home, their tops line up with each other (and look the same on both ends of the table). I did most of this fitting with a very sharp hand plane clamped upside down in the vise, taking very fine shavings off until the fit was just right. When I was satisfied with the fit of everything, I took the table apart and prepared for staining.

If I had to pick one thing that I dislike the most in woodworking, it would be staining an already assembled piece of furniture. There is practically no way to get an even coat of stain on an assembled piece unless you apply a sprayed toner coat, and even that doesn't look so great. I much prefer to stain all of the parts separately and then assemble them into the final product. It requires careful handling, and sometimes just can't be done—but I take this approach whenever possible.

My first staining step was to take a damp sponge and raise the grain on all pieces. When the parts had dried, I sanded them all to 220-grit. I paid special attention to putting a slight break on all edges that needed it.

I used General Finishes' EF wood stain in the Early American color on this table. Prior to staining, I pounded three

Figure 4: *The author chops the wedge mortises from both sides of the shelf. It is a meticulous and time-consuming process that pays dividends in spades.*

small finishing nails for each piece into the top of my bench in a triangular pattern. That provided me with a place to set each piece to dry after I had stained it, so I could stain both sides at the same time. I very carefully stained each piece separately and wiped it down with a lint-free cloth before moving on to the next piece. The stain is really great, but you do not want to let it dry before it is wiped down or you will end up with a streaky appearance. Water-based stains dry fast. So, just do one piece at a time, unless you are going for an antique look.

Assembling the Table

To start the assembly of this table I first put on a pair of rubber gloves. One of the drawbacks of water-based stains is that any water will dissolve them. Sweat on your hands or drops from your brow can damage your stain job. I then secured the shelf to the ends by putting a small amount of glue on the cut back ends of the shelf and clamping the whole thing together. The glue is just a little extra insurance, but I made sure it wasn't enough to result in squeeze-out. Water-based stain won't interfere with glue the way an oil-based stain will. With the assembly clamped up, I clamped the rails in place and attached them with pocket screws. I then attached the corbels with some glue and spring clamps. One of the great things about water-based stain is you can glue directly on it with Titebond and experience no loss of strength.

I finished the table with three coats of sprayed catalyzed lacquer, although polyurethane or some type of varnish would work about as well. I prefer to use a finish that has a medium rubbed or satin look to it. I don't think that a glossy finish looks appropriate on Arts and Crafts–style furniture.

The final assembly of this table was pretty simple. I first laid the top upside down on a furniture blanket, centered the base on it, and marked the attachment holes through the holes in the rails. After pre-drilling the attachment holes, I attached the top with four 1½" screws. The last step was to tap the wedges home. Even though I had fitted the wedges before, I found I needed to do a tiny bit more shaving on the back of a couple of them so they would line up exactly.

The table is a great project for somebody who is fond of the Arts and Crafts style. It requires a small amount of wood, and it incorporates some of the hallmarks of Arts and Crafts styling. In addition, it is not such a huge project that a person would become overwhelmed by it—three or four nights of work should pretty much take care of it.

I stopped at my parents' right after Christmas to give them their present, and my mother had me immediately carry the side table they had used for the last 25 years to the basement. Guess I can build them another one to replace their other side table next Christmas.

Figure 5: *Using a plane inverted in a bench vise, the author carefully fits the wedges in their mortises.*

Figure 6: *During final assembly (above), the wedges are coaxed home with a few gentle taps from a rubber mallet.*

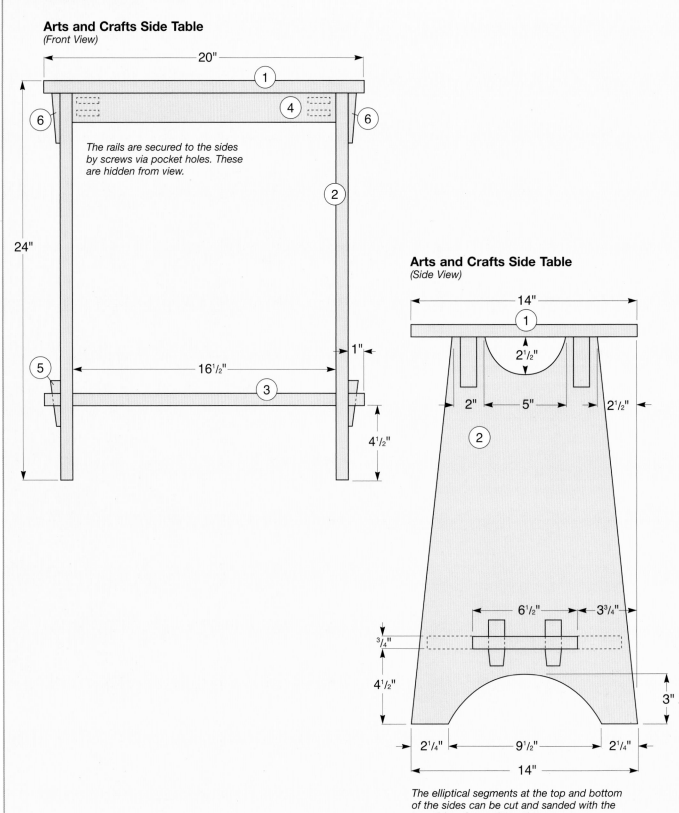

Arts and Crafts Side Table
(Front View)

20"

The rails are secured to the sides by screws via pocket holes. These are hidden from view.

24"

16½"

1"

4½"

Arts and Crafts Side Table
(Side View)

14"

2½"

2" 5" 2½"

6½" 3¾"

¾"

4½"

3"

2¼" 9½" 2¼"

14"

The elliptical segments at the top and bottom of the sides can be cut and sanded with the two sides clamped together.

Shelf
(Top and Side Views)

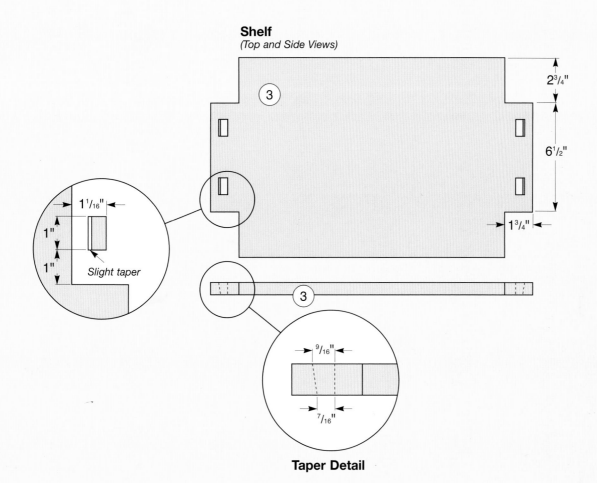

2³/₄"

6¹/₂"

③

1¹/₁₆"

1"

1"

Slight taper

1³/₄"

③

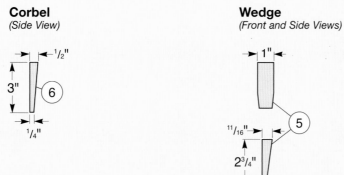

9/₁₆"

7/₁₆"

Taper Detail

Corbel
(Side View)

¹/₂"

3"

⑥

¹/₄"

Wedge
(Front and Side Views)

1"

⑤

¹¹/₁₆"

2³/₄"

¹/₄"

A Bedside Table

It's fun and educational to pause once in a while and make a small traditional piece of furniture like this bedside table. You can combine traditional methods with contemporary techniques, and you'll end up with a faithful reproduction that our forebears would have appreciated.

by Tim Johnson

Small, single drawer tables have been a favorite of furnituremakers and their patrons for generations. The tables range in style from prairie primitives to city sophisticates. It's the broad capacity for variation that attracts many of us to the tables in the first place, not to mention their compact size fits into virtually every home. Tables are also the type of project that make a great gift, because they don't take weeks of time to complete, yet reflect sincerity of purpose. If you have basic lathe skills, you can tackle it in a weekend.

The table requires only seven board feet of ¾"-thick cherry and four 30"-long leg blanks. When choosing your material, look for 6"- to 7"-wide boards so the sides, back and drawer front will be single planks and the top is a three piece lamination. Look for color and grain similarities in all your wood. For the leg stock, I recommend cutting your pieces from one continuous length of lumber.

You'll also need three board feet of secondary wood for the hidden drawer parts. Traditionally pine, poplar or basswood were used because they're easily worked by hand. Unfortunately, these woods wear quickly. I used oak for the drawer sides and back instead, and pine for the bottom.

Getting Started
Begin by gluing up three pieces of cherry for the top (piece 1) and cutting stock for the carcass, which includes

the front rails (pieces 3), the sides and back (pieces 4), the drawer runners (pieces 5), filler strips (pieces 6) and drawer stops (pieces 7). Label each piece and set them aside.

Cut your legs (pieces 2) to size and lay out the shoulders on each piece. Press masking tape along the shoulder lines at this stage. If you get a little tearout while turning, the tape holds onto the small pieces so they're easy to glue back in place. Now use a compass to lay out a 2" circle on the foot end of each piece. Tilt your bandsaw table 45° and trim the corners on each leg up to the 2" circle layout (see Figure 1). Cut from the foot end of the legs to within ½" of the shoulders. Trimming the legs now makes turning the stock easier.

The next step is to make a template, or story stick, to assist you during the turning operation. Use a copy machine to enlarge the leg template on page 131, and glue it onto some hardboard. Trim the hardboard to match the box around the leg pattern, then use a bandsaw to notch the template just a hair at each of the major layout lines.

Chuck a leg blank in the lathe so its square end is near the head stock. With the lathe speed at 800 rpm, turn the blank round using a large gouge, then switch to a parting tool to nibble up to the taped shoulders. Now hold your story stick against the blank while the lathe is running and set a pencil in each notch to lay out the major points on the leg (see Figure 2). Adjust the lathe

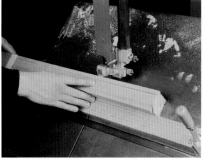

Figure 1: *To make your legs easier to turn, tilt your band saw table 45° and trim the edges off each blank from the foot end to the shoulder lines.*

speed to 1,200 rpm and, using a parting tool and a caliper, turn the reference marks to their proper diameter (see Figure 3). At reference points between the beads, leave the turning a little fat so you can cut deeper with a skew chisel later. Once the reference points have been cut, use a small gouge and rounded scraping tools to shape the vase and the coves (see Figure 4). Trust your eye to create evenly rounded rings and smooth transitions. Remember that like an antique, part of the Bedside Table's charm is having legs that aren't perfectly matched and show the hands of the maker.

When the leg is fully shaped, reduce the lathe speed to its slowest setting and sand with 100-grit paper to remove any tool marks, then use 120-grit paper to smooth the surface.

Drilling the Mortises
On many old furniture pieces you'll see marks at the bottom of mortises left by center point drills. In keeping with the

Figure 2: *Once you've turned the blank round with a large gouge and nibbled up to the shoulder lines with a parting tool, use your story stick to lay out the major parts of the leg.*

Figure 3: *The story stick lines represent the high and low areas of the leg. Use your caliper and a parting tool to cut the low areas to a slightly larger diameter than their finished dimension.*

Figure 4: *A small gouge and a diamond-shaped scraper work well for cutting the beads and coves on the legs. A large gouge and a skew chisel are best for shaping the long tapers.*

craftspeople of yesterday, follow this same method. Arrange the legs in the order that suits you, and label them for each position on the table. Be sure to hide sapwood or turning flaws by positioning that spot away from view on the table. Lay out the mortises as shown in the Elevation on page 131, and scribe a line down the middle of each mortise layout to help you position the entry point for the drill bit.

Clamp a fence to your drill press table to center each mortise under the bit and set the drilling depth at ¹⁵⁄₁₆". Now drill holes at each end of the mortise layout, then drill out the rest of the waste (see Figure 5). I leave about ³⁄₁₆" between the first set of holes, then come back and drill out the small bridges. Drilling this way keeps your mortises straight and square. Chisels

will make quick work of cleaning up the mortises. While you're at the drill press, lay out and drill the 1¼"-deep drawboring holes in the legs as shown in the base elevation drawings.

Machining the Sides and Back

Cutting tenons on the sides and back (pieces 4) is done with a table saw and a ½" dado blade raised ¼". Set the fence ⅜" from the blade to yield ⅞"-long tenons. Make test cuts in scrap until you get a nice slip fit in a leg mortise, then cut your table pieces. Once the cheeks are cut, raise the blade height to ½" and cut the edge shoulders.

To cut the double stub tenons on the front rails (pieces 3), set your dado blade height at ⅜" and cut the outside cheeks (see Technical Drawings on page 131). Cut the ⅝"-wide gap between each pair of tenons with a hand saw and chisel.

Now install a ¼"-wide dado blade and raise it ¼" to rip a groove in each side piece ¼" from the bottom edge. Next, clamp a wood face to your fence, slide the fence up to the blade and rip the edges of each drawer runner (pieces 5) to form ¼"-thick tongues.

Assembling the Base

It's time for a test assembly of the table base. Fit the major pieces together and, if the joints are too tight, check

the tenon edge shoulders first—that's usually where the problems are. If the joints are loose, shim the tenons to achieve a slip-fit. Mark the members of each joint with a letter to make reassembly easier.

With the table fully assembled, use a ¼" center point drill bit to mark the drawboring holes in the tenons. Slip the bit into each leg hole and tap it with a hammer. Disassemble the table and you'll see the marks left by the bit. Now use an awl to make new marks next to the old ones ¹⁄₃₂" closer to the tenon shoulders, and drill these locations with the ¼" bit (see Peg Detail on page 131). Use your drill press to assure straight holes.

To mimic the old time look of square pins, use a ¼" chisel to square the holes in the legs to a depth of ⅜".

Figure 6: *Marking gauge layout lines, slightly irregular dovetails and square drawboring pegs are telltale signs left by the hand of a craftsman.*

Figure 5: *To rough-in a mortise, first drill at the ends of the layout, then bore holes every ½". Finish up by drilling out the stock between the holes.*

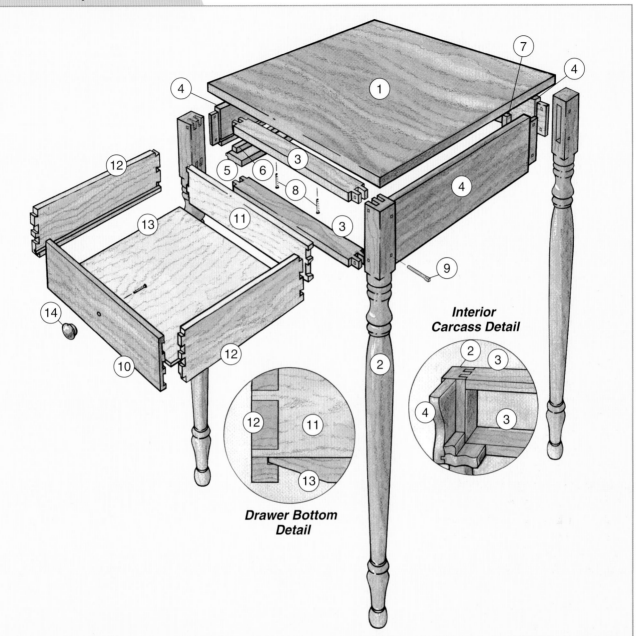

Interior Carcass Detail

Drawer Bottom Detail

Material List

	T x W x L		T x W x L
1 Top (1)	¾" x 17⅜" x 17⅜"	8 Screws (8)	#6-1¼" Flathead
2 Legs (4)	1⅞" x 1⅞" x 27"	9 Square Pegs (16)	¼" x ¼" x 1⅜"
3 Front Rails (2)	¾" x 1⅞" x 14"	10 Drawer Front (1)	¾" x 3¾" x 12¹⁄₁₆"
4 Sides and Back (3)	¾" x 5⅜" x 14"	11 Drawer Back (1)	¾" x 3" x 12¹⁄₁₆"
5 Drawer Runners (2)	¾" x 1⅞" x 12⅛"	12 Drawer Sides (2)	¾" x 3¾" x 13⁹⁄₁₆"
6 Filler Strips (2)	¾" x ¾" x 12⅛"	13 Drawer Bottom (1)	¾" x 13¾" x 11⁵⁄₁₆"
7 Drawer Stops (2)	¾" x 1" x 3½"	14 Knob (1)	1¼" Diameter

Half-blind Dovetails

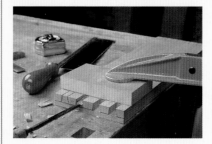

Cutting half-blind dovetails is very much like cutting through dovetails. Use a marking gauge to lay out the depth of the joint on the ends of the drawer front, then lay out the half-blind pins. Cut halfway down each pin wall with a fine hand saw, making sure to cut on the waste side of the lines (left). Next, remove the waste from between the pins, making light blows with your chisel and mallet (right). Protect the pin corners by limiting the size of the waste pieces to about ¹⁄₁₆" thick by half the width of the opening (see above).

The way to prevent tearout is to make a scrap tenon that fits in the leg mortises and be sure to back up the tenons with another scrap piece.

When the joints are reassembled the holes won't line up. However, when the pegs (pieces 9) are driven in, they will draw the tenoned pieces tightly into the legs. These are drawpinned joints. To make the pegs, rip stock into ¼" x ¼" strips and cut the strips into 1⅜"-long pieces. Leave the first ⅜" of each piece square, then whittle the rest of the peg round (see Elevation Detail on page 131). Taper the end of each peg to make driving them easier and so they won't force all the glue to the bottom of the holes.

Before assembling the table base, drill expansion holes in the sides and back, then fixed holes in the upper front rail for attaching the top. Use a ¾" Forstner bit to form pockets for the screw heads in the sides and back, drilling at a 10° angle, followed by ³⁄₁₆" pilot holes. In the upper front rail, drill countersunk ⁵⁄₃₂" pilot holes for attachment screws.

Gluing Up the Carcass

Now glue up the carcass in three stages: first the front legs and rails, then the back assembly, and finally pull the two assemblies together with the sides. As soon as you get each joint assembled, put a little glue on each peg and drive them in. Complete the base by adding the drawer runners and fillers (pieces 5 and 6). Remove any excess glue with a chisel when it becomes rubbery.

Cut the top to its finished dimensions and sand it thoroughly, then turn it upside down and center the base on it. Clamp the pieces together and extend the pilot holes from the base into the top with a ³⁄₃₂" bit. Now secure the top to the base with #6-1¼" screws (pieces 8).

Building the Drawer

The last thing to build is the drawer. Cut the drawer front (piece 10), back (piece 11) and sides (pieces 12) to size, but be sure to double-check your actual drawer opening with the drawer sizes in the Material List. Next, lay out the dovetail pins. For cutting the half-blind pins on the front, saw the walls partway, then remove the waste with a ¼" chisel as described in "Half-Blind Dovetails,"

above. Once the half-blind pins have been formed, cut the through pins on the back, then hold the sides in position against the pins and mark the tails.

Use a dado blade to cut ¼"-wide by ¼"-deep grooves in the sides and front (see Exploded View Detail on page 129) for holding the bottom panel (piece 13). Dry-fit the drawer box, and make sure it slips into the carcass opening easily—remember, wood expands in the summer. Also, check to see that the bottom edges of the sides and front sit flat on the drawer runners. If the drawer is twisted, shave the offending side until all edges slide smoothly on the runners.

Glue up pine stock for the drawer bottom, then cut it to size and sand it smooth. Next, tilt your table saw blade 12° to bevel the underside of the panel on its side and front edges so it fits the drawer dadoes. Slide the bottom into place and drill a ⁵⁄₃₂" countersunk pilot hole to drive a screw through the bottom and into the back. With the same setup, drill a pilot hole for the knob (piece 14) as well. Add the drawer knob next. After the drawer fits properly, customize the stops (pieces 7) so your drawer front sits flush with the front rails, then glue them to the inside surface of the carcass back.

Finishing Up

Sand everything to 180-grit, then apply a wash coat of shellac as a sealer because otherwise, cherry can be blotchy. Follow it with at least two coats of varnish and a final rubbing. After the varnish dries, wax the drawer runners to make them a little slippery.

As the details and methodology of this project attest, all woodworkers have some degree of connection with craftspeople of the past. There are easier and faster ways to produce a bedside table, but sometimes a traditional approach just seems fitting. Now, set your new table next to a deserving bed and watch it age gracefully over the years to come.

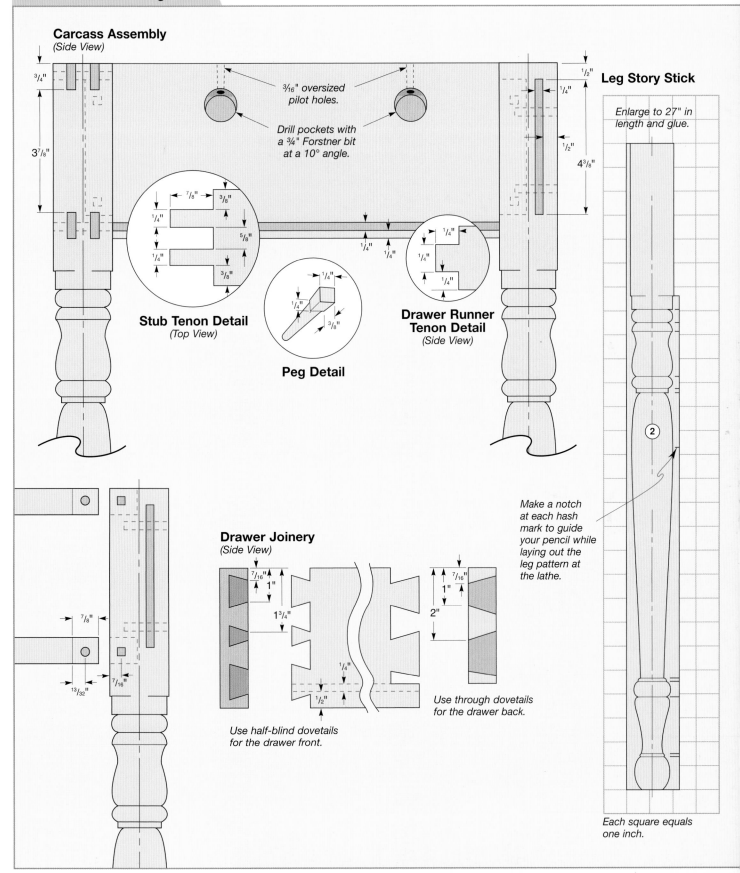

Carcass Assembly
(Side View)

3/4"

3 7/8"

3/16" oversized pilot holes.

Drill pockets with a 3/4" Forstner bit at a 10° angle.

1/2"

1/4"

1/2"

4 3/8"

Leg Story Stick

Enlarge to 27" in length and glue.

Stub Tenon Detail
(Top View)

7/8"

3/8"

1/4"

5/8"

1/4"

3/8"

1/4"

1/4"

1/4"

Peg Detail

1/4"

1/4"

3/8"

Drawer Runner Tenon Detail
(Side View)

1/4"

1/4"

1/4"

②

Make a notch at each hash mark to guide your pencil while laying out the leg pattern at the lathe.

7/8"

7/16"

13/32"

Drawer Joinery
(Side View)

7/16"

1"

1 3/4"

1/4"

1/2"

7/16"

1"

2"

Use through dovetails for the drawer back.

Use half-blind dovetails for the drawer front.

Each square equals one inch.

Edo Table

Inspired by the interlocking joints of Asian furniture, the Edo Table combines simple notches with four stout lag screws. Novices can make it using nothing more complicated than a table saw.

by Tom Caspar

By and large, tables are made the same way. Mortises are chopped out of the legs, tenons are cut on the aprons, and after you put them together, you add a top. Not long ago, however, I reconsidered the approach as I was building several copies of a Chinese table.

This Edo table (the Samurai-era name for the city of Tokyo, Japan) is the product of this re-thinking. Its construction is unlike the Chinese example I was copying, but it's also unlike any Western table I know of. What sets the Edo table apart is a new system of joinery that eliminates all the handwork of cutting and chopping mortise and tenon joints, yet it results in a very stable, attractive design. In fact, all the joints can be formed on a table saw by a beginning woodworker.

Making the Legs

Cut eight 2⅜"-wide by 26"-long rift-sawn pieces for the leg laminations. Plane these pieces to a thickness of 1⅛" and arrange them into four pairs. To get the best match for each pair, make sure the end grain runs in the same direction. Glue the pairs together, then rip them down to the final dimensions (pieces 1). Take a few minutes now to identify how the legs will be arranged on the table, and mark one end of each to make the orientation clear. That way you

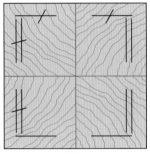

Front

won't accidently put a leg in the wrong place or show its poorer side. Arrange your legs so similar faces are neighbors and try to have their growth rings point to the outside corner. As an apprentice, I learned a nearly fool-proof system for making furnituremaker's marks. If you arrange the legs and pencil in marks like those at left, you'll find they always go together the same way.

Once the marks have been made, tilt your table saw blade 45° and rip a 1⅛"-wide bevel along the inside corner of each leg (see Figure 1). Depending on the brand of your saw, you may have to switch the fence to the opposite side of the blade to do this operation. Clean up the bevels with a hand plane.

Now enlarge the pattern of the leg on page 137 and make a hardboard template. Trace the template shape onto the outside faces of each leg, as shown in Figure 2. Be sure the toe of each layout points to the outside corner of the legs. Now band saw along the line on one face of each leg, then tape the waste back onto the stock and cut along the line on the second outside face. Use a hand plane and a scraper to smooth the leg faces.

Figure 1: *Bevel the inside corner of each leg with your table saw blade tilted 45°, then smooth the bevels with a hand plane.*

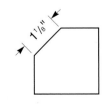

Leg Detail

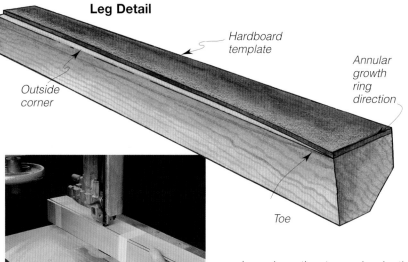

Hardboard template

Outside corner

Annular growth ring direction

Toe

Figure 2: *To cut the tapered curves on a leg, first band-saw one face, then tape the waste back into place and band-saw the second face.*

Making Edo Joinery

The mainstay of the Edo table is its joinery system. Instead of using traditional mortise and tenon joints commonly found on Western furniture, the table gets its stability by using pinned lap joints. By bracing the rails with a network of crossmembers, the table base gains tremendous rigidity, and all of the joints can be cut on a table saw.

Choose the best wood for the rails (pieces 2 and 3) and the less desirable pieces for the joint connectors (pieces 4 and 5). Mill the pieces to the thicknesses listed in the Material List on page 137, then trim them to overall size, but don't cut the arches on the lower rails just yet.

Begin working on the joints by carefully laying out the dadoes on your rails, as shown in the Rail Dado Details on page 136. Now cut the angled ends of the outside dadoes. Raise a ¾" dado blade ³⁄₁₆" and turn your miter gauge 45°. Clamp a stop to the fence to align a dado layout with the blade. Make the cut in each rail, then rotate the miter gauge to the opposite 45°

mark, re-clamp the stop and make the angled cut in the other outside dadoes. To remove the remaining waste from the angled dadoes and to cut the middle dadoes, set the miter gauge at 90° and re-adjust the stop. A chisel will quickly take care of any clean-up.

You've already trimmed the joint connectors to overall size, but now you need to fit them to the rail dadoes. For accuracy, make a fixture that will hold the upper rails in position while you plane the joint connectors to fit the dadoes exactly. To make the fixture, cut a 23¾" square of plywood and some positioning blocks (four 1" x 12" blocks and four 2⅞" squares), then nail the four long blocks to the plywood, as shown in Figure 3. Next, clamp the four upper rails, with dadoes facing up, to the long blocks and nail the 3" blocks in the leg positions. Fit the rails tightly between the leg blocks.

Now fit the middle joint connectors into the rail dadoes. Plane any piece that is too large, or, if a piece is too small, cut another one and plane it down to size. It's important the connectors fit snugly and their ends protrude ³⁄₁₆" beyond the rails.

Once the middle joint connectors are fitting properly, cut half laps in the center of each one with a dado blade. Next, make the corner joint connectors. Set your miter gauge at 45° to cut the ends of the corner connectors, using a stop block for each series of cuts to guarantee consistency. Cut the long miters first, then the short ones. Fit the corner connectors into their dadoes and then chamfer the ends of all the joint connectors using a router table and a chamfering bit, and a file or rasp.

Details, Details, Details...

Even though you haven't made the top yet, you need to provide a method of fastening it to the base that allows for wood movement. First drill ¼"-deep counterbores for fender washers (pieces 6) in each joint connector, as shown in the Corner Detail on page 137.

Now drill tight-fitting pilot holes for the screws (pieces 7) in one middle joint connector and oversized pilot holes

Snug-fitting lap joints reinforced with screws give the Edo table its unique appearance and outstanding stability.

in the other middle joint connector, as well as the corner connectors. When you assemble the table, be sure to position the middle joint connector with the tight-fitting holes so it runs parallel with the grain of the top. That will keep the top centered on the base, while the oversized holes will allow for seasonal wood movement.

Each leg is held to the rail assembly with a lag screw (pieces 8) that passes through a corner joint connector. First drill a 1¼"-deep counterbore in each joint connector for a washer (pieces 9), then drill a loose-fitting pilot hole for the lag screw—large pilot holes make assembly a lot easier.

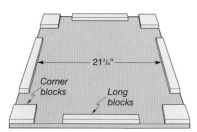

Figure 3: *Make a fixture to hold the upper rails in position while you fit the joint connectors. Once all the pieces fit together, drill a counterbored pilot hole through each joint.*

Enlarge the lower rail pattern to full size and trace the shape onto your stock. Be sure to mark the locations of the counterbored pilot holes on each rail, then drill the pilot holes and band saw the pieces to shape. Smooth the freshly cut edges with a spokeshave or drum sander, then position the lower rails on the assembly and extend the pilot holes through the joint connectors and into the upper rails. Try driving the joint connector screws (pieces 10) to ensure the sandwich pulls tight. When everything fits according to plan, remove the base from the fixture and hold the legs to the assembly. Mark and drill the pilot hole locations for the lag screws, but don't install the legs until the finishing has been completed.

Adding the Top

To get a good balance of color and grain, try making the top (piece 11) from sections of one board. A glued-up panel of three pieces will look best, so choose a board that's about 9" wide. Mill and joint your stock, then glue it up and leave it in the clamps overnight.

Trim the top into a 24½" square, then tilt your table saw blade 9° and set the fence 23⅞" away. Turn the top upside down and trim all four edges to form the gentle under-bevels. Take the table apart to give it a final sanding, but be careful to avoid rounding the dado shoulders on the rails (it's better to have crisp-looking joints). On the top, pay close attention to easing the bevels—not enough sanding and the top edges will remain too sharp, but too much will reduce the impact of this delicate accent.

Adding Finish

It's much easier to finish the table while it's disassembled. To reach all sides of the smaller pieces, drive a thin screw in each one (locating these in hidden spots), and hang them from some notched strips (see Figure 4). Remember, however, to avoid finishing the joint areas on the rails and on the joint connectors, otherwise the glue won't adhere to them during the final assembly.

Brush on a wash coat of white shellac and two coats of satin varnish, sanding lightly between each coat to remove any dust nibs or raised grain.

With the finishing completed you can assemble the table. Use the fixture to hold the rails and joint connectors in position while you glue and screw all the lap joints. Apply the glue sparingly so you won't have a lot of squeeze-out to clean up in the process. Once the rail

Figure 4: *Drive a screw into each piece of the table base and hang them from a wood strip so you can apply finish to all the sides at the same time.*

assembly has been completed, remove the fixture and use a socket wrench to secure the legs with the lag screws. Finally, center the base on the tabletop, extend the pilot holes from the joint connectors into the top, and drive the hold-down screws into place to secure the parts.

As you'll quickly find out, this table is as strong as any table built with mortise and tenon joints. While unconventional, the Edo joinery system does draw from traditional Eastern and Western techniques, proving that the best innovations often bring together ideas from vastly different places.

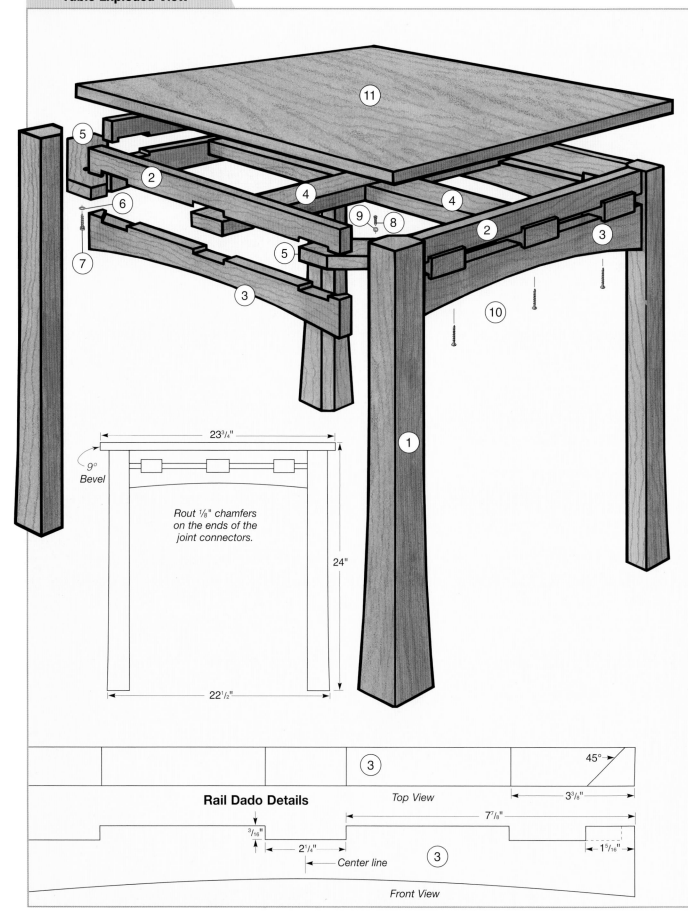

23³/₄"

9°
Bevel

Rout ¹/₈" chamfers
on the ends of the
joint connectors.

24"

22¹/₂"

Rail Dado Details

Top View

45°

3³/₈"

³/₁₆"

7⁷/₈"

2¹/₄"

Center line

1⁵/₁₆"

Front View

Leg Template
(Front View)

①

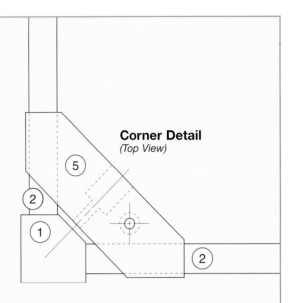

Corner Detail
(Top View)

⑤
②
①
②

Lower Rail **Upper Rail**
(Front View) *(Front View)*

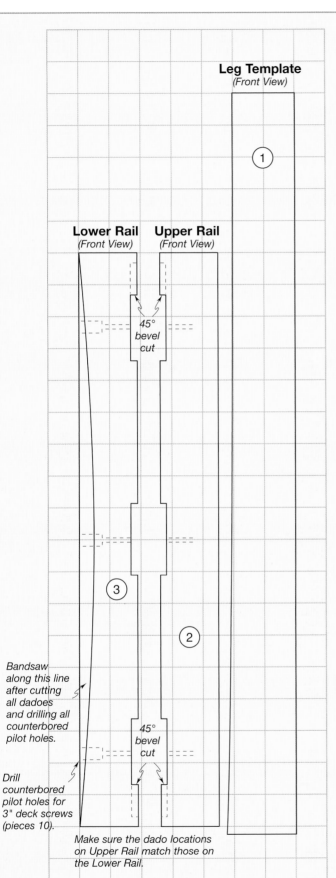

45°
bevel
cut

③

②

45°
bevel
cut

Bandsaw along this line after cutting all dadoes and drilling all counterbored pilot holes.

Drill counterbored pilot holes for 3" deck screws (pieces 10).

Make sure the dado locations on Upper Rail match those on the Lower Rail.

Material List – Table

		T x W x L
1	Legs (4)	2¼" x 2¼" x 23¼"
2	Upper Rails (4)	1" x 1¼" x 18"
3	Lower Rails (4)	1" x 1⅞" x 18"
4	Middle Joint Connectors (2)	1⅛" x 2¼" x 22⅛"
5	Corner Joint Connectors (4)	1⅛" x 2¼" x 8"
6	Fender Washers (8)	¼" Inside hole dia.
7	Screws (8)	#10-2½" Pan head
8	Lag Screws (4)	⅜" x 2½" Hex head
9	Washers (4)	⅜" Inside hole dia.
10	Screws (12)	#8-3" Deck screws
11	Top (1)	¾" x 23¾" x 23¾"

Enlarge patterns to full-size, make hardboard template and trace onto outside faces of each Leg (pieces1).

Each square equals one inch.

Shaker Sewing Stand

Hand-sewing may be a skill that's largely forgotten these days, but the Shakers did it on a daily basis as the use of electric sewing machines was against their religious principles. Consequently, furniture intended to make sewing easier came in many forms, including this sewing stand. It provides a good chance to spend some time at the lathe, and a handsome little table that's useful whether or not you sew.

by Ralph Wilkes

This classic sewing stand design was inspired by one made in the Shaker community of Mt. Lebanon, New York, around 1850. Many Shaker furniture items came from that area in the 19th century, the designs often emphasizing that simple things are the most beautiful. Practicality was important in their furniture designs as well, although in later years, Shaker craftspeople relaxed their austere beliefs a little, especially in furniture made for outsiders.

This sewing stand was designed for use by two people at the same time. The drawer is shared and pulls in both directions.

Start with the Pedestal

Since the three legs and the entire top assembly attach to the pedestal (piece 1), it is logical to turn it first. If you have to glue together two or more pieces to get the required size, check carefully to match the grain and wood color as closely as possible.

Turn the entire length to 3" in diameter and leave it at that size until after completing the three dovetail sockets at the lower end, which should be the live center end when mounting it on the lathe. That way, the other end, or dead center end, can later be turned to fit the 1½" hole in the upper assembly. It's also easier to clamp the piece when it's all the same size.

Making the Dovetail Sockets

As shown in the Pedestal Drawing on page 140, lay out the live center end for the dovetail sockets using a protractor to keep them 120° apart. Draw a line to the center point to aid in eyeballing the location of each of the router cuts. Using a ½" straight bit in a table-mounted router, make your first passes ¼" deep by 3" long. Use a stop block clamped to

Figure 1: *Turn the pedestal to a diameter of 3" and remove it from the lathe. Before completing the turning, form dovetail sockets for the legs, starting out on the router table.*

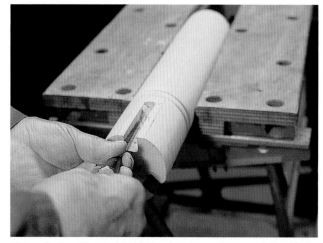

Figure 2: *Once the straight bit has done its work, use a sharp chisel to complete the dovetail walls and to flatten the areas that will later be covered by the ends of the legs.*

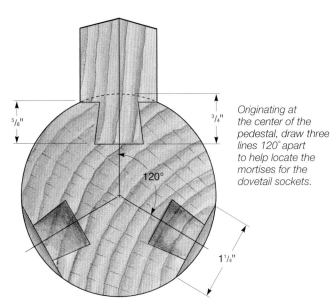

Figure 3: *To join the legs to the pedestal seamlessly, flatten the curvature of the pedestal and the dovetail sockets with a sharp chisel.*

⁵⁄₈"

³⁄₄"

120°

Originating at the center of the pedestal, draw three lines 120° apart to help locate the mortises for the dovetail sockets.

1¼"

the fence of the router table, as shown in Figure 1, to establish the length of cut.

To ensure the dovetail sockets stay straight while you rout them, take a few moments to make a cradling jig by cutting an arc into some scrap that perfectly fits the 3" diameter of the pedestal. Face it with some double-sided tape. By pressing the jig against one side of the pedestal, you can easily hold the other side tight against the fence, preventing the pedestal from rotating. After your first pass for each socket, successively increase the depth to ½", and finally to ¾" for your final passes.

Once you've reached the right depth, you'll need to complete the dovetail cuts with a sharp wood chisel, as shown in Figure 2. But first, you'll need to flatten the curvature of the pedestal around each dovetail socket. Do it by centering a 1¼" x 3½" piece of cardboard over the socket (representing one of the legs) and tracing around it with a pencil. By flattening the area, you ensure a tight fit of the leg against the pedestal. Use a sharp wood chisel, first making the cut across the top end 3½" from the bottom. Sandpaper, backed by a flat block, may be used for final flattening. When you're done with this task, the grooves should measure ⁵⁄₈" deep.

Lay out the guideline markings for the dovetails on the bottom end of the pedestal (see Figure 3) and chisel to the

dimensions shown. In any chiseling job, keep the blade edge sharp by honing frequently and, for your own safety, keep the hand not doing the work well away from the business end of the chisel.

Shaping the Legs

Use 1¼"-thick stock for the legs (pieces 2), choosing wood free of knots or blemishes. Use the Scaled Drawing at right to create a pattern and transfer it to your stock, paying careful attention to the grain direction. For the neatest and quickest sawing job, use your band saw, although it also can be done with a scroll saw or jigsaw if you don't have a bandsaw. Sand the upper and lower edges until smooth, using the end of a belt sander or a drum sander, as shown in Figure 4. Follow up with a ¼" roundover bit, as shown in the inset photo on page 143.

Creating the Leg's Dovetails

If you plan to make the dovetail depth cuts by hand, start by marking the guidelines and clamping a straight piece of scrap wood across the leg to guide the saw and protect the blade. Make the cuts ⁵⁄₁₆" deep, preferably with a back saw.

I found we could do a neater and more accurate job on the table saw. Trace out two jigs, one for each side of the leg, to hold it in position during the cut, as shown in Figure 5 and Figure

Pedestal
(Front View)

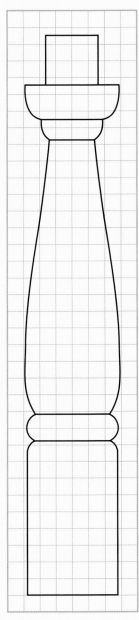

Each square equals ½ inch.

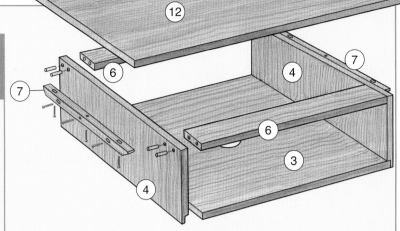

Material List – Sewing Stand

	T x W x L
1 Pedestal (1)	3" Dia. x 16¾"
2 Legs (3)	1¼" x 5" x 14"
3 Drawer Box Bottom (1)	¾" x 17" x 13"
4 Drawer Box Sides (2)	¾" x 17" x 5"
5 Stabilizer (1)	¾" x 4" Diameter
6 Drawer Box Rails (2)	¾" x 2½" x 12"
7 Cleats (2)	¾" x ¾" x 15"

NOTE: *Make pieces 3 and 4 from a single piece of glued-up lumber. To avoid exposed end grain, the grain in pieces 3, 4, and 6 should run around the opening at 90° to the table's drawer.*

Leg
(Face View)

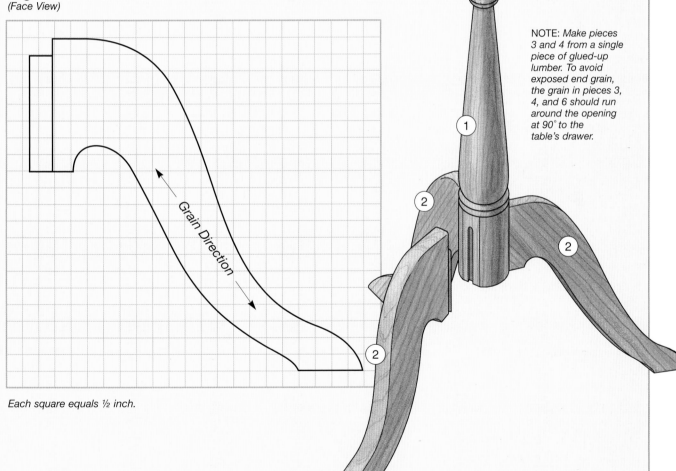

Grain Direction

Each square equals ½ inch.

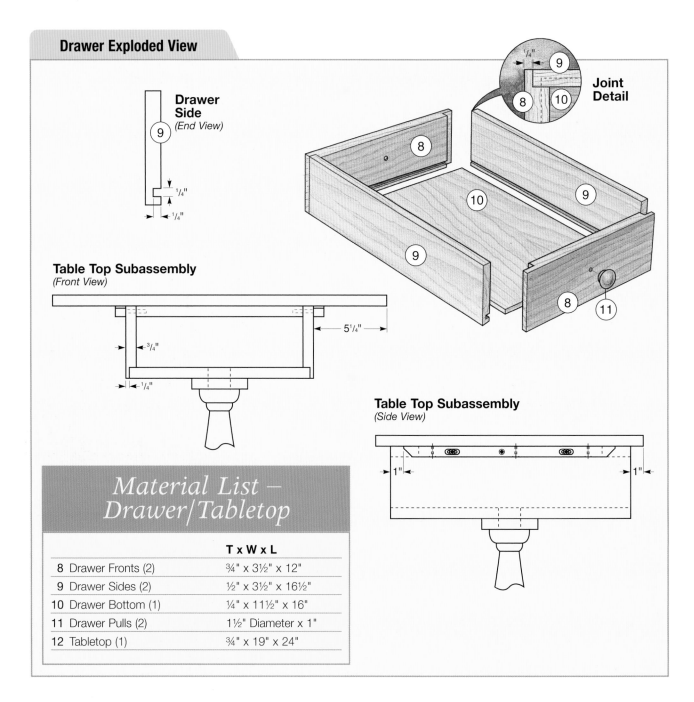

Drawer Exploded View

Drawer Side *(End View)*

⑨

¼"

¼"

⑧

Joint Detail

¼"

⑨

⑧   ⑩

⑧

⑩   ⑨

⑨

⑧   ⑪

Table Top Subassembly *(Front View)*

5¼"

¾"

¼"

Table Top Subassembly *(Side View)*

1"   1"

Material List – Drawer/Tabletop

	T x W x L
8 Drawer Fronts (2)	¾" x 3½" x 12"
9 Drawer Sides (2)	½" x 3½" x 16½"
10 Drawer Bottom (1)	¼" x 11½" x 16"
11 Drawer Pulls (2)	1½" Diameter x 1"
12 Tabletop (1)	¾" x 19" x 24"

6. Using ¾" scrap stock, hold the scrap and one leg (the end you will be dovetailing) squarely against your table saw's rip fence and accurately transfer the leg's curves with a pencil.

On the table saw (for legs that are 1¼" thick), set the blade to a depth of ⁵⁄₁₆", then make the shoulder cuts on each side of each leg to define the back of the tail. If you are short on experience with this type of joint, try shaping a complete dovetail on a piece of scrap stock first.

Consult the dimensions in Figure 7 to complete your dovetails, testing the fit in the sockets as you go. To shape the dovetail to fit the pedestal socket, use a padded clamp to hold the leg firmly in place on a bench and make the chisel cuts in the direction of the grain, not across it. Round the tail's upper corners to match the shape of the socket.

After sanding through the grits on each leg, you can set them aside for now, until after the pedestal turning is completed.

Some Drawer Frame Details

You won't want to see end grain when looking at the sewing stand, so orient the grain of the drawer box bottom and sides (pieces 3 and 4) so it runs crosswise to the direction the drawer will slide. Glue up one 17" x 24" panel to create these three pieces, joining the edges with glue and biscuits and then cut them each to size.

Form the rabbets on the sides (see drawings above) and join them to the bottom with glue and #4 finishing nails.

Now locate the center of the bottom piece and glue the stabilizer (piece 5) in place. Once the glue dries, drill the pedestal hole with a hole saw or expansion bit. As you can see from the drawings on page 141, the box rails (pieces 6) are held in place with two ⁵⁄₁₆" diameter x 1½" dowels at each end.

Before moving on to the drawer and pedestal, take a moment to form the two cleats (pieces 7) that attach the tabletop to the drawer box. Drill three holes in each direction on these two pieces, (see the Exploded View on page 142), slotting the outside ones to allow for seasonal movement of the sides and top. Because round-head screws with washers were employed here, use a Forstner bit to set the screw heads below the surface.

Completing the Pedestal

You can return to the pedestal and bring it to final shape. Start by dry-fitting the legs and lightly marking their uppermost locations. Raise the first bead above that point, as shown in the drawing on page 141. Then move to the top end and

Figure 4: *Sand the upper and lower edges of the three legs on an oscillating or drum sander or, in their absence, try clamping your belt sander upside down. Then use a ¼" roundover bit (inset photo) to complete the machining.*

QuickTip

Sharpening Station

You'll be more likely to sharpen chisels and plane irons when they need it if you have a sharpening station. Begin by cutting 6" off the bottom of a 5-gallon bucket and use it to keep your stones immersed in water or oil. Cut a 20"-square plywood base and rout a circular groove in the bottom to turn it into a lid for the bucket. Nail strips of wood around the top so water or oil won't escape while you work. Nail a small strip at either end of each stone to hold them when they're not immersed and a final strip under the front edge to catch the edge of your bench: the strips will hold the station steady while you're sharpening.

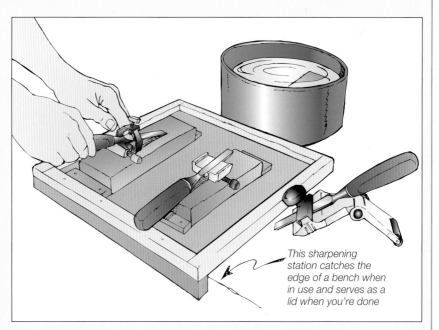

This sharpening station catches the edge of a bench when in use and serves as a lid when you're done

Figure 5: *To ensure straight shoulders on the tails, create two jigs to hold each leg exactly square as you form the shoulder of the dovetail. The curve in the leg is matched by the shape of the jig (inset photo) to hold the legs securely as they are being machined.*

Figure 6: *Once the shoulder cuts are made, use a chisel to shape the dovetails to fit the sockets in the pedestal perfectly. Chisel in the direction of the wood grain and use a padded clamp.*

turn it down to fit the hole in the center of the drawer box bottom. With the two ends done, follow the drawing to turn the pedestal's gently curving shape. Sand the pedestal while it's turning, ending with #220 or finer. When you're just about done, turn off the lathe and sand lengthwise by hand to remove any cross-grain scratches that may still show. Don't sand the upper tenon that fits into the drawer frame.

Attaching the Legs

Before gluing the legs permanently in place, fit them into their sockets and set the assembly on a level table. Use a carpenter's square to check that the pedestal rises at exactly 90° from the surface, (see Figure 9). Even the slightest error here can give you something akin to the Leaning Tower of Pisa. While a variation might be almost invisible to the eye, mark the exact place where the upper edge of each leg meets the pedestal when it is vertical. If you've worked accurately to this point, each leg should be perfectly in line around the base of the column, with the pedestal rising perfectly plumb.

Glue the first leg and use a padded C-clamp and several heavy rubber bands to hold it tightly until dry. The goal is to apply equal pressure along the entire length of the glued joint. Use a wood chisel or knife to scrape away any fresh glue that squeezes out of the joint, then go over the surface with a wet cloth. After each joint dries, proceed to the next.

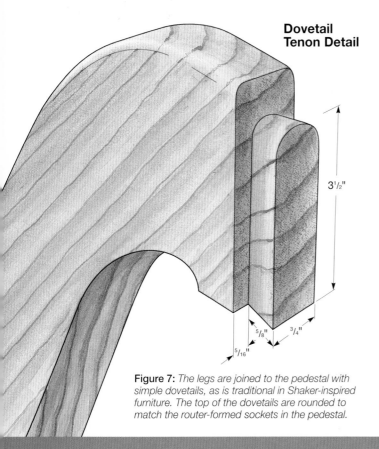

Dovetail Tenon Detail

3¹⁄₂"

⁵⁄₈"   ³⁄₄"

⁵⁄₁₆"

Figure 7: *The legs are joined to the pedestal with simple dovetails, as is traditional in Shaker-inspired furniture. The top of the dovetails are rounded to match the router-formed sockets in the pedestal.*

Making the Drawer

The double-ended drawer (pieces 8 through 10) is made with rabbeted corner joints and a plywood bottom that slides into grooves before attaching the second front (see drawings on page 142 for machining details). Do not use glue to secure the drawer bottom. Center the drawer pulls (pieces 11) vertically and horizontally. Drill a hole for each and countersink it on the inside for the screw. Shaker-style drawer pulls may be made on the lathe or purchased locally. Try to find (or make) some that match the wood species you use for the rest of the project. Traditionally, the Shakers frowned upon contrasting wood species used for the sake of ornamentation.

Time for the Final Assembly

You're now ready to bring all the components together. Start by placing the pedestal on a level surface and applying glue to the top tenon. Press the drawer box in place, using your level to ensure it dries flat. While the glue dries, select some of your best boards (with matching grain) for the tabletop (piece 12). The pieces are fitted with three biscuits at each joint before edge-gluing and clamping. Trim the ends to size and sand the edges and top. Soften the edges with sandpaper, but just enough to break the sharpness.

Finishing Up

Before attaching the tabletop, apply at least one coat of varnish to the inside of the drawer frame and to the underside of the tabletop to prevent uneven moisture absorption.

Stain your sewing stand, if you wish. After it dries, apply two or three coats of your favorite finish, sanding between coats. A bit of wax applied to the outside of the drawer will help it slide easily. Now you have an elegant, yet simple gift.

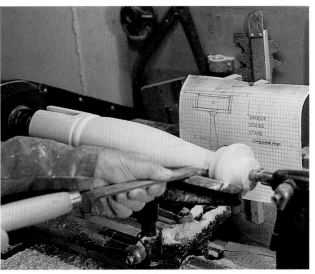

Figure 8: *After the dovetail slots are completed, return the pedestal blank to the lathe to wrap up the turning process. Complete all but one sanding step on the lathe as well, saving a final pass to do by hand, sanding with the grain.*

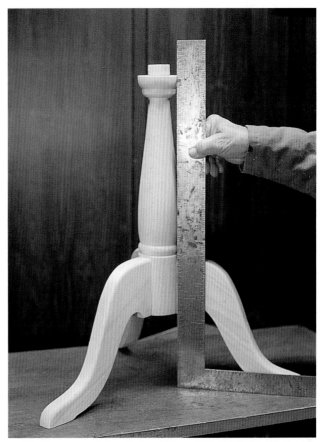

Figure 9: *During the final glue-up of the legs to the pedestal, check for plumb with a carpenter's square to be sure there will be no tilt to the top.*

Arts and Crafts End Table

Necessity is the mother of invention for some projects. If you're always searching for a heat-safe surface to park the morning coffee cup, a granite-topped end table provides a perfect spot. Plus, this project will provide an opportunity to use your jointer for some decorative profiling and try your hand at simple machine-cut inlay.

by Linda Haus

Figure 1: *The band saw makes short work of slicing the apron pieces of the mahogany leg blanks.*

This project started as the solution to a simple need—a place to set a steaming-hot cup of coffee while reading the paper. One thing led to another, and the result was the Arts and Crafts End Table. The granite top is impervious to heat, and the height keeps it above the level of a curious pooch's nose or an infant's easy reach. I chose straight-grained mahogany for the structural members of the table, but other hardwoods would also do just fine. Hard maple strips and ebony plugs create the accents that call the Arts and Crafts movement to mind.

Making Extra-Thick Leg Blanks

To begin the project, I used 1¾"-thick mahogany, cut to the length and width of the legs (pieces 1) as a starting point. Then resaw a ½"-thick slice from each leg blank (see Figure 1). The ½" stock is used to make the aprons (pieces 2 and 3). If you cut all of the leg blanks from one board and slice the apron stock from the leg blanks, the grain and figure will be consistent…so important with a natural oil-and-wax finish.

Plane the saw-marked face of the pieces smooth and step over to your jointer for a bit more machining.

Performing Some Jointer Magic

Jointers provide a nifty way to shape stock and cut down on sanding. Set the infeed bed of your jointer to remove a ¼" cut. Stick a piece of masking tape on the fence 2¾" back from the center of the knife roller. That is where you will stop your cut on each leg, to create uniformly shaped feet. Test your set-up by making practice cuts using scrap lumber trimmed to the proper

Figure 2: *Create the feet by taking a deep jointer cut in the leg blanks, stopping the cut short of the end of the wood (white tape marks the spot).*

dimensions. It is a one-pass cut, so your jointer knives need to be sharp. Use a push block with a top handle to keep your feeding hand completely safe (see Figure 3). The top end of the leg pushes past the far end of the outfeed table at the conclusion of the cut. That way, you can simply push down on the top end to lift the foot end clear of the cutter. When you are satisfied with the cut you are making, go ahead and shape all four legs.

Now mark a line to define the angled shape of the feet. Create each foot's angle on a disc sander— a simple way to get great results (see Figure 3).

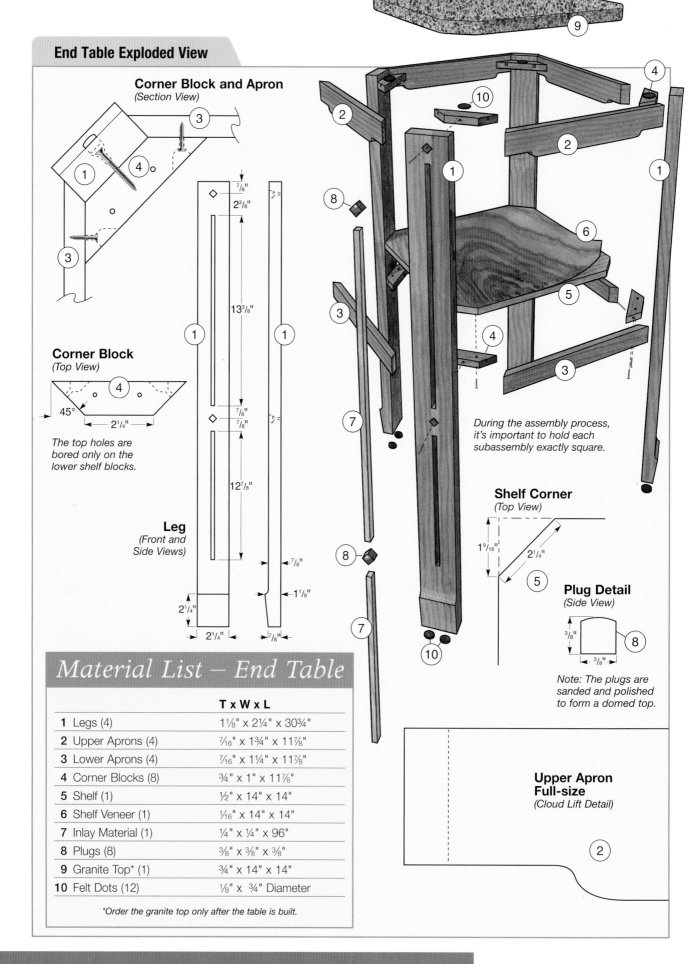

Corner Block and Apron
(Section View)

Corner Block
(Top View)

45°

2¼"

The top holes are bored only on the lower shelf blocks.

Leg
(Front and Side Views)

⁷⁄₈"

2³⁄₈"

13³⁄₈"

⁷⁄₈"
⁷⁄₈"

12⁷⁄₈"

⁷⁄₈"

1⅛"

2¼"

2¼"

⁷⁄₈"

During the assembly process, it's important to hold each subassembly exactly square.

Shelf Corner
(Top View)

1⁹⁄₁₆"

2¼"

Plug Detail
(Side View)

³⁄₈"

³⁄₈"

Note: The plugs are sanded and polished to form a domed top.

Upper Apron Full-size
(Cloud Lift Detail)

Material List – End Table

		T x W x L
1	Legs (4)	1⅛" x 2¼" x 30¾"
2	Upper Aprons (4)	⁷⁄₁₆" x 1¾" x 11⅞"
3	Lower Aprons (4)	⁷⁄₁₆" x 1¼" x 11⅞"
4	Corner Blocks (8)	¾" x 1" x 11⅞"
5	Shelf (1)	½" x 14" x 14"
6	Shelf Veneer (1)	¹⁄₁₆" x 14" x 14"
7	Inlay Material (1)	¼" x ¼" x 96"
8	Plugs (8)	³⁄₈" x ³⁄₈" x ³⁄₈"
9	Granite Top* (1)	¾" x 14" x 14"
10	Felt Dots (12)	⅛" x ¾" Diameter

Order the granite top only after the table is built.

Figure 3: *A one-cut jointer trick will do the majority of the machining on the legs (below). It's a simple but sophisticated technique. Then shape the feet by sanding an angle on the remaining lower leg stock (above).*

On to More Machining

In a nod to the Greene brothers, the upper aprons (pieces 2) have a cloud lift cut along their bottom edge. Form the shape on your band saw (using a ⅛" blade) and then stack the aprons for their final sanding, to ensure uniformity. Miter-cut the ends of all the aprons and set them aside. While you're at it, make all eight corner blocks (pieces 4). They are identical in shape, but the four lower blocks will have a couple of additional holes predrilled into them. You'll drive screws up through the holes to secure the shelf.

Building the Veneered Shelf

Like inlaying, veneering has the reputation of being tricky and hard to do. Not the way we'll do it. Cut the shelf and its veneer (pieces 5 and 6) to size. To achieve best results, cut the veneer piece a full 1½" large overall. Apply yellow glue to one side of the shelf and one face of the veneer and allow it to dry completely. Then place the shelf (glued side face up) on a solid work surface and place the veneer (glued-side face down) on top of it. Get a regular household iron (most shops have one), set it to "high" and allow it to get fully hot. Now iron the veneer to the plywood shelf. Start the process at the center of the shelf and move in a circular motion to the edges. That's it. To trim off the excess veneer, use a sharp shop knife and slice from the back of the shelf to avoid tearout.

Adding Details

The decorative inlay and ebony plug steps come next. They are not required, but I think they really make the piece. For instructions on my "simple as pie" inlaying method, read "Tackling the Inlay Fear Factor" on the next two pages. I used a mortising machine to make the plug mortises and to square up the inlay grooves. Don't cut the inlay or plugs (pieces 7 and 8) until your grooves and plug mortises are machined—matching the inlay and plugs to the exact groove and mortise sizes only makes sense.

Use the same logic when it comes to the granite top (piece 9). There is no give in granite, and you can't sand it down a bit if it's too big to fit. So don't order your granite until after the table has been made and assembled. Then fit a template to the opening and give that to the folks making your granite top. There are many countertop companies who fabricate granite these days, so finding a source for your tabletop shouldn't be too difficult.

Figure 4: *Inlay made simple. Square up the ends of your inlay grooves with a mortising machine (or attachment on your drill press). For the complete process, turn to page 150.*

Assembling the Table

Although at first glance assembling the table may appear to be a walk in the park, it does require attention to detail. Because the smallish corner blocks do the lion's share of the joinery work, it's easy to get the assembly out of square. Exactly mark the positions of the corner blocks and then glue and screw all eight blocks in place, dead square to the legs' edges. The four corner blocks with the extra holes are placed in the lower position. Attach two legs to their upper and lower aprons with glue and screws, in effect creating a side assembly. Note the upper aprons are flush to the top of the legs and the bottom aprons are proud of their corner blocks by the thickness of the veneered shelf. Check for square, then duplicate the process and allow the glue to cure. Finish the assembly by securing the remaining four aprons and shelf. Again, allow the glue to cure. When all is square, install the ebony plugs and sand the project all the way through 320-grit paper. Then gently round and break all of the exposed edges. Now is the time to make your top template and order the granite top.

As a final touch, I recommend applying three coats of natural Watco oil or a similar product, followed by a rubdown of wax. Attach the felt pads (pieces 10) to the bottom of the feet and add a few more to keep your granite from wobbling. Now you're ready to brew that coffee and grab the paper!

Decorative inlay, an age-old technique that enhances the appearance of woodworking projects, dresses up the flat outer surfaces of these table legs. Unfortunately, some woodworkers shy away from inlaying because they think it's too difficult and time-consuming. It's not, if you follow this simple approach.

The heart of decorative inlay is the use of contrasting but complementary species of wood. Done well, the contrasting textures and colors will create beautiful designs that highlight shapes and shadows. The Arts and Crafts End Table was milled from mahogany. I chose a strip of plain hard maple (light colored with little visible grain or figure) broken by ebony plugs to contrast with the rich red mahogany. The maple strips are long slender rectangles like the legs, and the plugs, although square, were turned 45° to appear diamond-shaped. Both accents were chosen to enhance the look of the piece, and the approach I used is easy to duplicate.

Jigs and Power Tools: The Perfect Combo

After you cut the legs to size and complete the basic machining, chop the plug mortises and plow the grooves. To cut the grooves, build the jig shown at right to hold the legs securely in place while you guide a router exactly down the center of the leg. I used a trim router...but the jig can accommodate any size router you have.

Using a mocked-up leg made from scrap lumber, test the cuts and lay out where you'll start and stop each groove. There are two per leg. Once you've marked the jig with the starting and stopping points, you are ready to rout. Form two ¼"-wide by ¼"-deep grooves on each leg. As you know, the end of a groove formed by a router is rounded. In order to make the inlay strips rectangular, square up the grooves at each end. You can do it by hand with a chisel, but a ¼" mortising chisel will square up all 16 grooves in a snap—and you'll use the same chisel to chop the plug mortises.

Now, on to the plug mortises. As mentioned, use your mortising machine to chop the ⅜"-square holes that accept the ebony plugs. Drill pilot holes through the legs—centered in the mortise holes—because the plugs actually hide screws that attach the table's corner blocks to the legs. Beautiful and practical.

Making the Inlay and Plugs

If you hate to do things twice, form the grooves and plug mortises before you make the inlay strips and plugs. By routing the grooves first, you can cut the maple inlay strips to fit them perfectly... the first time. The same rationale applies with the plugs.

Ripping skinny little pieces of hardwood on the table saw can be dangerous if you don't take the proper precautions. For starters, be sure to use a zero-clearance insert. Plane oversized, ¼"-thick slabs of maple and rip the strips to width using a good

Figure 1: A simple shop-made jig holds the table leg and helps make the inlay grooves. Note the markings indicating where to start and stop the router cuts.